Atlas of
Medieval
Europe

LE·ROY·CLOVIS

Les allemans meetent e fuyte
Aureben et en pourluyte
Croy au dieu au quel croyt ta feme
Reuient fur eulx et les diffame

Clouis et les gens dōt lexclame
Dift au Roy pour euiter blasme
Ce qual faict pins acoups de taille
Et soubdain gaigne la bataille

·S·REMY

LE·ROY·CLOVIS·

LA·ROYNE·CLOTILDE

LE·ROY·

Clotilde Reyne a sainct remy ēuoye
Dilligēmēt pour le cueur elmouuoir
Du Roy clouis afin quil le pouruoie
De saincte foy que chacū doibt auoir

Alaunct Remy e
Et le Repēt dau
Dieu tout puisse
Semblablemar

Atlas of
Medieval
Europe

Angus Konstam

Checkmark Books™

An imprint of Facts On File, Inc.

Atlas of Medieval Europe

Text and Design © 2000 Thalamus Publishing

Checkmark Books
An imprint of Facts On File, Inc.
11 Penn Plaza
New York, NY 10001

Konstam, Angus.
Atlas of medieval Europe / Angus Konstam ; [maps, Roger Kean].
New York : Checkmark Books, c2000.
p. cm
G1791.K6 2000
911/.4 21
0-8160-4469-4 (acid-free paper)
Includes index.
Civilization, Medieval—Maps—Europe—Historical
geography—Maps.
Geography, Medieval—Europe—Maps.
Kean, Roger.
12111863

Checkmark Books are available at special discounts when purchased in bulk quantities for businesses, associations, institutions or sales promotions. Please call our Special Sales Department in New York at: (212) 967-8800 or (800) 322-8755.

You can find Facts On File on the World Wide Web at:
http://www.factsonfile.com

For Thalamus Publishing
Commissioning editor: Lucian Randall
Project editor: Neil Williams
Maps: Roger Kean
Illustrations: Oliver Frey
Four-color separation: Prima Media Ltd and Thalamus Studios

Printed and bound in India by Thomson Press

PICTURE CREDITS
Picture research by Image Select International Limited
AKG Berlin: 58, 102, 119 (bottom), 130, 134, 136, 149 (top); AKG Berlin/ S. Domingie: 180; AKG London: 1, 2/3, 12, 13, 15 (bottom), 21, 24, 25, 31, 48, 49, 50, 53, 55 (bottom), 60, 61, 67 (both), 69, 70, 74, 76, 80, 84, 87, 104, 108, 109, 110, 112, 123, 127, 135, 142, 151 (top), 154 (top), 155, 160, 162, 164, 169, 174, 183; AKG London/ British Library: 7, 42, 66, 71, 113 (top), 120, 132; AKG London/ Erich Lessing: 22, 29, 35 (top), 38/9, 40/1, 86, 91, 95 (top), 115 (bottom), 126, 129, 137 (bottom), 141 (bottom), 151 (bottom), 152, 177, 184; AKG London/ Jean-François Amelot: 77, 96/7; AKG London/ S. Domingie: 153; AKG London/ Stefan Drechsel: 95 (bottom); AKG London/ Tarek Camoisson: 78; Ann Ronan Picture Library: 68, 85, 98, 106, 113 (bottom), 115 (top), 147, 182; ARPL: 16, 17, 19 (bottom), 51, 59, 90, 163, 171; BPCC/ Aldus Archive: 6 (left), 103; British Museum: 43; ET Archive: 15 (top), 111; Exley Publications: 181; Image Select International: 20, 30, 36 (left), 36/7, 46, 63, 88, 89, 99, 105, 107, 119 (top), 128, 131, 133, 137 (top), 161, 165, 168, 170 (bottom), 175 (top), 178, 179; Image Select International Limited/ Ann Ronan: 92, 93, 121, 143, 144, 145, 146, 148, 149 (bottom), 156, 157, 167, 186; Image Select International Limited/ CFCL: 33; Image Select International Limited/ Exley: 47; JS Library International: 56, 176; Mirror Syndication International/ British Museum: 8; Pictures Colour Library: 32, 57, 122, 140/41; Sarrazin/Kreis Coesfeld: 6 (right); Spectrum: 19 (top), 55 (top), 125; Thalamus Publishing: 35 (bottom), 72, 73, 154 (bottom), 175 (bottom); Thalamus Studios: 23, 62, 62, 170 (top); The Board of Trustees of the Armouries: 114

Half title page:
King Louis IX of France (who later became St. Louis), sets off on the Sixth Crusade (1248–54), a book illustration of c.1330 from Vie et miracles de Saint Louis by Guillaume de Saint Pathus.

Title pages:
Clovis I, King of the Franks, who united the tribes of Roman Gaul and adopted Christianity at the end of the fifth century AD, is baptized by Bishop Remigius, later St. Remi of Reims.

CONTENTS

Foreword

Below: This late
14th-century
illustration from Les
Très Riches Heures du
duc de Berry (April),
sums up the romantic
myth of the medieval
period—turreted
castles and beautifully
dressed ladies and
their elegant lords.
The reality was
usually far less
peaceful.

The medieval world—the world of knights and of chivalry—has long fascinated young and old alike. The gallant riders in shining armor and the beautiful ladies who owned their hearts were the subject of many romantic tales, particularly in the 19th century. Hollywood and television created their own medieval world where harnesses were never rusty, the heroes

never too exhausted to rescue those in danger, and where all castles were mighty strongholds that offered a level of comfort similar to that which we are used to in the modern world.

Careful investigation and evaluation of documents, building structures, and other material remains, and in particular the development of new methods in modern archeology, have since shown us another picture. The reality of medieval life is beginning to emerge from behind that veneer of glamor. What we now see is a world full of hardship, a world in which food was often scarce, and fatal diseases frequent; of cramped living

without much privacy even for the lords and their ladies. And as we begin to learn about real life in medieval times and the struggle for survival, we start to appreciate the motivations behind some of the desperate and bloodthirsty wars which characterized the era.

As we understand more of the Middle Ages, the era appears more colorful and our fascination with the time increases. Medieval castles register an ever-increasing number of visitors, and children are now as fascinated by the stories of knights as they once thrilled to tales of the age of dinosaurs. But in contrast to the romantic interest in medieval times during the 19th century, we now want to know more about the field of serious research into the Middle Ages. Ahead of you in this book is the door to the forgotten world of the real medieval times: the domestic and monastic life; the dynastic struggles and deadly rivalries; the sophisticated innovations in weaponry; a harsh way of life that permeated all classes; and ultimately a society that laid the very foundations of our life in the 21st century.

Dr. Jenny Sarrazin

Right: Keeping the
medieval chivalric
tradition alive:
knights of the "Ars
Militia" pose in front
of the 13th-century
castle Burg Vischering
in Germany.

The Medieval Myth

The medieval period has often been portrayed as a backward era, when Europe was plagued by incessant warfare, disease, and spiritual ignorance. In recent years historians have come a long way toward regarding the era as being, not in fact a "Middle Age," but one that saw the development of modern European civilization.

Until comparatively recently, our view of the medieval period suffered at the hands of historians. The word *medieval* (or *mediaeval*) is defined as "of the middle ages," implying a transitional era, linking the Dark Ages to the Renaissance. Like the "Dark Ages," which preceded it, the era has been depicted as one of barbarism and cruelty, and the Renaissance is credited as the epoch that ushered in the era of modern man, together with modern forms of culture, government, and thinking; all emerging fully-developed at the end of the 15th century. Although the collapse of the Roman Empire in the fifth century AD was an immense setback for the development of European civilization, in the period that followed Europe was reborn as a thriving cultural and even a political entity. This took place in the very period termed the "Dark Ages"—an age now regarded as one in which the foundations of Europe can be traced.

Until recently, the millennium between the fall of Rome and the dawn of the Renaissance in Italy was seen as a stagnant age. Most modern historians now believe this is far from the truth. While before, historians demarcated the start of the middle ages from either the reign of Charlemagne or from the development of the feudal system a century later, many now argue that, following the calamitous events of the fifth century AD, Europe followed a gradual curve of development that culminated in the cultural explosion of the 15th century.

Dividing the course of history into defined periods is even more problematic than geographical partitions. The medieval world as defined in this book is essentially that of western Europe, but it did not exist in a vacuum—trading links with the Middle East and, through Arab merchants, with Africa, central Asia, and the Far East played a part in the continent's development. Of paramount importance was the influence of the Roman Church, although to a lesser extent, other religious views had an impact on European development, particularly those of the Islamic world and the Greek Orthodox (or Byzantine) Church. While some historians portray the medieval period as one where religious beliefs were largely fixed, the truth was very different.

The theological debates described in this book helped to create the Christian beliefs of today, and laid the groundwork for the Protestant Reformation. Similarly, although scientific knowledge was constrained by a high level of illiteracy, mechanical and technological breakthroughs were made and formed the framework for later Renaissance inventors. The medieval period, then, was a time of constant and often dynamic development—and this is reflected in the maps in this book, as the the continual flow of power rewrote the borders of Europe.

However, life in medieval Europe was harsh, and the feudal system maintained the supremacy of a minority of the population over the rest. With endemic warfare, poor sanitation, and primitive medical knowledge, life expectancy was short. Nevertheless, medieval Europeans built some of the most impressive religious structures in the world, established a political system that stood the test of time, and eventually exported their civilization to the rest of the world. Ironically, the constant warfare was part of the reason for Europe's growth and development—a virile by-product of the harsh Dark Ages during which the civilization was formed. While historians have linked the emergence of modern Europe—and ultimately western civilization—to the Renaissance, the first blooms of its growth were visible hot on the heels of the fall of the Roman Empire.

Above: *By contrast to the picture on the facing page, this illustration for January, from a Flemish calendar, depicts the work of farming folk. It is still a romanticized view; life under the feudal system for disenfranchized peasants was harsh, and often short.*

The Darkest Age: Barbarian Invasions

The half-millennia following the fall of the Roman Empire has long been known as the Dark Ages. In recent times, this period has been redefined as comprising only the fifth century AD. Traces of the old Roman civilization survived, and the Christian religion actually expanded in Europe even during the most adverse of times. From the sixth century AD, Europe entered the "early medieval" period, which saw a revival of its cultural and political dynamism.

Below: *Even before the fall of Rome to barbarian armies, the East Anglian coast of Britain came under threat of Saxons from across the North Sea, who raided the river estuaries of what became known as the Saxon Coast.*

During the fourth century AD, the Roman Empire in the West was anything but exclusively Roman. In the Empire's provinces of Gaul (France) and Britain, the Romans integrated with the existing Celtic cultures to produce a distinct Romano-Gallic or Romano-British society. Similarly, even in the lands beyond the natural frontiers of the Rhine and Danube rivers, local peoples were introduced into the Roman Empire as slaves, and eventually as soldiers and artisans. The Roman Army was the cornerstone of the Empire, but increasingly its ranks were filled by conquered peoples rather than by Roman citizens. By the mid-fourth century AD, many of the garrisons guarding the Roman frontiers in northern Britain and Germany were staffed by the same people they were intended to guard against. The inevitable consequence was an exchange of cultures across Roman frontiers, a union augmented by trading and political links.

Many of the non-Latin peoples had shared cultural roots, but had evolved into distinctive groups; the tribes closest to the Roman frontiers and those further to the east. The western Germans (including the Saxons, Angles, Jutes, and Franks) were truly Germanic, while the Visigoths, Ostrogoths, Lombards, and Vandals probably originated in the steppes of what is now the Ukraine. These various Germanic peoples maintained little unity above the tribal level. Their unification into the wave of migration known as the Barbarian Invasions was forced on them by external factors.

Demise of the west

The impetus was the arrival of the Huns; a nomadic Mongolian people one Roman historian described as a "race savage beyond all parallel." In AD 375 the Visigoths petitioned the Emperor Valens (364–378) for permission to cross the Danube into the Roman Empire in an effort to escape from the Huns, and although the request was granted, the Emperor attacked the Visigoths, but was killed at Adrianople (AD 378). The situation was restored, but the precedent had been set. About AD 400 the Visigoths united under King Alaric and conquered Greece and Illyria, and in 402 they attacked Italy. Ironically, a Vandal general commanded the largely Germanic Roman army that checked the Gothic advance and saved Rome. In 406 the Vandals and other Germanic peoples crossed the River Rhine into Gaul, reaching as far south as Spain and northern Italy.

In 410 the Visigoths captured

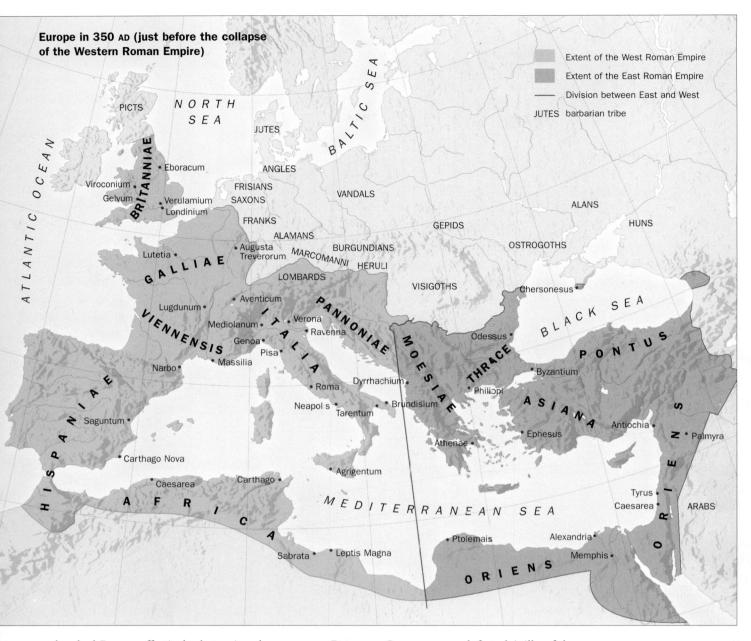

Europe in 350 AD (just before the collapse of the Western Roman Empire)

Extent of the West Roman Empire
Extent of the East Roman Empire
Division between East and West
JUTES barbarian tribe

and sacked Rome, effectively destroying the empire. The Vandals continued into North Africa around 429, while the Visigoths followed behind them and occupied Spain. In Britain, waves of Angles and Saxons crossed the North Sea from northern Germany during the fifth century and rolled back the Romano-British Celts, who were also attacked by Scots-Irish and Pictish raiders from the north and west.

The Roman Empire in the west, which had endured for over five centuries, had fallen in just three decades. In the east the Empire survived the debacle, and consolidated its control over its Middle Eastern provinces while strengthening its western defenses around Constantinople. An alliance between the Romans and the Visigoths was forged under Emperor Valentian III (425–55), with Imperial power centered around Ravenna, and on his death Rome was sacked again, this time by the Vandals.

A second wave of invasion was precipitated by the westward migration of the Huns, who crossed the Rhine in 452. A combined Romano-German army defeated Atilla of the Huns (433–53) at Chalons (452), and although Rome itself was threatened, the Huns retreated after the death of their leader. These second waves of invaders were the Franks and Ostrogoths, who occupied Gaul and the Danube valley respectively. By the start of the sixth century the Roman Empire in the west was ruled by barbarians, and almost all traces of Roman civilization had been destroyed, including the church, central administration, cities, trade, and the legal system.

But the Germanic successor states embraced some aspects of the Roman culture they had destroyed. King Clovis of the Franks embraced Christianity, and waged war against the pagan Visigoths, driving them into Spain. He established links with the Pope, and with the surviving remnants of Roman authority, as did Theodoric the Ostrogoth, ensuring the protection and survival of crucial elements of the Roman church and state. The stage was set for a revival of European fortunes

CHAPTER ONE

The Recovery of Europe

Following the fall of the Roman Empire, Europe faced its bleakest period for centuries. While the eastern Roman world survived the disaster and re-emerged as the vibrant Byzantine Empire, western Europe was occupied by successive waves of invaders. Christianity was almost extinguished, but the faith kept alive by Celtic and Mediterranean monks ensured its survival. By the sixth century, the Roman Church had extended its influence among the barbarian overlords of Europe while growing increasingly distant from the Orthodox Church in Byzantium (Constantinople).

A series of Gothic, Frankish, and Saxon states emerged in western Europe, and while Byzantine and Moorish armies vied for control of the eastern Mediterranean, the dominance of the Franks in northwestern Europe created some degree of political stability. The conversion of the Franks to Christianity occurred just as the Muslims were invading Spain. The Merovingian and Carolingian dynasties of the Frankish kingdom halted the Muslim advance, and under Charlemagne (768–814) the Franks created an Empire that unified western Europe into a single cultural and political entity. Although this political unity was short-lived, the cultural cohesion introduced by Charlemagne was encouraged by the Church, and allowed western Europe to survive the ravages of a fresh wave of Viking, Magyar, and Moorish invaders.

The Barbarian Kingdoms AD 500

▇ Byzantine Empire

▤ Reconquest of Italy by Belisarius between AD 536–540

JUTES

SAXONS

BALTIC SEA

THURINGIANS

LOMBARDS

AVARS

OSTROGOTHS

● Ravenna

● Rome

● Naples

SICILY

BLACK SEA

● Byzantium
(later Constantinople)

SASSANID
KINGDOM

● Antioch

CYPRUS

● Damascus

CRETE

M E D I T E R R A N E A N   S E A

● Jerusalem

ARABS

Alexandria ●

The Empire of the Franks

Following in the wake of the Goths who decimated the Western Roman Empire were the Franks, a Germanic tribe of settlers and farmers. Over the next three centuries they created a Frankish State, supportive of the Church and of existing Romano-Gallic systems of government. Although the era of the Merovingian Franks was characterized by civil war and weak leadership, it gave rise to the stable rule of the Carolingian dynasty. Under the Carolingians, the Franks would emerge as the dominant people of Europe.

At the end of the fifth century AD, the Frankish ruler Clovis united the tribes of Frankish Gaul into a unified kingdom, which he ruled from his capital in Paris. He founded the Merovingian dynasty, which ushered in a period of dynastic strife and warfare. Clovis became a Christian, winning the support of many of his Romano-Gallic subjects, and he supported many

of the late Roman institutions, preserving their laws while interspersing them with his own Salian Frankish system of justice.

When he died in 511 the Merovingian kingdom was divided between his four sons. The Frankish heartland was Austrasia, the territory straddling the River Rhine, and stretching from Paris in the west to the River Main valley in the east. The divided Frankish lands were expanded by the sons, who incorporated Thuringia, Neustria (the new territories) and Burgundy. In 536 the Franks conquered Provence, extending their kingdom as far south as the Mediterranean Sea.

Later additions included Aquitaine, although this province spent some time as an independent state in the sixth and seventh centuries. In 562 the divided lands were further divided between the sons of Clothar I, the last surviving son of Clovis. What followed was a period of near-anarchy, where the brothers, their wives and offspring fought against each other, and frequently resorted to poison and assassination to improve their position. Some of these Merovingian characters appear larger than life, such as Queen Brunhilde, whose long reign was characterized by claims of witchcraft, murder, and intrigue. In AD 613 she was captured by a nephew, and dragged to death behind a horse. Her executioner, Clothar II, emerged as the sole surviving claimant to the Frankish kingdom. The last of the Merovingian kings to rule effectively was Clothar's son Dagobert, who died in 638. The Frankish kingdom appeared in danger of breaking up, as a series of weak Merovingian successors vied for power.

By 650, Frankish power lay in the hands of the nobility, presided over by the king's senior minister, the Mayor of the Palace. Under Dagobert, the hereditary post was held by Pepin of Landen. About 680 the post was given to Pepin's grandson, Pepin of Heristal, who ended a vicious civil war between Austrasia and Neustria by conquering both provinces in the name of his king. On his death in 714, his son Charles Martel became Mayor. Charles was a skilled soldier, and during his term he united the Frankish nobles by calling on them to fight, attacking Frisia to the north and Saxony to the east.

His remodeling of the Frankish army was significant in that he emphasized the use of armored cavalry, laying the seeds for the later development of the medieval knight. In 732 his army defeated the Moors at the Battle of Tours, saving Christian Europe from Muslim domination. When he died in 741, he was succeeded as Mayor by his son Pepin, who promptly deposed the last Merovingian puppet-king, Childeric III. King Pepin the Short (741-68) was anointed by the

Pope, emphasizing the strong links which had developed between Church and State in the Frankish kingdom of the Carolingian dynasty. Pepin worked closely with the Church to adopt the reforms proposed by St. Boniface, and encouraged the establishment of Benedictine monasteries inside his kingdom.

Charlemagne

When Pepin died in 768, he was succeeded by his two sons, Charles (768-814) and Carloman (768-771), who divided the kingdom according to Frankish custom. When Carloman died four years later, Charles ignored the claim of his brother's infant son and siezed control of the entire Frankish kingdom. King Charles was now Carolus *Magnus Rex*, the Great King, a title that developed into *Charlemagne*, or Charles the Great. The kingdom inherited by Charlemagne was a Christian one, surrounded by pagan or Muslim enemies. His achievement was to unify his lands, expand them through a series of brilliant military

conquests, and unite most of Europe under his leadership. His military, administrative, and legal achievements were recorded by his biographer Einhard, and are described in detail on page 22.

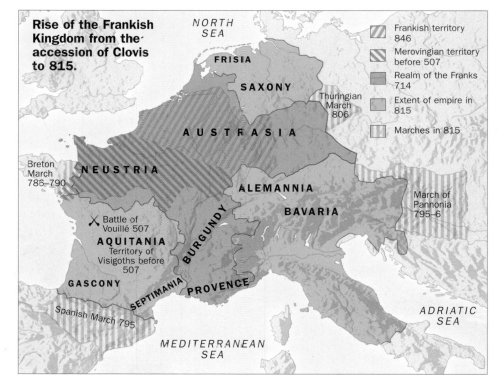

Rise of the Frankish Kingdom from the accession of Clovis to 815.

- Frankish territory 846
- Merovingian territory before 507
- Realm of the Franks 714
- Extent of empire in 815
- Marches in 815

NORTH SEA
FRISIA
SAXONY
Thuringian March 806
AUSTRASIA
Breton March 786–790
NEUSTRIA
ALEMANNIA
BAVARIA
March of Pannonia 795–6
BURGUNDY
✕ Battle of Vouillé 507
AQUITANIA Territory of Visigoths before 507
GASCONY
SEPTIMANIA
PROVENCE
Spanish March 795
ADRIATIC SEA
MEDITERRANEAN SEA

Byzantium Triumphant

The fall of the Roman Empire at the hands of barbarian invaders in the fifth century AD was only partial. The eastern part of the Empire survived intact, and established a new center at Byzantium (Constantinople). The Byzantine Empire saw itself as the successor to the Roman Empire and a bulwark against further invasions.

Even before Rome fell, the Empire had been divided for administrative purposes. Emperor Zeno (AD 474–91) became the first "Byzantine" Emperor. By 518 effective power was held by Justinian (527–65), who became the official emperor just over a decade later. For almost 50 years, Justinian remained dedicated to the reconquest of the Western Empire, and the restoration of Roman rule throughout the Mediterranean.

Justinian was not a military commander, but employed sound military tacticians to carry out his wishes. In 533 his general Belisarius recaptured the African provinces held by the barbarian Vandals. Two years later he landed in Sicily and captured the island, using it as a springboard for an invasion of the Italian peninsula. Rome was taken in 536 and, after enduring a two-year siege by the Ostrogoths, Belisarius left the city to conquer all of northern Italy.

In 540 the general was withdrawn to the east, and his successors continued the subjugation of the Goths. These Gothic wars all but ruined Italy, and by the mid-sixth century Rome was a ghost city. From that point on, Constantinople became the last bastion of the Roman Empire. The wars also strained the human and fiscal resources of the Byzantine Empire, and its troops were unable to prevent the conquest of most of Italy by the Lombards in 568. By the start of the seventh century, Byzantine power in Italy was confined to the far south and to Sicily.

From Roman to Byzantine

Justinian's administrative achievements outlasted his military successes. Together with his Empress, Theodora (a former prostitute), he reinforced the supremacy of an Imperial throne that had long been subject to damaging attacks from both the general population and the Byzantine nobility. He worked on the codification of Roman law, combining the *jus vetus* (old law) of the Roman Empire with the new, imposed by Imperial edict. In 528 his *Codex Justinianus* codified the body of *jus novum* (new law), and this was eventually followed by the *Digest*, with both bodies of law summarized in the legal manual of *Institutes*. Justinian's objective was to reinforce his own Imperial position by re-establishing the laws by which he governed. He was the last true Latin Emperor, and his successors were Greeks, influenced by Greek language and customs.

In the decades following Justinian's death, internal disputes weakened the emperor's authority, and the Eastern Roman Empire was attacked by fresh waves of invaders; Lombards from the west, Sassanid Persians from the east, and nomadic Slavs and Avars from the north. In the early seventh century Persians conquered Egypt and Palestine, while Avar raiding parties reached the walls of Byzantium. Under the Emperor Heraclius (610–41) the old borders were re-established, and the Persians were decisively defeated in battle (Niniveh, 627).

The Empire had survived relatively intact, maintaining its borders and the administrative

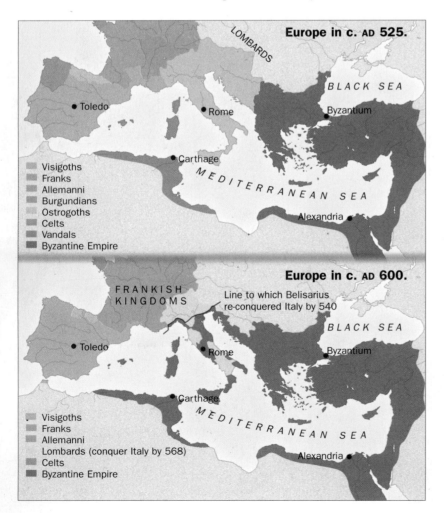

Europe in c. AD 525.

LOMBARDS

BLACK SEA

Byzantium

• Toledo

• Rome

• Carthage

MEDITERRANEAN SEA

Alexandria •

Visigoths
Franks
Allemanni
Burgundians
Ostrogoths
Celts
Vandals
Byzantine Empire

Europe in c. AD 600.

FRANKISH
KINGDOMS

Line to which Belisarius
re-conquered Italy by 540

BLACK SEA

Byzantium

• Toledo

• Rome

• Carthage

MEDITERRANEAN SEA

Alexandria •

Visigoths
Franks
Allemanni
Lombards (conquer Italy by 568)
Celts
Byzantine Empire

Left: A 14th-century mosaic by an unknown artist adorns the dome of a Byzantine church (now the Kariye Camii) in Istanbul (formerly Byzantium and then Constantinople). The mosaic depicts stories from the life of the Virgin Mary.

Below: A contemporary psalter shows Emperor Basilios II (976–1025) surrounded by angels, dressed in his armor and carrying sword and spear—head of Church and State.

institutions of the old Eastern Roman Empire. What changed following the death of Justinian was the virtual abandonment of the lands of the Western Roman Empire. It was deemed militarily impossible to reconquer these territories from the barbarians, and the largely Greek emperors now concentrated on protecting their own provinces. At this point it became a Byzantine Empire, not an Eastern Roman one.

By the mid-seventh century a distinctive form of Byzantine culture developed, founded on Hellenistic and Middle Eastern roots, which was reflected in all aspects of Byzantine civilization: art, architecture, administration, even economic and political practices. While western Europe united Germanic and surviving Roman culture, Byzantium looked eastward for inspiration. The large, complex bureaucracy was centered on the sanctified Emperor, ruler of both Church and State.

A thriving commerce ensured an opulence unknown in western Europe, and led to further patronage of the arts (principally in the form of mosaics and illuminated manuscripts), and the creation of masterpieces of church architecture. Greek theologians redefined the Christian faith as they saw it; and although the Roman Church grew apart from that of Byzantium, their influence dominated religious thought for much .of the early medieval period. While western Europe was trying to emerge from the Dark

Ages, Byzantium remained a stable, well-run, and culturally vibrant society.

The Spread of Islam

During the period of the Roman and early Byzantine Empires in the eastern Mediterranean, Arabia held no strategic importance. It formed a barrier between the lands of the Byzantine and Persian Empires; an inhospitable desert containing small trading cities and tribes of nomadic herdsmen. In the seventh century this dramatically changed with the birth of Islam.

The Prophet Mohammed (c.570–632) was born in what was then the small Arabian trading city of Mecca. About 615 he experienced a series of revelations that he took to be messages from God (Allah), and these were later recorded in the Koran, which became the holy book of the Muslim faith. This was a monotheistic religion, and had Old Testament roots. God communicated with mankind through a series of prophets, including Abraham, Moses, Christ, and Mohammed. It followed certain Judaic

Below: *Musicians and standard-bearers of a Saracen army on the march, from an Arabian manuscript.*

practices and included a Christian-style emphasis on works of charity. Mohammedan teachings said that the duty of mankind was to carry out the will of Allah. Failure to do so resulted in eternal damnation, while his faithful servants entered eternal heaven. Islamic followers were prepared to fight for their faith, and death in a *Jihad* (Holy War) ensured a place in heaven.

In 622, Mohammed was exiled from Mecca by the local authorities. This date marks the start of the Muslim calendar. The Prophet moved to Medina, converted its inhabitants, and became the local leader. By 630 Mohammed and his followers had conquered Mecca, and by his death in 632 the Prophet united most of Arabia under Islamic rule. During this period, secular and religious governments were combined into one, and all followers were subjects of the Prophet.

A series of caliphs (deputies, or successors) succeeded Mohammed, and Caliph Omar (634–644) launched a Jihad against the Byzantine province of Syria in the first year of his reign. The Byzantines were decisively defeated at Yarmuk (636) and by 640 the entire province was in Muslim hands, including the cities of Antioch, Jerusalem, and Damascus. In the following two years Egypt was added to the growing list of conquered territories. Military victories over the Persians extended Islamic rule into the fertile crescent of the Tigris and Euphrates rivers.

Under the Caliph Uthman (644–55) the unpopular Umayyad dynasty gained control, creating a religious and political split between supporters of Ali, the son-in-law of the Prophet and the aristocratic Umayyads, ending in the assassination of both rival leaders. Dissident Islamic groups which developed from the followers of Ali include the Shi'ite Muslims, but Umayyad dominance continued until the mid-eighth century. While these internal disputes temporarily slowed down the Arab conquests, the Islamic expansion continued

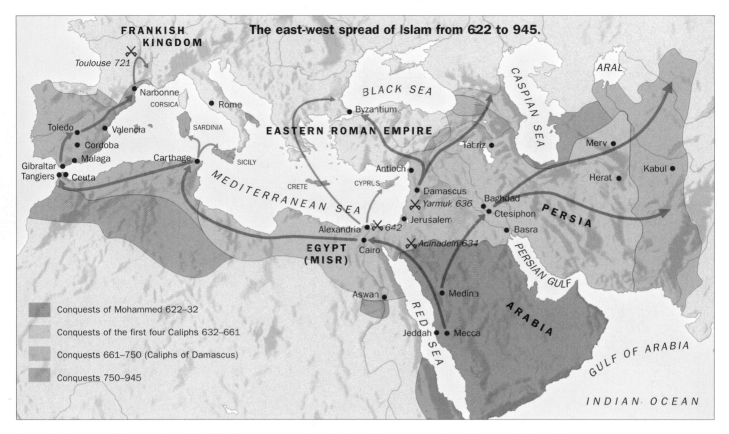

The east-west spread of Islam from 622 to 945.

Conquests of Mohammed 622–32

Conquests of the first four Caliphs 632–661

Conquests 661–750 (Caliphs of Damascus)

Conquests 750–945

through the rest of the century. By 650 the Persian Empire had fallen to the Muslims, and the holy warriors continued even further east, reaching the Indus River, the border of India. By the end of the Umayyad dynasty in 750, the eastern border of Islam extended north along the Indus valley to the level of the Aral Sea, in the heart of Central Asia.

Dynamic expansion

Further to the west, the Islamic armies continued to attack the eastern provinces of the Byzantine Empire. Cyprus was captured by an Arab amphibious invasion in 649, and the Byzantine provinces in North Africa fell in quick succession; Libya in 642 and Tripolitania in 647. By the time Caliph Uthman was assassinated in 655, the entire eastern and southern Mediterranean coast from Antioch to Tripoli was in Muslim hands. While in the period from 661 to 750 there were only minor increases in Umayyad territory in Central Asia and along the border of Asia Minor, the most spectacular gains were in the western Mediterranean.

Muslim conquests continued along the African coast during the latter half of the seventh century, as Arab armies pushed into the Magreb region of what is now Tunisia and Algeria. At first, the native Bedouin tribesmen opposed the invaders, but in time they converted to Islam and joined in the Jihad themselves. The leading Byzantine city of Carthage fell in 698, and within a decade the Muslims controlled the entire North African coastline of the Mediterranean, and were poised to cross over into Spain. A raid into the Byzantine Empire from 673–78 was stopped short of Constantinople and an uneasy truce led to the relative stabilization of the Byzantine-Muslim border by the early eighth century.

In less than a century, the Islamic caliphs had carved out an empire stretching from India to the Atlantic, and their leadership had been proved in a series of brilliant conquests followed by effective administration of the new territories. Further expansion could only occur at the expense of the struggling states of western Europe.

Below: *The first half of the first Sura of the Koran, from a manuscript dating from the 16th century.*

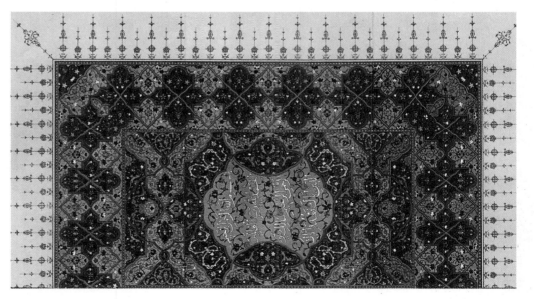

The Moorish Conquest of Spain

In the early fifth century, the Roman province of Spain was conquered by Visigoth barbarians. Visigoths continued to rule Spain for three centuries, until the tide of Islamic conquest reached their shores. In AD 711 an Arab army crossed from Africa and conquered most of Spain, ushering in a period of peace and prosperity for the peninsula.

For more than seven centuries the Iberian Peninsula had been the Roman province of Hispania. In AD 409, Visigoth barbarians crossed the Pyrenees and conquered Spain within a decade. For the next three centuries it remained the Kingdom of the Visigoths. In AD 507 the Franks in turn conquered Visigoth territory north of the Pyrenees, but south of this mountain range the Visigoths thrived, acting as overlords while maintaining the existing form of Hispanic-Romano government they had found when they first arrived. Under the reign of King Leovigild

(568–86), Visigothic rule was extended into northwestern Spain; a territory that had been held by the Germanic Suevi people since the collapse of Roman rule. Leovigild also contained a Byzantine invasion of southern Spain, and established a permanent capital in Toledo.

Much of southern Spain was Christian and, under King Recared (AD 586–601), the Visigoths adopted Christianity. This instituted a period of close co-operation between Church and State in Spain, and significant legal improvements were made, particularly under King Receswinth (649–72). One great weakness of the kingdom was the lack of a system of succession. During a divisive feud over succession in 711, Arab (Moorish) armies crossed from North Africa and landed in Spain. The place where the Berber Moorish commander, Tariq ibn Ziyad, landed was named *Jebel Tariq* (Mount Tariq). Today the name has evolved into Gibraltar.

The Moors defeated the Visigoths in open

The Moorish conquest of Spain from 711 to 732.

Between 409–20, the Visigoths invaded Roman Spain across the Pyrenees. After their defeat at the hands of the Merovingians at the battle of Vouillé in 507, the Visigoths were pushed into the Spanish peninsula.

Land conquered by Visigoths, 409–420

Frankish conquests to 507

Land conquered by Moors from Visigoths and Franks, 711–732

ATLANTIC OCEAN

ASTURIAS

FRANKISH KINGDOM

Tours

732 Second Moorish wave defeated at Tours

778–814 Frankish invasions held off by Moors

EMIRATE OF CORDOBA
(FORMERLY VISIGOTHIC KINGDOM)

Toulouse

Toledo

714 Moors take Toledo

721 Moors cross Pyrenees, turned back at Toulouse

Nimes

Narbonne

Seville

711 Moors take Jerez

Cordoba

711 Moors take Cordoba

711 Moors take Gibraltar

Tangiers

Gibraltar

Ceuta

Valencia

MEDITERRANEAN SEA

IBIZA Captured by Moors from Byzantine Empire in 798

MAJORCA

MINORCA Both captured by Moors from Byzantine Empire in 903

AFRICA

battle at Jerez (711) near Seville, and fanned out to the north, capturing Cordoba and making it the Moorish capital of Spain. By 714, the Islamic invaders had captured Toledo and had pushed the Visigoths north into the mountains along Spain's northern coast. The Moors were never able to completely eradicate the Visigoth toehold in Spain, which became known as the Kingdom of Asturias from the mid-eighth century. Elsewhere, the Moors consolidated their hold over the conquered Spanish territories, which became the Emirate of Cordoba.

In 720 the Moors crossed the Pyrenees into the Kingdom of the Franks and, although they were defeated at Toulouse (721), they managed to establish control over Frankish lands south of the city. In 732, after some success, a second Moorish drive was halted when a Frankish army under Charles Martel defeated the Muslims at Tours (732). Tours marked the greatest penetration of Islam into Europe. The Moors were forced back into Spain, and an uneasy peace settled over the region.

Spain's integration

Inside the Emirate, religious tolerance and a benign government led to a slow process of assimilation. Spanish merchants traded extensively throughout the Mediterranean Muslim ports and, after Islamic troops captured Sicily, Sardinia, and Corsica in the mid-ninth century, the safety of Arab sea trade was assured. Under Charlemagne (771–814), the Carolingian Franks made several incursions into the Emirate of Cordoba, one of which (in 778) led to the engagement at the Pass of Roncavalles that was celebrated in the medieval poem, *The Song of Roland*.

Divisions within the Arab Empire led to the Umayyad Emir Abd-er-Rahmann ibn Mu'awiya breaking away to make the Emirate of Cordoba independent in 756, when Umayyad dynastic control ended elsewhere in the Empire. The Abbasid dynasty, which gained control of the Arab kingdoms, moved their capital to Baghdad, and left Moorish Spain to its own fate.

The eighth and ninth centuries were a time of relative stability for Spain. Those who remained Christians were known as Mozarabs, and were allowed to practice their religion in peace, as was the sizeable Jewish population. These minorities survived, but most people converted to Islam. Centers of learning spread through Spain where Arabic, Greek, Roman, and Persian works were studied. It was a period of prosperity, borne on the back of Mediterranean trade, and as the Spanish coastal cities such as Valencia grew so did the prosperity of the Spanish population. This period of peace continued until the start of the 11th century, when religious fervor in Christian Europe led to a new wave of attacks on Moorish Spain.

Above: *Throughout Spain the Moorish inheritance is clearly visible. This is the Mezquita Cathedral, formerly an Arabic mosque, in Cordoba.*

Below: *The votive crown of Visigothic King Suintila (621–631).*

FOCUS: RELIGION
The Survival of Christianity

Following the fall of the Western Roman Empire, the fate of Christianity hung in the balance. By the fifth and sixth centuries AD, a resurgent papacy and the work of Celtic missionaries saved the religion from extinction.

Opposite page:
Gregory I, the Great, Pope and Saint, is depicted seated at his writing desk, from an ivory panel carved at the end of the tenth century

Below: *an illuminated page from the beautiful Celtic* Book of Kells, *written in Ireland c.650–90.*

The Eastern Roman Empire provided a safe haven for the Byzantine Church, which was already evolving along different lines to the Roman one. The Pope saw himself as the successor of St. Peter, while the Byzantine Emperor was head of both the Byzantine Church and its State. Theological conflict was inevitable, and Imperial attempts at providing all-embracing solutions were singularly unsuccessful. For the next 60 years, popes and emperors fought for supremacy, and the emperor supported his rhetoric with action; exiling some popes and replacing them with his own supporters. This was set against a swirl of barbarian invasion, settlement, and warfare in the Italian peninsula, culminating in the Lombard conquest of Italy in 568.

In 590, Pope Gregory I the Great (590–604)

was elected, and almost single-handedly saved the Roman Church. While maintaining his distance from the emperor, he attempted to re-establish the authority of Rome over the scattered remains of the Church in western Europe. In 597 he sent a mission to England to convert the Saxons, allegedly after seeing Anglo-Saxon child slaves in Rome. Gregory, who saw himself as a teacher, popularized the doctrines of St. Augustine and wrote his *Book of Pastoral Care*, which laid down the responsibilities of priests and bishops within the structure of the Roman Church. He constructed a framework that allowed the Church to survive in the turmoil of a barbarian and pagan Europe.

The ecclesiastical framework that already existed was badly damaged during the barbarian invasions, and Christianity survived in western Europe largely as a result of the work of monks and monasteries; isolated islands of religion in a pagan sea. The first monasteries arose in Egypt, and these early hermetic desert outposts developed in the fourth century into monastic communes under the guidance of St. Pachomius and St. Basil. During the sixth century, St. Benedict (480–543) established a monastic community at Monte Cassino, to the south of Rome. In 520 he wrote his *Holy Rule* for fellow monks, emphasizing poverty, chastity, and obedience. His rigidly structured monastic system became the basis for the Benedictine Order.

Celtic Christianity

A distinctly separate development was the Celtic Church, a body that did much to ensure the survival of Christianity through monasticism and missionary work. At the same time as the Celts in Britain were being driven back into the Scottish and Welsh mountains by the barbarian invaders, missionaries such as St. Patrick (c.390–461) ensured that the Celts embraced Christianity.

Monastic life in the Celtic centers was primitive, but their monks produced some of the finest manuscript work of the age, linking traditional Celtic art with the new religion to produce illuminations for works such as the Irish *Book of Kells*. In 563, St. Columba (521–615)

410	411	453
Rome is sacked, marking the end of the Western Roman Empire	St. Augustine describes Rome as the "City of God"	Attila the Hun dies

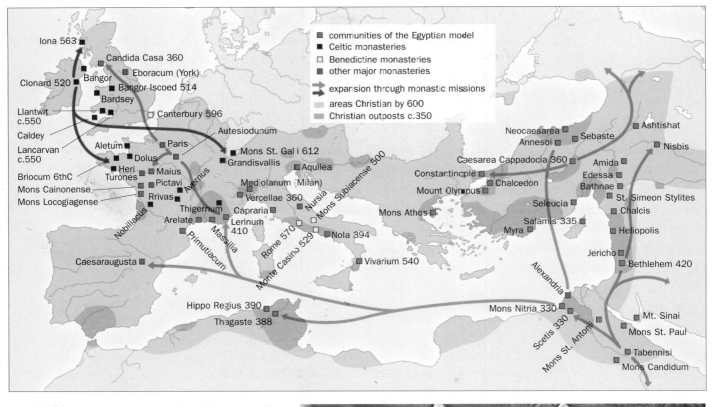

established a monastery on the Scottish island of Iona, and his conversion of the Pictish (early Scottish) kings led to further missionary work by his disciples in England, Burgundy, and among the Saxon English. This work by Celtic missionaries from Ireland and Scotland led to a wave of fresh monasteries in western Europe, and the conversion of the entire population. By the time the authority of the Roman Church and the monastic order of the Benedictines reached the Franks, Saxons, and Goths, much of the spiritual groundwork had already been accomplished.

During the seventh century the Roman Church established its own system of regional ecclesiastical centers in France and England, and in 664 at the Synod of Whitby, the Celtic Church elected to align itself with that of Rome. While the Benedictine monks provided centers of religious order and contemplation, Celtic monks converted the peasantry of the continent, and handed over their converts to Rome. By the eighth century, the Church in western Europe was strong enough to survive the chaos brought about by Frankish civil wars and the anarchy and lawlessness that occurred in its wake. Similarly, although most monastic settlements in Britain, Ireland, and northwest France were devastated by the Vikings, the popular Christianity these centers helped to create ensured the survival of organized religion in Europe.

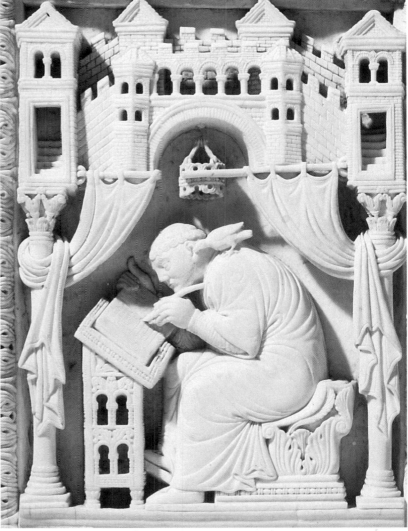

507	520	528	536	537	563	568	570
Franks conquer Visigoth territories outside Spain	St. Benedict writes his *Holy Rule*	The Emperor Justinian revises Roman law	The Byzantine general Belisarius captures Rome	The Church of St. Sophia is completed in Byzantium	St. Columba establishes a Celtic monastery at Iona, Scotland	The Lombards conquer Italy	Mohammed is born

Charlemagne The Great

During the late eighth century, the Frankish kingdom was ruled by King Charles the Great, or "Charlemagne." A series of brilliant conquests extended his rule from the Pyrenees to the River Elbe, and from Italy to the North Sea. In the process he created an empire and provided the stability that European civilization needed to develop. His administrative and religious reforms laid the groundwork for the medieval states that were to follow, and helped earn Charlemagne his posthumous reputation as "the founder of Europe."

Below: *While few visual references to Charlemagne are known, we do have his marble throne in the Palatine Chapel of Aachen Cathedral; an impressively plain seat for the great monarch.*

King Charles (768–814) was the son of Pepin III the Short (741–68) and was 26 when he acquired half his father's realm. Power was shared with his brother Carloman, and relations between the two young kings were strained until Carloman's death in 771. Carloman's family fled into exile in Lombardy, and Charles took control of the entire Frankish kingdom, becoming *Carolus Magnus* (Charlemagne, or Charles the Great). In 773, Charlemagne conquered

Lombardy, captured his brother's family and safeguarded both the Papal State and his own southern border.

Charlemagne's life was dominated by what amounted to a crusade against his pagan and Moorish neighbors, particularly the Saxons beyond the River Rhine. Saxon raids conducted while Charlemagne was fighting the Lombards in Italy provided the excuse he needed to launch an all-out invasion. In 775 he returned to Saxony and began what was to be a decade of fighting, which ended in the complete subjugation of the Saxons and their conversion to Christianity. The Saxons proved to be tough opponents, and Charlemagne had to resort to brutal tactics, massacring thousands of Saxon prisoners in 782, and destroying all traces of their pagan religion. In 785 King Widukind of the Saxons surrendered to Charlemagne and adopted Christianity.

Charlemagne was described by his biographer Einhard as being a tall, powerful man, who was a skilled soldier, hunter, and administrator. He was also a singularly forceful man, capable of dominating his nobles and warriors with ease. He had a great admiration for learning, and under his patronage a standard form of script was adopted, which became known as "Carolingian miniscule." It was used extensively in early medieval annals, manuscripts, and records from the late eighth century onward.

Determined reformer

He issued *Capitularies* or instructions, which standardized his form of government, and enforced his bureaucratic reforms through a class of royal administrators, the *Missi Dominici*. Church reforms were also encouraged; monasteries were founded, theological points clarified in the *Libri Carolini*, and the supremacy of the Church in Rome emphasized rather than the older Gallo-Celtic Christian institutions.

Charlemagne's religious views

590	622
Pope Gregory elected, and reforms the Church	Mohammed exiled from Mecca

encouraged his campaigns against his non-Christian neighbors. In 778 he led an army into Spain to fight the Muslims, a campaign that produced a reversal at the Pass of Roncesvalles, immortalized in the *Song of Roland*. A further foray into Spain was launched in 809.

A conquest of Brittany was followed by a campaign against his cousin, Duke Tassilo of Bavaria (742–94). Tassilo was defeated and accepted Charlemagne as his king, then promptly revolted again. This time he was assisted by the pagan Avars, a nomadic Asiatic people who had settled in what is now Austria after being driven west by the Turks. By 796, Charlemagne had conquered both the Bavarians and their Avar allies. For the next 18 years, he continued to push back the eastern Frankish frontier, campaigning against the tribes beyond the River Elbe and the Czechs of Bohemia.

In 799 a revolt broke out in Rome, and Charlemagne marched south to restore Pope Leo III (795–816) to power. As a reward, Charlemagne was crowned as Roman Emperor (Carolus Augustus) in St. Peter's on Christmas Day, 800. Einhard claimed that the coronation was unsolicited by Charlemagne, partly since it implied Papal superiority over the Frankish king. This was a recognition of his achievements in reuniting Europe under the Church, and the power it embodied set him apart from all who went before, or after. This new Roman Empire

was the forerunner of the Holy Roman Empire of the 12th century.

During his last decade, Charlemagne strengthened the security of his frontiers by creating border *marches*, or fortified military districts, and reorganizing his Carolingian army into a powerful mobile force. His administrative system of issuing *capitularies* and *missi dominici* provided control of both ecclesiastical and temporal matters. This was augmented by a class of regional royal administrators called *grafs* (counts), each responsible for a particular *comitatus* (county).

Improved administration led to an increase in income through taxation. By the end of his reign, Charlemagne's capital at Aachen was home to scholars, craftsmen, and leading churchmen, prompting the cultural movement known as the Carolingian Renaissance. This patronage did much to ensure the survival of classical manuscripts and the creation of new religious structures. By the time of his death in 814, Charlemagne had transformed Europe from a fractious collection of warring states into a unified entity.

Left: *This illustration is taken from the bronze equestrian statue of Charlemagne at Metz, and it was originally gilded. The oldest known representation of the emperor, it is probably not an accurate likeness. He holds an orb in one hand, and the other probably held a scepter. In the background is his royal cipher, an abbreviated form of the Latin "Karolus," which he used to authorize documents. Charlemagne was well educated and spoke Latin as well as understanding Greek.*

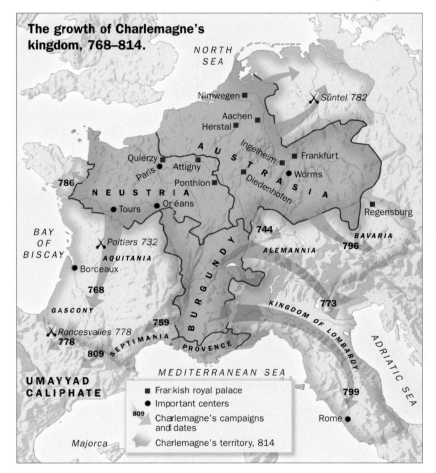

The growth of Charlemagne's kingdom, 768–814.

NORTH SEA

Nimwegen ■
Aachen ■
Herstal ■
✕ Süntel 782
Quierzy ● Attigny
Ingelheim ● Frankfurt
Paris ● Ponthion ■ ● Worms
786 Diedenhofen
NEUSTRIA
● Tours ● Orléans
744
Regensburg
BAY OF BISCAY
✕ Poitiers 732
AQUITANIA
BAVARIA
ALEMANNIA 796
● Borceaux
768
BURGUNDY
773
GASCONY
759
KINGDOM OF LOMBARDY
✕ Roncesvalles 778
778
809 SEPTIMANIA
PROVENCE
ADRIATIC SEA
UMAYYAD CALIPHATE
MEDITERRANEAN SEA
799
Rome ●

■ Frankish royal palace
● Important centers
809 Charlemagne's campaigns and dates
➤ Charlemagne's territory, 814

Majorca

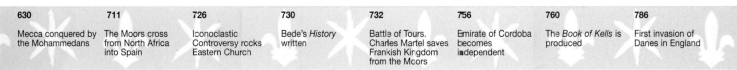

630	711	726	730	732	756	760	786
Mecca conquered by the Mohammedans	The Moors cross from North Africa into Spain	Iconoclastic Controversy rocks Eastern Church	Bede's *History* written	Battle of Tours. Charles Martel saves Frankish Kingdom from the Moors	Emirate of Cordoba becomes independent	The *Book of Kells* is produced	First invasion of Danes in England

23

FOCUS: WARFARE

The West Besieged: Vikings and Magyars

A divided Frankish Empire was unable to prevent the devastation caused by waves of barbarian invaders attacking Europe from all sides during the ninth century. The most catastrophic attacks were launched by the Scandinavian Vikings (or Norsemen), and for a time it seemed as if Christian Europe would be unable to survive.

Below: *A Viking rune stone c. AD 1000, from the region of Copenhagen.*

Following the death of Charlemagne in 814, the Frankish Empire passed intact to his son, who became Louis the Pious (814–40). Louis was an educated monarch, but no soldier like his father, and maintaining the unity of the Empire by force seemed beyond him. When Louis died in 840, a three-year civil war ended in stalemate, and the brothers Charles the Bald, Lothair, and Louis the German divided the Empire between them, following lines of linguistic division. King Lothair died in 855, and his middle kingdom was divided between the two surviving brothers.

This lack of unity came at a critical time for Europe. During the ninth century the Frankish Empire came under increasing attacks from waves of invaders; first the Muslims to the south, then the Vikings (or Norsemen) from the north and west, and finally the Magyars from the east. By the mid-ninth century the threat of a Moorish invasion from Spain had subsided, but elsewhere Muslim raiders threatened Italy and southern France. In 827 the Moors landed in Sicily and began a conquest of the island

that would last a decade. Other expeditions captured Sardinia, Corsica, and the Balearic Islands. Although Spain remained the only lasting Muslim territory on the European mainland, raiders threatened Rome in 846–50 while the Franks were distracted by civil war, and a Muslim army occupied the Rhône Estuary in 890.

The Viking era begins

An even more devastating series of raids began along the northern shores of the Frankish Empire from the late eighth century. In 787, Viking raiders first appeared off the English Saxon coast, and by the end of the century the Vikings had pillaged coastal monasteries such as Iona and Lindisfarne, settled in the northern isles of Scotland, and conquered much of eastern Ireland.

In 814 Viking fleets raided as far south as the estuary of the River Loire. For the next 50 years, summer brought Viking raids in western Europe that devastated coastal communities and caused mayhem. Often these Viking bands were small; the crew of a mere handful of longboats. In 841, during the crisis of Frankish succession, a large Viking fleet sailed up the River Seine and plundered Rouen. A similar fate befell the Gallo-Frankish city of Nantes, at the mouth of the River Loire. Not only were these expeditions far larger than before, but this time the Vikings stayed over the winter.

In 844 the Viking fleet plundered far up the Loire and Garonne rivers, then ravaged the northern coast of Spain. Moorish Spain also felt the brunt of Viking attacks, and the same expedition sacked the city of Seville. By 860, most cities in northeastern France had been sacked, and Viking raiders had entered the Mediterranean, wintering in the Rhône estuary. Paris was spared from capture after a lengthy siege by a relief force led by Charles "the Fat" (884–87), but this was the exception.

A period of consolidation followed. Viking raiders had conquered and settled northeastern England, despite the resistance of the Saxon king Alfred (871–99), and in 911 the Viking leader Rollo was granted lands in what would become

792	800	907	911	955	964	1014	1016–35
Viking raiders attack Lindisfarne monastery on the English coast	Charlemagne proclaimed Roman Emperor	The Magyars enter Germany	The Duchy of Normandy is created by the French king	Battle of Lechfeld ends Magyar threat to western Europe	First record of mining in Germany's Harz mountains	The Danes conquer England	Cnut reigns in England, Denmark, and Norway

Normandy. As the raids subsided, a process of assimilation led to the re-establishment of the Carolingian status-quo, although the Norsemen retained control of much of Scotland and parts of Ireland for the next few centuries.

Just as these attacks were abating, a fresh wave of nomadic invaders attacked the East Frankish State (Germany). In 895 the Magyar people from central Asia arrived in what is now Hungary, where they joined with the remnants of the Avars. In about 900 they swept up the Danube valley into Bavaria, pillaging and looting as they went. Over the next 30 years Magyar raids devastated Saxony and Thuringia, and even crossed the River Rhine, sacking Reims in 937. These attacks were slowly contained by East Frankish forces, and in 955 Magyar power was crushed at the Battle of Lechfeld. The only beneficial outcome from all these raids was the realization that society had to reorganize itself for its own protection. The result was the introduction of the feudal system.

Above: *Although the iron components of this Viking sword have corroded, the ornate silver and gold work bear testimony to the Norsemen's cultural development.*

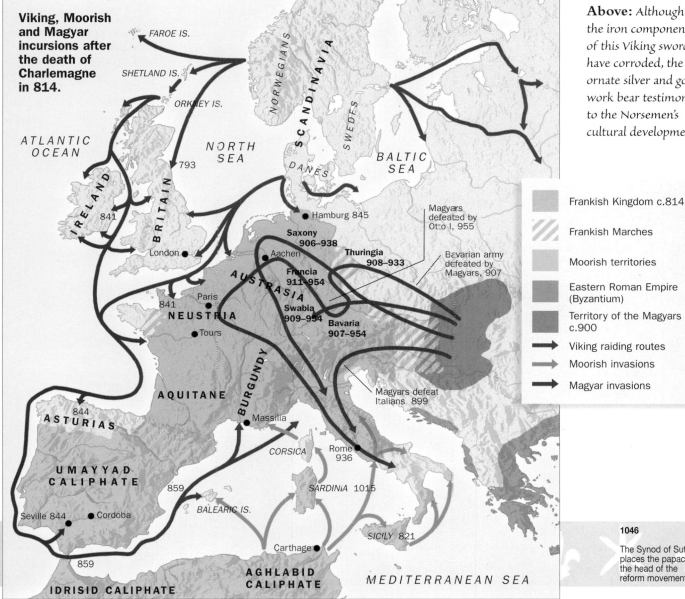

Viking, Moorish and Magyar incursions after the death of Charlemagne in 814.

Frankish Kingdom c.814

Frankish Marches

Moorish territories

Eastern Roman Empire (Byzantium)

Territory of the Magyars c.900

→ Viking raiding routes

→ Moorish invasions

→ Magyar invasions

FAROE IS.
SHETLAND IS.
ORKNEY IS.
ATLANTIC OCEAN
NORWEGIANS
SCANDINAVIA
SWEDES
NORTH SEA
793
DANES
BALTIC SEA
IRELAND
841
BRITAIN
London
Hamburg 845
Magyars defeated by Otto I, 955
Saxony 906–938
Aachen
Thuringia 908–933
Bavarian army defeated by Magyars, 907
AUSTRASIA
Francia 911–954
Paris
841
Swabia 909–954
Bavaria 907–954
NEUSTRIA
Tours
BURGUNDY
Magyars defeat Italians 899
844
ASTURIAS
AQUITANE
Massilia
CORSICA
Rome 936
UMAYYAD CALIPHATE
859
SARDINIA 1015
BALEARIC IS.
Seville 844 Cordoba
SICILY 821
Carthage
859
AGHLABID CALIPHATE
MEDITERRANEAN SEA
IDRISID CALIPHATE

1046

The Synod of Sutri places the papacy at the head of the reform movement

CHAPTER TWO

NORTH SEA

SCOTLAND

IRELAND

NORTHUMBRIA

Stamford Bridge

EAST
ANGLIA

MERCIA

WALES

ESSEX

WESSEX

KENT

Hastings

CORNWALL

ENGLISH CHANNEL

1066

BAY OF BISCAY

DUCHY OF
LOWER
LORRAINE

DUCHY OF
FRANCONIA

COUNTY OF
FLANDERS

DUCHY OF
UPPER
LORRAINE

Paris

COUNTY OF
CHAMPAGNE

DUCHY OF
SWABIA

DUCHY OF
NORMANDY

MAINE

DUCHY OF
BRITTANY

ANJOU

POITOU

DUCHY OF
BURGUNDY

COUNTY
OF
BURGUNDY

DUCHY OF AQUITAINE

AUVERGNE

COUNTY
OF
ROUERGE

COUNTY OF
PROVENCE

COUNTY
OF
TOULOUSE

MARCH
OF GOTHIA

DUCHY OF
GASCONY

NAVARRE

ARAGON

COUNTY OF
BARCELONA

The Norman Achievement

I n the early 10th century, a Viking named Rollo was granted control of the lands around the mouth of the River Seine by the French king. His Viking settlers extended their territory to the west, creating a new and extensive province. The region was given the name of Normandy, "land of the Northmen" (or Vikings). By the start of the 11th century, the Dukes of Normandy controlled a duchy that stretched along much of the French coast; a region that was nominally part of the Kingdom of France, but which was in most respects an independent state.

Normandy was not particularly prosperous, and many Norman nobles encouraged their sons to become adventurers: young Norman knights who served as mercenaries throughout Europe. Although Norman adventurers served from Scotland to Hungary during the century, these mercenaries made their most significant mark in Italy. At first acting as mercenaries, the Norman knights began to operate for their own gain, carving out and expanding feudal domains based on the Norman model. By the end of the 11th century these men had created the Norman Kingdom of Sicily, encompassing the southern Italian mainland as well as the island itself.

In 1066, Duke William of Normandy led an army across the English Channel and into Anglo-Saxon England, where his troops defeated the English in pitched battle and won the kingdom. The conquest of England was one of the most daring military operations of the medieval age, and was only overshadowed by the skill with which William the Conqueror established Norman authority over his new territories.

By the end of the 11th century Norman noblemen maintained a firm grip over both England and Sicily, and were busy creating a third kingdom in the Middle East. The "Norman achievement" is a term that has been applied to both their military and their social and economic successes. In addition to conquering new lands, the Normans adapted French feudalism, then applied the Norman model to these new territories. The century that encompassed these achievements, and their knights' domination of warfare, can truly be described as The Norman Century.

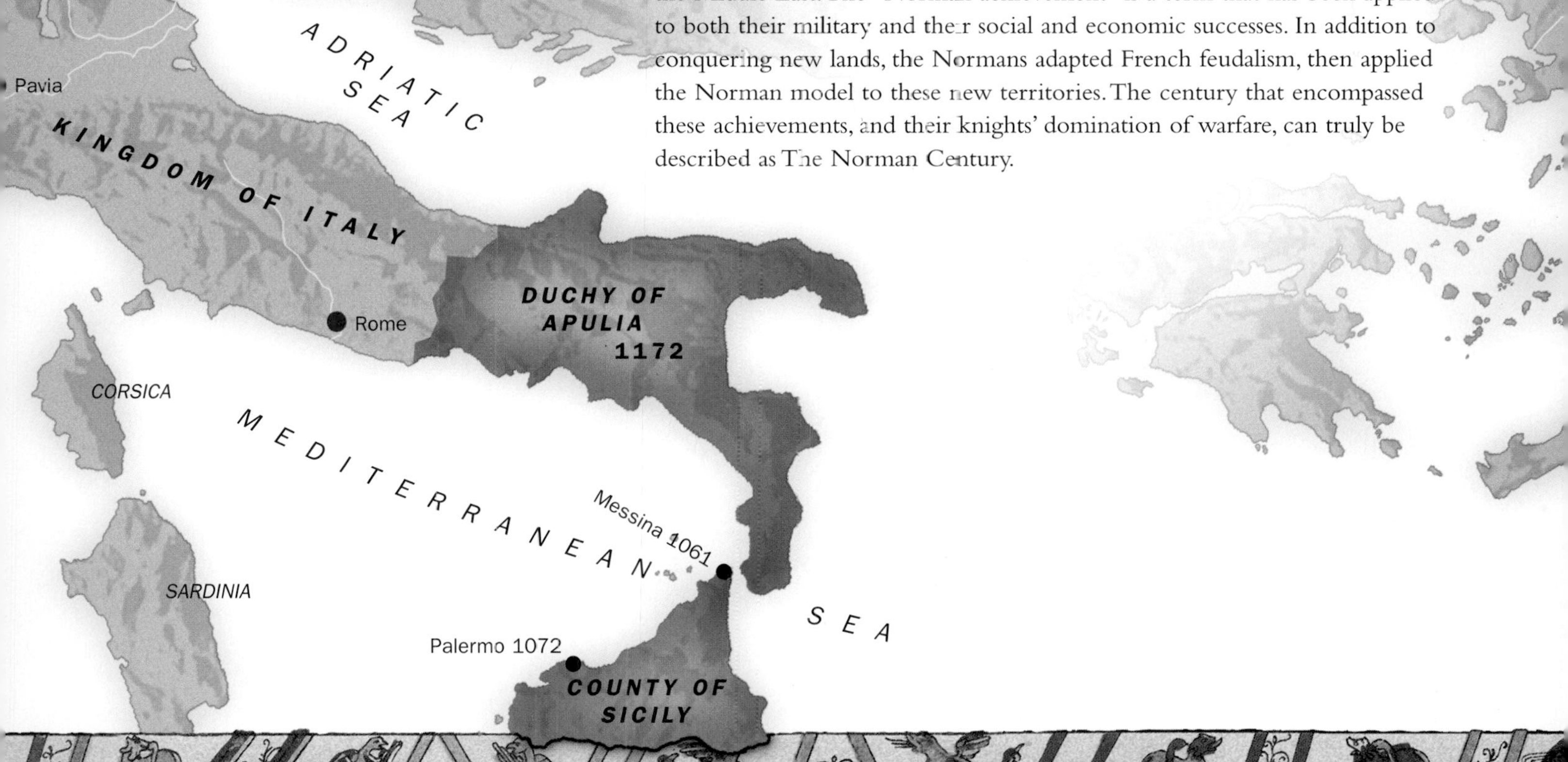

Pavia

ADRIATIC SEA

KINGDOM OF ITALY

DUCHY OF APULIA 1172

Rome

CORSICA

MEDITERRANEAN

Messina 1061

SARDINIA

SEA

Palermo 1072

COUNTY OF SICILY

The Norman State in France

The region of France that became Normandy was originally populated by Gallo-Romans, and after the fall of the Western Roman Empire by Frankish settlers and their overlords. During the early Carolingian period the region formed the administrative province of the ecclesiastical See of Rouen, and by the late ninth century Vikings had begun to establish bases and settlements in the region. In 911 a Norseman named Rollo was recognized by King Charles III of France as the overlord of eastern Normandy.

Facing: *A partial view with a peel tower of Falaise Castle in Normandy. Former palace to the Dukes of Normandy, Falaise was, in 1028, the birthplace of William the Conqueror.*

By AD 923 Rollo had extended his control to include the western part of the province, renamed Normandy in French accounts. His successors turned Rouen into a flourishing trading center, and extended the borders of the province into Brittany to the west. Even as late as the early 11th century the Normans were still regarded as Scandinavians but, unlike their northern ancestors, they adopted a feudal system to ensure their firm control of the duchy.

During the tenth century the Duchy of Normandy prospered, while the feudal retinue of dukes and their vassals became increasingly proficient in battle through the practice offered by border disputes and minor rebellions. Ducal authority was more pronounced in Normandy than in other regions of France, and a rebellion against teenaged Duke William the Bastard's growing authority was crushed in 1047. William realized that his lesser knights and nobles were eager for power, and Normandy itself was one of the less wealthy regions of France.

Previous dukes had solved the problem by allowing their knights to campaign in the Mediterranean as mercenaries, and by the mid-11th century they had created a new kingdom, independent from the Norman realm in northern Europe. An even greater opportunity presented itself to William the Bastard in 1066 that provided the opportunity to supply his nobles with a whole new country to administer. The Norman invasion of England succeeded through a combination of luck, military superiority, and superb organization. Duke William's vassals and allies were awarded tracts of land, and replicated the Norman feudal system in England, albeit modified to create fortified borders with Wales and Scotland. The illegitimate son of Duke Robert became King William I of England, while retaining his ducal title to Normandy.

A Channel bridge

He still remained a vassal of the French king, Philip I (1060–1108), and his semi-autonomous position was safeguarded by the support of Pope Alexander II (1061–73). This support reflected what was to become a close relationship between the Norman rulers of England, Normandy, and the Church. As a virtually independent ruler, William the Conqueror was free to develop relations with other neighboring rulers, and an alliance with the adjacent Duchy of Brittany brought this province also under Norman rule.

The authority of the French Capetian Kings reached its lowest point during the reign of Philip I, where the Dukes of Normandy, Burgundy, Aquitaine, and Gascony all operated almost autonomously. These nobles were technically vassals of the Crown, but their feudal obligations were minimal. The Capetians were also Dukes of France (the Île de France, centered on Paris), which remained their sole area of effective control for more than a century

This decentralized state continued until the reign of Philip II Augustus (1180–1223), who defeated the rebel Count of Flanders at Bouvines (1214), and then the provinces of Anjou, Normandy, and parts of Aquitaine passed directly to the French Crown by right of military conquest. For all of the 12th century, the Duchy of Normandy was an Anglo-Norman possession, together with the adjacent provinces of Brittany, Maine, and Anjou, which were effectively under Norman control (as were Scotland and Wales). Although William the Conqueror had become King of England, the political situation he left behind in France was divisive, and became the direct cause of centuries of Anglo-French rivalry and conflict.

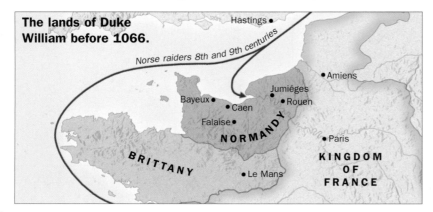

The lands of Duke William before 1066.

Norse raiders 8th and 9th centuries

Hastings
Amiens
Jumiéges
Bayeux
Rouen
Caen
Falaise
NORMANDY
Paris
BRITTANY
Le Mans
KINGDOM OF FRANCE

Origins of the Feudal System

The collapse of Charlemagne's Frankish Empire and the invasions by Magyars, Moors, and Vikings all contributed to a change in the social order of western Europe. In order to survive, the Franks developed a social and military system that offered them comprehensive protection against external threat. This structure is now known as the feudal system.

Feudalism is a term created by modern historians to describe a social system based on the Latin word *feudum* or *fief* (estate). A fief was a parcel of land held by an individual in return for his allegiance and military commitment to a feudal superior. There is no evidence that the Europeans of the 11th century even gave it a name, since it was so familiar and natural to them.

Many of the roots of feudalism can be traced back to the barbarian invasions during the last years of the Western Roman Empire, and to the subsequent period of Germanic settlement. The holding of a parcel of land in return for certain obligations was common under Roman law (the *benefice* system of tenure), while the fealty of

sworn vassals to their superiors was a Germanic tribal tradition. Feudalism simply amalgamated the two practices.

The feudal system was based around military service. Unlike most other European peoples, the Carolingian Franks made extensive use of cavalry. These mounted warriors needed to have the resources to supply horses, armor, and equipment, and were required to devote most of their time to military service. The eighth-century Frankish monarch Charles Martel granted his cavalrymen *benefices* in return for their sworn allegiance to him. This created the *vassi dominici* (vassals of the lord), or the forerunners of medieval knights.

Following the disintegration of the Carolingian Empire and the civil wars and barbarian invasions that ensued, military protection became a vital prerequisite for survival. Many of the more prominent *vassi dominici* commanded their own bands of troops, and post-Carolingian rulers hired these bands to protect their lands against attack by external invaders or rival claimants to the throne. They were paid in grants of royal land, made using the

Below: *The Banquet—this illustration from an 11th-century psalter shows three lords being served a feast by their squires or pages.*

benifice system. The large armies of the Carolingian heyday were unable to survive the disintegration of central power, and were too unwieldy to respond rapidly to Viking raids or Magyar incursions. This inevitably led to a decentralization of military power, devolving from royal hands into those of the leading warlords. The nature of this local military power was directly responsible for the rapid spread of feudalism.

Feudal hierarchy

In the ninth and tenth centuries, a farmer or villager lacked the means to defend his own lands, so he sought the protection of a knight, in exchange for the loss of his freeholding status. Serfdom of this kind ensured protection and survival. These petty knights were unable to defend against larger incursions, so they in turn surrendered the lands they acquired to a more powerful warlord. The lord granted the lands back to the knight, who became his vassal.

This continued upward: a villager became the serf of a knight; the knight became the vassal of a more powerful man (possibly a baron); he owed allegiance to a provincial warlord (possibly a count), who in his turn became the vassal of an even more powerful lord (possibly a duke). This top tier in theory comprised the vassals of the king, but for much of the early medieval period royal authority was severely limited.

Another aspect of feudal privilege found its roots in an earlier form of special dispensation. Under the Carolingian system, Church lands had often been granted *immunity*; special privileges that allowed them to operate separately from royal authority (the medieval tradition of churches offering *sanctuary* for criminals escaping from royal authority originated from this *immunity* dispensation). During the turmoil of the ninth century, many of these religious centers turned toward the Frankish warlords for protection, and their lands were often amalgamated with those of the warlord, who then transferred many of the special privileges to the rest of his lands.

Other lords simply adopted their own system

of privileges and powers, since royal authority was too weak to challenge their actions. By the 11th century many leading nobles ruled territories that were largely autonomous, these dukes having the right to raise armies, tax subjects, and impose law and order.

In the tenth century this hierarchical system developed rapidly, particularly in the western Frankish State (Neustria, or France). By the start of the 11th century, feudalism was firmly established, and only a few isolated parcels of land remained free of feudal obligations. This system would continue until the growth of towns and the re-establishment of royal power led to a re-evaluation of the feudal system.

Bastions of Power: Norman Castles

During the 11th century wooden castles began to appear throughout western Europe, a symbol of feudalism and the uncertainty of the times. By the end of the century these castles started to be replaced by imposing stone structures; bastions of feudal power and political dominance.

Facing: *Built during the reign of King Henry II, Hedingham, in the county of Essex, England was built in 1130. A five-story keep, it has no motte, and only two of its four towers survive.*

Below: *Corfe, in Dorset, England was built in the late 11th century. Its circular keep was constructed on the site of an earlier Saxon fort.*

Fortifications had been in use in Europe since prehistory, but usually consisted of fenced villages, hill-forts occupied in times of threat, or even special strategically placed forts, occupied by a military garrison. During the introduction of the feudal system into western Europe in the ninth and tenth centuries, castles emerged as a symbol of the power of a feudal overlord. Wooden fortifications sprang up throughout the continent following the collapse of the Carolingian Empire, and during the attacks by Magyars, Moors, and Norsemen. The main castle-building area was in northern France, where the local feudal lords suffered the worst of the Viking attacks. These were not simply fortifications, but provided accommodation for a feudal lord, his family, and their retinue.

Many of these wooden fortifications took the form known as the motte-and-bailey castle, a style so common in northwestern France (and England after 1066) that it became closely associated with the Normans. These castles consisted of a *motte* (mound), usually about 15–30 feet high, surrounded by a ditch (or moat if flooded). The top of the mound was flattened, then surrounded by a wooden palisade and wall-walk.

Inside the palisade stood a tall wooden tower, either free-standing or raised on stilts. Where the palisade was pierced by a gate, a second area of enclosed ground formed the *bailey*. A ditch and palisade surrounded the bailey, and the two fortifications were connected by a wooden walkway or ramp. The bailey contained stables, a well, domestic quarters for retainers and servants, and other necessary buildings. The exact layout of these motte-and-bailey castles varied considerably, and when natural rather than man-made mounds were used, the defenses conformed to the local terrain.

Some were even constructed inside the remains of pre-medieval earthworks, such as old Celtic hillforts, which provided additional outer rings of ditches and banks. The mounds and enclosures of these castles can still be seen throughout England and France.

More affluent times

The economic boom of the 11th century allowed a vast program of church- and castle-building. The feudal system created a degree of stability for European society, while the increasing benefits of a money economy, trade, and the growth of towns meant that feudal overlords had wealth to spend. This was as true for the lower levels of the knights and minor nobility as it was for the kings and dukes at the top of the feudal pyramid. They were able to purchase luxuries, such as quality clothes, arms and armor, exotic foods and spices, and improved forms of accommodation.

While before, early feudal overlords had traveled around their domain, from the early 12th century most were established in a fixed location. This center provided a place from which the overlord could control his lands, accommodation suitable for his wealth and standing, and a means of defense if attacked. Where before, the overlord might have several motte-and-bailey castles, the 12th-century nobleman established only one fortified residence, building its walls from stone rather than timber.

Sometimes stone walls surrounded the mottes of existing castle mounds, forming ring keeps. In most cases, castles were built on unoccupied level sites, where a large stone *donjon* (keep, or tower, and from which we derive the word "dungeon") was sometimes surrounded by an outer stone or timber wall (or *curtain*). These inner keeps were usually square, and could be massive structures, like the White Tower inside the Tower of London, or Rochester Castle in Kent, England (*see page 36*). They had a second-floor entrance accessed by a removable staircase, and the keep contained living quarters, storerooms, and a well. The interiors were spartan, drafty, unsanitary, and cold, but until the 14th century, comfort was a lesser consideration than protection.

These stone keeps remained the standard form of castle until the 13th century when moves were made to improve outer wall defenses by adding towers and even concentric rings of curtain walls.

During the Norman period, these tall, dark structures dominated the surrounding countryside, creating a powerful base for the nobility to impose its control over feudal Europe, or to dominate occupied territory. Warfare amounted to a contest for the control of castles. Since most monarchs lacked the resources to undertake extensive sieges, the security of the lesser nobility was assured until royal power increased in the late 11th century.

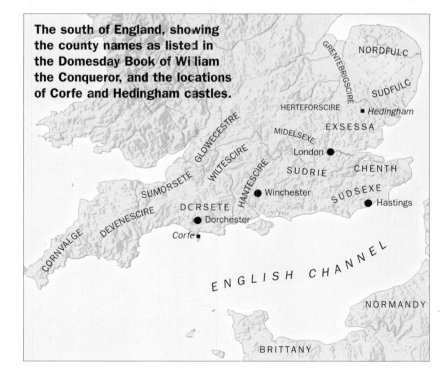

The south of England, showing the county names as listed in the Domesday Book of William the Conqueror, and the locations of Corfe and Hedingham castles.

Norman Adventurers in Italy

Norman knights, returning from pilgrimages to Jerusalem, passed through southern Italy. They saw a desirable land and wanted to possess it. During the 11th century Norman adventurers battled with Moors and Byzantines to create a new Norman kingdom in Sicily and the heel of Italy.

At the start of the 11th century, the Italian peninsula south of Rome was split into a patchwork of small states; either administered by Lombard warlords, by the Byzantines, or by semi-independent city authorities. Nearby Sicily was held in Moorish hands, ruled by Arab emirs who

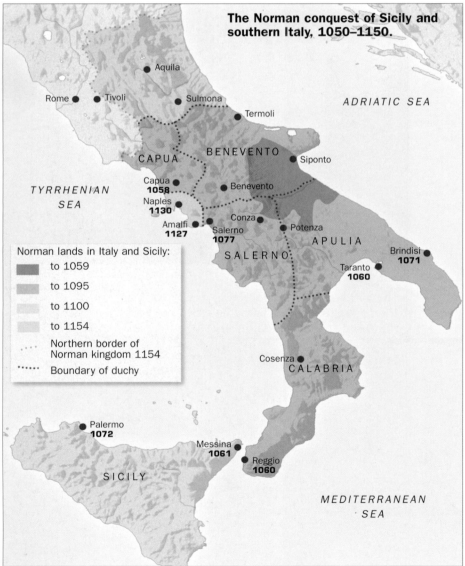

The Norman conquest of Sicily and southern Italy, 1050–1150.

Norman lands in Italy and Sicily:
- to 1059
- to 1095
- to 1100
- to 1154
- ······· Northern border of Norman kingdom 1154
- ······· Boundary of duchy

owed their allegiance to beys in Egypt or Tunisia. The first mention of Norman knights in the region was in 1017, when they acted as

mercenaries, supporting an Italian rule against Byzantine authority.

These mercenaries included three brothers, the offspring of a Norman lord named Tancred de Hauteville. When the brothers started carving out petty fiefdoms in their own name, they sent representatives back to Normandy to recruit more adventurers to help them. Many younger sons of the less wealthy Norman noble families enlisted. These adventurers included two other Hauteville relatives, Robert and Roger.

By 1038 Norman knights had occupied the area around Aversa near Naples, and in 1059 the Pope recognized the Norman knight Richard d'Aversa as the Lord of Capua, and Robert Guiscard (the cunning) de Hauteville as the Duke of Apulia. This was the climax of a decade of expansion by Norman adventurers, who gained control of large segments of southern Italy by conquest, annexation, and treaty.

Within a year, other Norman adventurers extended their influence by capturing much of Calabria, and in 1071 the Apulian ports of Bari and Brindisi fell to Robert de Hauteville. These were the last Byzantine strongholds in Italy; by the end of the tenth century southern Italy had become a Norman kingdom, distinct from the semi-independent Lombardic city-states of Naples and Amalfi.

About 1060 Norman adventurers launched an invasion of Sicily, capturing Messina in 1061. They were led by Roger, the younger brother of Robert de Hauteville, who matched his sibling by appointing himself Count of Sicily (1061–1101). The Moors were slowly pushed back to the south and west. Palermo fell in 1072 and provided an administrative capital for the new Norman Kingdom of Sicily. The Norman conquest of the island was completed by 1091, and Roger set about reorganizing his domains, which technically formed part of the lands of the Duke of Apulia.

Roger de Hauteville was succeeded by his son, who became Roger II, Count of Sicily (1103–54). When Robert's grandson died in 1127, Roger II seized control of the Duchy of

Apulia, and three years later in 1130 Pope Innocent II granted him the title of King of Sicily. This Kingdom of Sicily grew to include the other small Norman states in southern Italy, and by 1154 it extended as far north as the border of the Papal State, providing the papacy with a loyal semi-independent vassal to the south of Rome, and a Christian bulwark against Moorish or Byzantine invasion.

A successful Norman state

King Roger II of Sicily maintained tight centralized control over his kingdom through a system of courts and professional administrators, based in Palermo. His leading nobles administered his five duchies under firm royal supervision and, by being a direct vassal of the Pope, Roger II was able to directly control his bishops. The kingdom was a triumph of the Norman system of government, and as its economy improved through trading links with the Muslims and Byzantines, it became one of the richest Frankish states. From 1123, Roger began to dabble in the political affairs of his neighbors, but with no lasting success. His troops conquered the North African coast from Tunis to Tripoli, but a Muslim revolt led to the collapse of this overseas domains by 1159.

The policy of expansion was furthered by his sons, William I (1154–86) and William II (1166–89).

Attacks on Greece and counter-raids by the Byzantines led to a Norman invasion of Byzantine Greece in the 1180s. Despite having Venetian help, King William II was forced to abandon the project in 1185.

The Kingdom of Sicily remained a unified state until it became embroiled in the struggle between Empire and Papacy. In 1194, Norman rule in Italy came to an end when the kingdom was occupied by the Hohenstaufen German Emperor, Henry VI. For more than a century, the most cultured of all the Norman states flourished on the Mediterranean coast; a model example of a centralized feudal kingdom.

Above: *Roger II of Sicily was unusual in his admiration of the Arabs and of Islam. His coronation mantle, woven in Palermo, incorporated Arabic inscriptions, as well as the Hegira date of 628.*

Below: *Norman castles in Sicily are often identifiable only by their original keeps, which were extensively added to in the following centuries.*

The Norman Conquest of England

When the Anglo-Saxon King Edward the Confessor died in 1066, the English throne was gravely weakened. The Anglo-Saxon nobles appointed Harold Godwinson as their new monarch, but William the Bastard, Duke of Normandy, gathered a force for what would be the last, and most influential, invasion of England in history.

Below: *The Norman stamp on Saxon England was made in stone. Rochester, built by William de Corbeil on the site of a Roman fort, is undilutedly Norman in style.*

When the Romans abandoned Britain in the early fifth century AD, the local Celtic peoples were left exposed to attack. Germanic invaders crossed the North Sea in ever-increasing numbers: Angles, Jutes, and Saxons. By the ninth century these invaders had homogenized to become Anglo-Saxons, and the Celtic Britons who survived sought refuge in the mountains of Scotland and Wales. Frequent Danish invasions ravaged the country, and one invader, Canute (1016–35), even held the high kingship for a period.

King Edward the Confessor of England (1042–66) had strong Norman links; his uncle was the Duke of Normandy, so he spent his early years in Normandy, and his court contained several Norman supporters. Many Anglo-Saxons resented this foreign interference, and Earl Godwin of Wessex acted as the focal point of opposition. Godwin was succeeded as Earl by his son, Harold Godwinson, in 1053. Harold continued to maintain his father's isolationist stance. He was shipwrecked off the Norman coast in 1064, and captured by Duke William of Normandy, who also maintained a claim to the English throne through his aunt, the wife of King Edward. In return for his freedom, Earl Harold swore to support William's claim to the throne. When Edward died in 1066, Harold ignored his oath, and accepted the kingship. Incensed, William began planning an invasion.

Since most Norman lords were not obligated to serve overseas, William called on Norman and French adventurers to join him; the younger sons of the feudal nobility. By the summer of 1066 he had collected an army of about 5,000 men and an invasion fleet. All he needed were favorable winds. In England, an invasion force led by King Harald Hardrada of Norway attacked in the north. The invaders were supported by Harold's brother Tostig. Harold was on the south coast, guarding against a Norman invasion. He raced north and defeated the Norwegians at Stamford Bridge (1066), in Yorkshire. Three days later, the Normans

landed on the south coast. Duke William stepped ashore at Pevensey, fortified the beach-head, then marched inland. Harold's army force-marched back south to meet him and, on October 14, 1066, the two armies clashed near Hastings. In a confused engagement, a series of Norman attacks were repulsed, but a feigned retreat drew the English from their hilltop position.

Overstretched forces

The Normans turned and charged the now disorganized enemy, who were cut down by the hundred. The English formed a final shield-wall formed around their king and, as dusk fell, a final charge by Norman cavalry broke the English line, which disintegrated. Casualties were heavy on both sides, but the dead included King Harold, reputedly pierced in the eye by an arrow, and most of his nobles.

For all practical purposes, England was conquered on the battlefield of Hastings. The Normans marched on London, and William was crowned King William I of England in Westminster Abbey. The conquest was an immense stroke of luck; the Norwegian invasion meant that Harold was unable to oppose the Norman landings, and the resulting battle ended all English opposition at a stroke. The last traces of Anglo-Saxon resistance, in the fenlands of East Anglia, were quashed by 1071, and the Normans extended their control west and north, enforcing their authority by constructing castles in each old Anglo-Saxon borough, then garrisoning them with seasoned troops.

William the Conqueror rewarded his adventurers by granting them fiefdoms, and large royal castles were built in London, Dover, and along the Sussex coastline to safeguard his communications with Normandy. His son

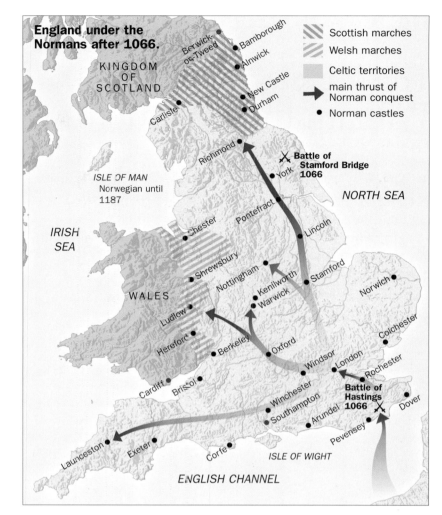

Robert became the new Duke of Normandy, thus ensuring a familial control of the entire Norman demesne, old and new. William realized that capturing a kingdom was easier than controlling it, and his subsequent organization of his new realm is discussed on pages 38–9. By his death in 1087, William the Conqueror had consolidated his Anglo-Norman kingdom into a largely unified political entity, safeguarded its Scottish and Welsh borders, and ensured its survival by imposing a feudal system based on the Norman model. Any further expansion would have to be at the expense of France.

Below: *This section of the Bayeux Tapestry depicts Norman knights charging onto the shore in the conquest of England. It also offers us the only contemporary illustration of what Viking longboats looked like, since they remained unchanged.*

FOCUS: LEADERS
William the Conqueror

In 1066, William, Duke of Normandy became King William I of England. Although he is always associated with the epithet "the Conqueror," his spectacular military achievements would not have been remembered today had it not been for his successful introduction of the Norman feudal system into England, together with its attendant social, ecclesiastical, and economic changes. A more accurate title might have been William "the Reformer."

Right: This section from the Bayeux Tapestry shows Harold Godwinson—sent on an embassy by King Edward the Confessor—meeting Duke William in Normandy in 1064. This contemporary account is at odds with other versions, which suggest that Harold was shipwrecked off the coast and captured by William.

William was born in 1028, the illegitimate son of Robert, Duke of Normandy and Herleve, daughter of a Falaise tanner. His father adopted him as his successor, forcing the headstrong Norman nobles to acknowledge him as his heir in 1033, when William was only five years old. The Duke then left on a pilgrimage to the Holy Land, only to die in Byzantine Anatolia during his return journey.

His death sparked a power struggle in which the young William became a pawn, with supporters and enemies fighting openly for the ducal crown. King Henry I of France (1031–60) interceded on William's behalf, and his accession was temporarily recognized. A second rebellion—led by William's cousin Guy of Burgundy—was quashed in 1047 when the teenage Duke defeated the rebels at Val-es-Dunes, again with the help of the French king. William was now firmly in control of his duchy, and between 1050 and 1064 he defeated an invasion from Anjou, extended his control into Brittany, and married the daughter of the Count of Flanders. This marriage was part of a deliberate policy of alignment with the northern French nobles; allies in any struggle with the more aggressive dukes to the south.

By the eve of his invasion of England, Duke William had developed Normandy into a powerful centralized duchy, his power supported by the Norman bishops and his claims to the English throne endorsed by the Pope. When the succession crisis developed following the death of Edward the Confessor of England in 1066, the Norman nobility were unwilling to participate in

an invasion of England, which, if unsuccessful, could threaten their own realms. Instead, William used his papal support to encourage adventurers from all over France to join him; mercenaries who would be paid with conquered land rather than money. His army consisted of knights and their feudal retainers from most provinces of France, as well as Normandy, and his invasion was accompanied by a body of clerics and royal administrators, ready to take over the reins of government in the conquered land.

Following the successful invasion, William was crowned King of England in Westminster Abbey

1000	1000	1012	1014	1015
Widespread terror created by dawn of new millennium	Leif Erikson discovers the North American continent	First persecution of heretics by the Church	Battle of Clontarf ends Viking domination of Ireland	Norman adventurers act as mercenaries in Italy

on Christmas Day, 1066, and by that time had already set into motion the occupation of all English provinces. At first, he allowed the English nobles who had survived the Battle of Hastings to keep their lands, especially since most were concentrated in the midlands and north, far from William's administrative base in London.

Norman-style government

His first concern was military security. While English rebels were hunted down, he instituted a feudal system by allocating lands to his supporters, but ensured that the most powerful lords occupied the lands adjacent to Scotland and Wales. The Earldom of Northumberland was created to guard northeast England, supported by a bishopric at Durham. To the west, other powerful nobles were established in Lancashire and Richmond, while the marchlands facing the Welsh were divided into three feudal districts; the Earldoms of Chester, Shrewsbury, and Hereford. While retaining the royal lands of King Harold for himself, William divided the rest among his remaining nobles and their Anglo-Saxon counterparts who swore allegiance to him.

Many of these feudal lands were widely scattered, and little information survived the change of power, so in 1086 William instituted a census. The survey, its results contained in *The Domesday Book* (from the Norse word *dome*, which means "a reckoning," and from which we derive the modern word "doom"), was the most comprehensive census ever undertaken up to that time. The attention to detail is still mightily impressive today, with every settlement in England, no matter how small, listed and described. William now had a detailed account of his realm, and could tax his population efficiently.

FOCUS: WARFARE

The Norman Military Structure

Feudalism was a social system based on military service, and a feudal army reflected the pyramidal hierarchy of the feudal system. During the 11th century the knight was the dominant force on the battlefield, and his kind gradually evolved into an exclusive military caste; the arbiter of victory or defeat.

The knight formed a vital part of the feudal system; one of the lesser vassals of the great noblemen, and a crucial component in any Norman army. His co-operation in warfare was a prerequisite of his feudal standing, and the power of a noble centered around the number of knights and supporters he could call upon for military service. The chief function of a feudal lord was to protect those beneath him; his vassals. In return, they performed military service when called upon to do so.

The system developed from a localized form of defense that had emerged in response to Viking and Magyar raids. A feudal retinue could be formed at short notice, with peasants dropping their tools and arming themselves, then forming into bands under the control of their direct feudal superiors. This banding together would continue up the feudal hierarchical pyramid until a sufficient force was gathered to deal with the threat. When military service was completed, the feudal army would return to their homes.

By the 11th century, a distinction was drawn between military service called in protection of feudal lands, and offensive attacks on enemy territory. In self-defense, the vassals were obligated to serve for the duration of the threat. When the feudal superiors were engaged in offensive action, service became limited to a certain period, such as a month, or 40 days. In these cases, to avoid disruption to the planting and harvesting of crops, military service was called in summer, between spring planting and fall harvest. In some instances, knights (and their retinues) could be asked to serve for an additional period of similar length, as long as the feudal

overlord supplied the retinue with provisions.

A modification of the requirement to defend feudal lands emerged as a result of the growing need to provide garrisons for castles. If no threat was expected, powerful nobles would call upon individual retinues to serve for set periods, ensuring a year-round garrison. For example, a count who had around 120 knights as vassals might call on ten of them and their peasant retinues to provide a castle-guard for a month, then another ten would form the garrison… and so on throughout the year.

Knights were granted fiefdoms to provide them with the economic support to afford the increasingly expensive military tools of their trade. This usually consisted of a hauberk (a mail shirt—

Right: The English Anglo-Saxon infantry wards off a charge of mounted Norman knights during the Battle of Hastings, 1066, from the Bayeux Tapestry, which was woven in the late 11th century.

1018	1027	1028	1050	1052
Alliance made between England and Denmark	Guido d'Arezzo introduces musical scales (solmizalto)	Castille annexed by Navarre in Spain	The Welsh epic poem the *Mabinogion* is written	Work begins on Westminster Abbey in London

a badge of rank and wealth), a helmet, horse, saddle, spear, sword, and shield. When not called upon for feudal service, the knight was expected to practice his military skills. As the 11th century wore on, training facilities were provided in many feudal castles, and the gathering of knights for sport and hunting provided an excellent opportunity to demonstrate military prowess.

Dominating the battlefield

By the 12th century this class of knights had become stratified by the economic necessities of providing equipment. Lesser knights became *sergeants*, and gradually evolved into a secondary level of mounted warriors, along with *squire*s and the rest of the knight's feudal retinue. An exception to the feudal rule were the adventurers or mercenaries, who were often better trained and equipped than their feudal counterparts, and were supported by a band of experienced professional troops. Unlike the feudal peasant levies, these infantrymen had marketable military skills. During

the conquest of England in 1066 Duke William made extensive use of Norman adventurers, and they supplied him with experienced archers for his army.

Developments in armor and equestrian equipment (especially stirrups) made the mounted knight a powerful military tool capable of dominating the early medieval battlefield. His principal weapon was the lance, carried couched underarm, and designed to overpower an enemy through the shock of impact; one body of troops crashing into another. These all-or-nothing tactics developed in concert with the rise of the knight as part of an exclusive military caste. On the battlefield, a knight would fight another knight, and combat took on an increasingly chivalrous nature. On an 11th century battlefield the foot soldiers were concentrated into blocks (*battles*), sometimes supported by mercenary archers. Little was expected of these troops, and a battle was won or lost by the vigor of the mounted knights.

FOCUS: SOCIETY
Early Medieval Agriculture

Early medieval society was agricultural; an agrarian economy that rarely existed above the level of individual villages. These settlements followed a method of agriculture dictated by climate and land quality. Feudal rural life remained unchanged for centuries, until it was transformed by improved farming methods during the 12th century.

The large urban centers of the Roman Empire had been swept away by barbarian invasions at the start of the Dark Ages and, following the collapse of the Carolingian Empire, even small towns were a rarity. Where they existed, they were usually based around religious and political centers such as large churches or noblemen's halls, but they were far from being

Above: *Fragment from an English manuscript calendar of c.1050, showing men reaping grain with scythes in August.*

urban communities. Their inhabitants still relied on the surrounding countryside for their livelihood, which made them little more than large villages. While Europeans struggled to survive, there was little impetus to look beyond the village for a livelihood. The introduction of feudalism provided security in exchange for the freedom of the peasantry to move elsewhere, stifling any impetus for change.

During the early Middle Ages this agricultural economy existed throughout most of Europe, although its style varied depending on location. In areas where the soil was poor or the terrain mountainous, for instance in Scotland, central France, the Alps, and Ireland, dispersed

settlements of isolated farms or hamlets were the standard economic unit. Elsewhere the village became the basis for medieval society. The system used by the village also varied with geography. In England and northern France (and to a lesser extent northern Germany), open-field farming was the standard method, where a village was surrounded by unfenced areas of arable land.

In most cases, these tracts were divided into fertile and fallow areas, allowing for an annual rotation of workable land. Tracts were subdivided into long strips, each allocated to particular households in the village, or to the lord of the manor in whose fiefdom the land lay. Italy and southern France relied on a closed-field system, where small rectangular fields or plots were allocated in the same manner as the strips of northern Europe, and divided into fallow and fertile fields.

This geographic variation was in response to climate. Small plows were needed in southern Europe, where a deep furrow would be harder to irrigate. In the north, where rain was more frequent, a system of deep ridges and furrows allowed for drainage. This called for heavy plows and several horses or oxen, so long strips reduced the need to maneuver these cumbersome things more than necessary. Animals were pooled by the village, and many tasks were shared communally.

In areas of more dispersed settlement, this solution was not possible. There, individual farms or small hamlets divided the arable land into an in-field area—which was kept fertilized by manure from farm animals—and an out-field area, where crops were grown until the land was exhausted. Then a new area was cleared and used. Whatever system was used, crop yields were far lower than today, with under ten bushels of grain per acre regarded as high. Nearby woodlands

1053	1054	1057	1064	1066	1066	1071	1072
Norman Kingdom established in southern Italy	Split between Roman and Greek Churches becomes permanent	Macbeth, King of Scots, is killed by his rival Malcolm	The Seljuk Turks establish control over Armenia	Norman Conquest of England	Appearance of Halley's Comet recorded in Bayeux Tapestry	Normans extend their control into southern Italy	Normans capture Palermo in Sicily

were used as a source for berries and to support pigs, while other livestock such as cattle or chickens were less common.

Agriculture supports towns

The growth of towns and commerce during this period went hand-in-hand with improvements in agricultural techniques. Improved farming methods provided surpluses that could be sold in town markets, rather than merely being consumed by the peasant population.

One simple improvement was the change from a two- to a three-field system, where one field was planted with winter grain, one with spring grain, and the third lay fallow, ready for use in the following year. In effect this crop rotation system improved a village's production during the year by about one third. Improved horse harnesses and the introduction of horseshoes increased the efficiency of plowing

teams, and horses became more widely used in agriculture. They were also used to help in the conversion of raw land to arable use.

Most villages boasted a mill, usually owned by the lord of the manor. The introduction of efficient water wheels and milling machinery improved the quality of ground grain, and the same technology was adapted to improve irrigation. The result was an increase in agricultural production that served to feed the growing towns through the sale of surplus produce.

By the late 13th century, Europe's agrarian economy had expanded, allowing the rise of a parallel economy based on commerce. Together these economic changes helped to transform Europe from a continent geared to a purely agrarian subsistence economy to one that used a far more complex model.

1075–1122	1078	1079-1142	1081	1085	1087	1098	1099
Investiture Contest damages the authority of the Holy Roman Empire	Construction begun on the Tower of London	Lifetime of Peter Abelard, philosopher and theologian	Trade agreement established between Venice and the Byzantines	Toledo recaptured from the Moors	*The Domesday Book* compiled, the first survey in Medieval Europe	First Cistercian Monastery founded	Death of El Cid, the Spanish national hero

CHAPTER THREE

Popes and Emperors: the Crisis of Church and State

During the 11th century, European monarchs began using the feudal system as a means to increase their power over their subjects. The most spectacular rise was in Germany, where a succession of German kings assumed the title "Emperor of the Romans," which created a large yet vulnerable political entity that dominated central and southern Europe well into the 12th century.

One of the cornerstones of Imperial power was the Church, and emperors appointed bishops from among their followers. This flew in the face of the mood of reform that had been sweeping through the Church in the 11th century. Increased Papal power, the revival of monasticism, and a stronger enforcement of Catholic doctrine all helped propel the Church from the doldrums it had fallen into following the collapse of the Carolingian Empire.

The scene was set for a titanic struggle between the emperor, representing political authority, and the Pope, fighting to ensure the primacy of the papacy in all spiritual matters. The conflict would divide Europe for the greater part of a century, distracting the Church from a wave of growing religious dissidence, and weakening medieval monarchs through internecine warfare. Italy was turned into a battleground between the feuding factions, and the Holy Roman Empire was almost brought down by the constant warfare and intrigue. The Church emerged as the victor, although the seeds were sown for the Protestant Reformation.

NORTH SEA

LÜBECK

Lübeck

Hamburg

POMERANIA

Bremen

SAXONY

Brandenburg

BRANDENBURG

KINGDOM
OF
POLAND

LOWER
LORRAINE

Dortmund

Cologne

FRANCONIA

Prague

BOHEMIA

Mainz

Worms

UPPER
LORRAINE

Nuremburg

Regensburg

SWABIA

The Holy Roman
Empire under
Frederick I
Barbarossa.

Augsburg

Basel

Munich

Vienna

AUSTRIA

Zurich

STYRIA

KINGDOM
OF
HUNGARY

BURGUNDY

CARINTHIA

FRIULI

Lyons

VERONA

CARNIOLA

Verona

Milan

LOMBARDY

Venice

KINGDOM OF ITALY

PROVENCE

Genoa

ADRIATIC SEA

Bologna

Marseilles

Ravenna

Pisa

CORSICA

TUSCANY

Siena

ROMAGNA

Rome

TYRHENNIAN SEA

Benevento

Naples

Brindisi

Gaeta

Taranto

SARDINIA

KINGDOM OF SICILY

Cosenza

MEDITERRANEAN

Palermo

SEA

Messina

Reggio

SICILY

Syracuse

Holy Roman Empire

Kingdom of Sicily under
Frederick II

Venetian territories

German invasions
1190–94

Genoese and Pisan
fleet of Henry IV 1194

The Reform of the Church

At the start of the 11th century, the Christian Church was in decline. Corruption, lack of central authority, and secular interference combined to bring it into disrepute, until a widespread burst of religious enthusiasm revitalized it and paved the way for its dominant role during the 12th century.

When Charlemagne's empire disintegrated in the mid-ninth century, the Church nevertheless continued to maintain some form of effective presence in society. French bishops

intervened in the policy of Frankish monarchs, and under Pope Nicholas I the supremacy of the Roman Church over the Byzantine was reaffirmed. Pope Nicholas also produced a forged set of documents (the false *decretals*), which cited precedents supporting the legal right of the Pope to appoint his own bishops, free of outside control. After the tenure of Pope Nicholas, the Church went into a decline that lasted for two centuries.

Muslim incursions into Sicily, Spain, and Italy, and Viking and Magyar attacks in eastern and northern Europe ravaged the lands and properties owned by the Church, threatening its stability. In Rome, the defense of the Papal States dominated the thoughts of the pontiffs of the tenth century, who became little more than the secular appointees of Italian landowners. To combat the crisis the Church was forced to look for assistance from the secular Frankish nobility. This gave the nobles a say in the appointment of clerics, and the policy extended to local priests, whose churches and incomes were provided by local landowners.

The Benedictine monasteries of western Europe provided some degree of temporal stability, but their introverted nature did little to help the Church regain control of its holdings. An exception was the Abbey of Cluny in Aquitaine, founded in AD 910. The Abbey was directly subordinate to the Pope, not to the local secular authorities, and the institution served as a springboard for later monastic reform. Secondary monasteries of the Clunaic order, or ones based on similar lines, spread throughout France and England, leading to a revival of monasticism in the late tenth century.

The Clunaic movement joined a larger continental movement of Church reform in the 11th century. Although Rome was still seen as the natural center for the Church, lack of pontifical leadership had undermined its authority. This changed with Pope Leo IX (1049–54), who proved to be a remarkable reformer and administrator. He created a body of reforming *Cardinals* to help him govern the Church; including Hildebrand, who would become Pope Gregory VI, the nemesis of the Emperor's son. A series of synods were held which framed vital Church legislation, and councils were held throughout western Europe, publicizing and enforcing the wishes of the pontiff. Simony (the buying or selling of religious artifacts) was outlawed, as was clerical marriage, while bishops unwilling to instigate the papal reforms were deposed. By the time Pope Leo died he had effectively reasserted the position of the Pope as the head of the Catholic Church.

The spread of monasteries

In the 12th century there were fresh movements of monastic reform, led by the establishment of new religious orders. While the religious revival of the 11th century led some to break from the Church in search of a purer form of Christianity, most harnessed their religious drive to the established structure. Hundreds of new religious houses were created throughout western Europe, some of which were extremely reclusive. The most extreme was the Carthusian order, whose founder had spent years living as a hermit. In 1084 he established the monastery of La Grande Chatreuse near the French city of Grenoble, and others followed.

Carthusian monks spent their days in private cells, meeting only on special occasions. Fasting, poverty, and silence all played a part in their devotional creed. In 1098 a monastery was established at Citeaux in France, inspired by St. Bernard, one of the leading monastic figures of the period. This Cistercian order expanded rapidly during the 12th century, as devotees were drawn by its strict enforcement of Benedictine rules, simplicity of life, and self-sufficiency. Houses were often founded in unfertile areas, to avoid direct links with their feudal surroundings.

These religious orders, while set slightly apart from the Church, helped to ensure its influence was felt throughout western Europe, and helped shape the development of the Church in the centuries to come. Similarly, the reforms of Leo IX laid the foundation for the challenge to the involvement of secular rulers in ecclesiastical affairs that would dominate much of the 11th and 12th centuries.

Left: *During the 12th century many new monastic foundations sprang from the inspiration of singular monks; perhaps the most famous is St. Francis of Assisi (1181–1226), who founded the Franciscan order. He is painted here by Italian artist Giotto, who was born the year St. Francis died.*

Facing: *The contemplative life of reclusive monasteries resulted in an outpouring of religious literary work. Eadwine the Scribe included a picture of himself at work on an English psalter, c.1150, written at Christ Church, Canterbury.*

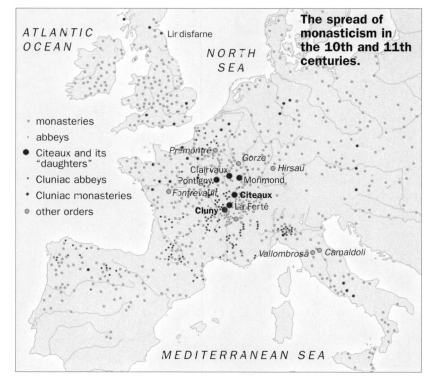

The spread of monasticism in the 10th and 11th centuries.

ATLANTIC OCEAN

NORTH SEA

Lir disfarne

· monasteries
· abbeys
● Citeaux and its "daughters"
· Cluniac abbeys
· Cluniac monasteries
◦ other orders

Prémontré
Gorze
Clairvaux
Hirsau
Pontigny
Morimond
Fontrevault
Citeaux
Cluny
La Ferté

Vallombrosa
Camaldoli

MEDITERRANEAN SEA

The Holy Roman Empire

In the ninth century semi-autonomous East Frankish Kingdoms formed the easternmost fringe of the Frankish Empire, its lands divided into provinces. The Empire survived the threat of Magyar invasion to emerge as a powerful political entity, capable of dominating northern Italy and its eastern neighbors. During the 11th and 12th centuries the Holy Roman Empire was gripped by a series of religious and dynastic disputes that eventually dragged it into political obscurity.

Following the death of Charlemagne's son in AD 840, the Carolingian Empire was divided into western, eastern, and central kingdoms. As the Eastern Frankish Kingdom incorporated territories that had only recently been captured

from the pagan Slavs and Saxons, it was considered less civilized, and consequently evolved along completely different political and social lines from the Frankish states to the west. The kingdom was divided into substantial duchies (Swabia, Franconia, Bavaria, and Saxony), and during the reign of the last Carolingian monarchs these duchies became all but autonomous.

The Magyar invasions of the tenth century forced these nobles to accede to a more unified system. In 919 the crown was passed to Henry I (919–936), of Saxony. Although viewed as only the "first among equals" by his fellow dukes, the new king gained their allegiance to promote himself to a higher secular authority, and added the province of Lorraine to his lands. Otto I the Great (936–973) increased the influence of this position by crushing the dukes in battle, and then by putting a permanent end to the Magyar threat at the Battle of Lechfeld in 955. In 951 he conquered Lombardy, and in 962 he was crowned Emperor of the Roman Empire, the new appellation given to the East Frankish Kingdom.

Although the Pope had crowned Otto, he fermented a rebellion against the new emperor. Otto responded by convoking a synod and deposed the Pope, replacing him with a more suitable candidate. A dangerous precedent had been set; Roman popes as well as German bishops were now appointed by a secular ruler.

On his death a series of less successful kings (and emperors if crowned by the Pope) would struggle to maintain control of the Empire. Following the death of Otto II in 983 the Slavs along the Empire's eastern frontiers rebelled, massacring thousands of German settlers before order was restored. Henry II (1002–24) was the last king of the Saxon dynasty and, on his death, the German dukes elected Conrad II (1024–39) of Franconia as king, starting a Salian dynasty (Franconians were known as Salian Franks). By developing a combined military and civil service (the *ministeriales*) throughout Germany, Conrad ensured some degree of control over his dukes. In 1037 he forced the Italian nobility to guarantee that the lordship of northern Italy would customarily be granted to the German king, whether anointed as emperor or not.

In 1056, the Emperor Henry III died, leaving an infant son to succeed him. The new situation provided an opportunity for dissenters to challenge imperial authority. German kings appointed their own bishops, and the Church began to show dissent over the fusion of spiritual and temporal power.

Debate grows heated

A Church Council in Rome instituted new rules for the election to the papacy in 1059, prompting a resultant Investiture Contest. Pope Gregory VII excommunicated Henry IV (1056–1106) for attempting to depose him and the Emperor was forced to perform penance before being pardoned. The German dukes took this opportunity to rebel. Henry was forced to fight a bitter civil war, with the Pope in support of his opponents. Although Henry won, the conflict with the papacy dragged on until 1122.

This contest developed into a political struggle between the Guelphs and the Ghibbellenes, political supporters of the Church and the Empire respectively. In Germany the Ghibbellenes were associated with the Hohenstauffen family, and when Frederick Barbarossa came to the throne in 1152, the Empire was politically divided. His attempts to restore the fortunes of the Empire are outlined on page 58. He left a legacy of a powerful feudal empire to his successors. Over the half century this legacy would be squandered through a continual erosion of imperial power.

Papal intrigue led to a decade-long civil war in Germany from 1197. Frederick II (1215–50) was constantly in conflict with both his nobles and the papacy, particularly when he extended his political intrigues to include Italy and the Latin State of Jerusalem. Frederick's successor was the last Hohenstauffen emperor, and on his death the Imperial throne was effectively left vacant for almost 20 years. By the time Rudolph of Hapsburg was crowned Emperor in 1273, his empire was a political union in name alone, with little or no military power at its disposal. Although it would remain on the European map until the early 19th century, the Holy Roman Empire was nothing more than a shadow of its former self.

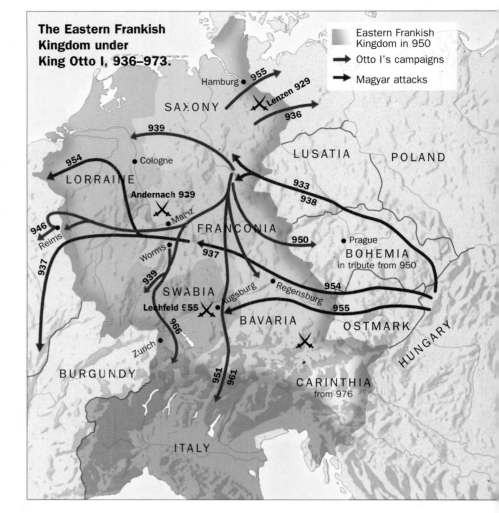

The Eastern Frankish Kingdom under King Otto I, 936–973.

Eastern Frankish Kingdom in 950
→ Otto I's campaigns
→ Magyar attacks

Hamburg • 955
Lenzen 929
936
SAXONY
LUSATIA
POLAND
939
• Cologne
954
LORRAINE
933
938
Andernach 939
• Mainz
946
Reims
FRANCONIA
950
• Prague
937
Worms
950
BOHEMIA
in tribute from 950
937
939
SWABIA
Augsburg
Regensburg
954
Lechfeld 955
955
• Zurich
BAVARIA
OSTMARK
HUNGARY
BURGUNDY
951
961
CARINTHIA
from 976
ITALY

Facing: *The failure of leadership at the end of the 12th century gave rise to opportunism—this illumination shows a lord leading his men-at-arms as they raid a neighbor's cattle. From the Codex Manesse, Heidelberg University.*

Left: *Frederick II; detail from the dedicatory picture for the manuscript of his* De arte venandi cum avibus *("from the Falcon Hunt").*

Pope versus Emperor: the Investiture Crisis

In the late 11th century, Church reformers attempted to curb secular influence within the Church. Secular rulers headed by the German Emperor saw this as an invasion of their right to govern. The medieval world was plunged into a crisis between the two sides, each using every available tool to win their case.

The reforms of Pope Leo IX (1049–54) strengthened the position of the Church and ensured that the Pope in Rome was seen as its recognized leader. They also paved the way for the Church to challenge the interference of Europe's secular rulers in ecclesiastical matters. During the late 11th century it became increasingly rare in France and England for secular rulers to appoint senior clergymen (mainly archbishops and bishops), although parish priests were for the most part appointed with the support of local feudal landowners. In Germany the emperor still appointed ecclesiastical leaders, and the Church was keen to challenge his authority to do so.

When the Emperor Henry III died in 1156 he was succeeded by his infant son, Henry IV (1056–1106). The Pope took advantage of the temporary lapse in imperial supervision to call a council of reformers in 1059. It was declared that in all future Papal elections, the pontiff would be elected by the College of Cardinals rather than by secular rulers. The first pope elected by this system was Alexander II (961–73), who expanded Leo IX's policy of reform by appointing papal legates to encourage the adoption of Church reforms in provincial sees. One of the most zealous reformers was Hildebrand, who succeeded Alexander as Pope Gregory VII (1073–85).

During the tenure of Henry IV, the authority of the German monarch was constantly undermined by the senior German nobles, and the young king needed the support of his own bishops if he was to re-establish his imperial authority. Henry and Gregory had incompatible views about the role of ecclesiastical leaders, and a conflict was inevitable.

The Pope's powers in law

Shortly after his election, Pope Gregory wrote to Henry IV demanding that he stop meddling in Milanese politics. Two years later, in 1075, Gregory presided over a Church council which decreed in the *Dictus Papae* that henceforth no bishop or abbot could be appointed by a secular ruler. It also stated that the Pope could not be judged by anyone, but had the right to depose the "Emperor of the Romans" if he saw fit. Henry ignored him, and continued to support a pro-Imperial city leader in Milan. Gregory threatened to excommunicate the German king, prompting Henry to summon a council of German bishops who declared Pope Gregory a usurper and unfit to hold office. In February 1076 Pope Gregory excommunicated Henry IV and invoked his right to depose the monarch.

The German bishops backed down and abandoned Henry. At the same time his leading nobles sensed King Henry's weakness, and rebelled against him. Henry was forced to meet his dukes at a council (*Diet*), held in Augsburg in 1077. The idea was that the Pope, together with the German nobles, would there decide whether to restore Henry to his kingdom. In what would today be termed a "publicity coup," Henry traveled to Canossa in northern Italy to meet the Pope in person. The penitent Henry approached the pontiff on bare feet, confessed his sins, and asked for absolution. Gregory had little option but to accede.

This was far from the end of the matter, however. Henry returned to Germany, gathered supporters, and spent the next three years defeating the rebel German lords. He then turned his attention back to the Pope. Declaring him a usurper, Henry appointed an "antipope," or rival pontiff, then invaded Italy and—briefly—captured Rome in 1084. Gregory died the following year, but his successors continued his struggle.

The Investiture debate raged on into the early 12th century, with ecclesiastic and lay supporters on both sides. It was a rivalry mirrored in Italy by the two dominant political parties: the Guelphs and the Ghibbellenes. The agreement that ended the crisis was the Concordat of Worms, penned in 1122. In a compromise agreement between Henry V of Germany (1106–25) and Pope Calixtus II (1119–24), the Church had the right to appoint its own bishops, but in Germany, the king could be present, and reserved the right to veto the decision. This compromise was significant, since it ended a slide toward royal theocracy, but removed the threat of direct Papal interference in secular affairs through politically motivated decrees of excommunication and deposition. The investiture contest created a form of uneasy dualism in government, separating temporal and spiritual power, but ultimately pleasing no one. Another contest in the late 12th century would eventually settle the argument one way or the other.

Above: *Saint Remi, as depicted in a tapestry at Reims Cathedral.*

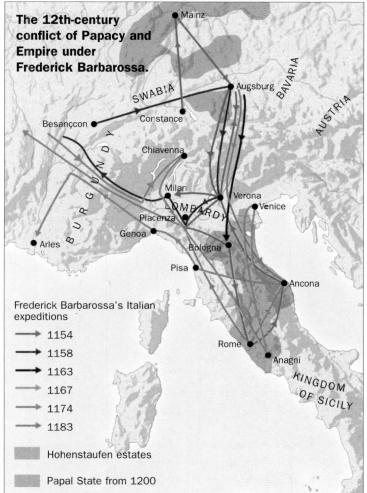

The 12th-century conflict of Papacy and Empire under Frederick Barbarossa.

Frederick Barbarossa's Italian expeditions

→ 1154
→ 1158
→ 1163
→ 1167
→ 1174
→ 1183

Hohenstaufen estates

Papal State from 1200

Facing: *Pope Gregory IX (see page 53) receiving the keys of the Vatican from St. Peter seated on his throne, as viewed in a 15th-century illuminated manuscript.*

Heresy

Organized religious dissent had been almost unknown in the Christian world since the fall of the Roman Empire, but during the late 11th century various sources of opposition to the established Church spread rapidly across Europe. What began as a protest against clerical worldliness became more threatening to the Church when some dissidents opposed long-established doctrinal views.

The Church declared all forms of dissent heretical in 1184, and instituted a policy of legal and theological repression. While some heretical groups abandoned their stance under this pressure, others, such as the Cathars, were only crushed through military conquest and inquisition.

In the late 12th century the Church emerged powerfully positioned from its struggle with the secular leaders of Europe. Its lands and holdings were extensive, and, at least in principle, its subjects were united under the spiritual protection of the Pope. Despite this position of strength, religious dissent had grown steadily for more than a century. Much of the discord centered around Christ's denunciation of worldly wealth. While poverty was a cornerstone of the monastic movements, regular clergy and the Church itself appeared to covet wealth and property, contrary to Christian teaching.

Increasingly, theologians and devout Christians began to stray from the established teachings of a Church they viewed as corrupt. The Church branded these religious dissenters as heretics, a word which means "error in faith"—a faith determined by the Roman Catholic Church. The two principal heretical movements of the period were the Waldensians and the Cathars, both of which were popular in southern France and parts of Italy (although other heretical communities flourished for brief periods in the Rhineland, Flanders, and the Loire valley).

The Waldensians followed a similar doctrine to that proposed by the Donatists, a fourth-century dissident movement. In 1173, Waldo, a prosperous merchant from Lyons, underwent a personal revelation and gave away his worldly possessions. He became a lay apostolic preacher, and his followers were first known as "the poor men of Lyons" and later as Waldensians. When the Waldensians continued to preach in defiance of the wishes of the Church, they were branded heretics in 1184.

Like the Donatists, Waldensians believed that that the sacraments could only be offered by priests who were free of sin. The official Catholic view was that as mere servants of Christ, any priest's moral failings were insignificant. The Waldensian argument proved popular, given contemporary criticism of the morality of the clergy. After 1184 the Church campaigned to win over the heretics in the Waldensian regions of southern France and northern Italy. Pope Innocent III (1198–1216) resorted to sterner measures, and by 1220 the inquisition courts had crushed almost all Waldensian dissent.

The pure in heart

The Cathars (named from the Greek word for "pure") developed during the 12th century and followed Manichean beliefs, an eastern theology that emphasized duality in life. Like the Waldensians, they were motivated by opposition to what they saw as the corruption of the existing Church, and opposed the authority of its clerics. Instead they created their own Cathar Church, where clerics, liturgy, and theology more accurately mirrored their beliefs.

Manichean dualism saw the world divided into two equal parts: good and evil. While spiritual matters and the soul were seen as good, materialism and the body were evil. Cathars were

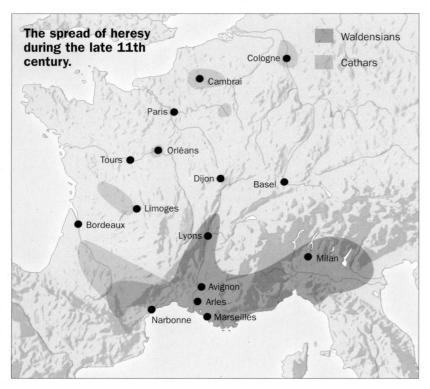

The spread of heresy during the late 11th century.

Waldensians

Cathars

Cologne
Cambrai
Paris
Orléans
Tours
Dijon
Basel
Limoges
Bordeaux
Lyons
Milan
Avignon
Arles
Narbonne
Marseilles

divided into the "perfect," who attempted to be the embodiment of worldly purity and chastity, and the "believers," who composed the rest of the Cathar faithful. Although all Cathars rejected material possessions and did not eat meat, the "perfect" were viewed as morally purer than the more worldly "believers." Cathars also rejected most aspects of the sacraments, and saw Christ as a spiritual messenger rather than the Son of God.

From the late 12th century, the Church launched a concentrated attack against heresy. At first, the spread of heresy was countered by reasoned debate, but soon Pope Lucius III (1181–85) established a papal inquisition to try heretics, an organization run by Dominican and Franciscan monks, but administered by regional Church diocese. Under Pope Gregory IX (1227–41) the Inquisition was used extensively to crush the Cathars in southern France. Those who repented were pardoned, but lapsed penitents or unrepentant heretics were burned at the stake. In 1209 Pope Innocent III (1198–1216) launched an intensive campaign against the Cathars and the nobility who sheltered them. A series of massacres destroyed most of the Cathar communities in southern France, and the Inquisition followed in the wake of the Crusades. By 1244 only very isolated pockets of Cathars remained, entrenched and isolated in the mountains of the Pyrenees.

Above: *The monk Domingo da Guzman (1170–1221) holds an Inquisition Court. Two condemned men await their turn, chained by the neck, while two others burn at the stake. Painted in 1496 by Pedro Berruguete.*

The Growth of Towns

During the 12th century Europe underwent an economic transformation. A revival of commerce, which had been greatly reduced following the collapse of the Roman Empire, encouraged the growth of urban centers. Within a century, towns would become a major force in the development of medieval Europe.

Facing above:

Towns sprang up in the shadow of great churches or castles, often clustered on the slopes of a defensive hilltop, like Calascibetta in Sicily.

Facing below:

This scene from a 14th-century manuscript is titled Building a town. *It could easily be taken for a lampoon, since the majority of the building work is ecclesiastical.*

To some historians, the growth of towns indicated the collapse of the feudal system. In reality the feudal system was based on an agrarian economy and each economy relied heavily on the other. Without a surplus of food produced in the surrounding countryside, towns were unlikely to grow. Towns provided a market for specialization, where merchants traded in specific commodities, and the rural peasants benefited from the resulting affordability of domestic items such as cooking pots and clothing. The feudal lord provided protection in exchange for revenue from tradesmen and, at least in theory, a pool of artisans who could produce arms and armor.

Towns and cities provided the medieval Church with powerful centers from which were administered rural areas. These Episcopal regions (or *diocese*) were almost always centered around a cathedral or other religious institution, which also served the needs of the town in which it was sited. By the late 12th century, secular rulers found they needed to house a growing staff of bureaucrats, and administrative centers developed, such as Paris and London (Westminster). This allowed greater freedom of movement—vital when courts moved around the country,

constantly securing the loyalty of the feudal nobility. In some regions, such as in what is today Germany, rulers encouraged settlement in fortified towns as a means of defense against incursions. Special economic privileges were offered as an incentive to encourage settlement, tax exemptions and judicial protection, for instance.

The economic revival and the renewal of commerce that led to the spread of towns during the 12th century had originated two centuries earlier. By the late tenth century, Venice shipped food and wines to the Byzantines in return for silks that were sold throughout northern Italy. Merchant centers on Italy's western coast like Genoa and Naples traded with the Arabs. For the inland towns of northern Italy, this provided a market for the sale of wool. The Norman conquest of Sicily and southern Italy helped to protect this growing maritime trade, and by the mid–11th century, Italian merchants traded throughout the Mediterranean.

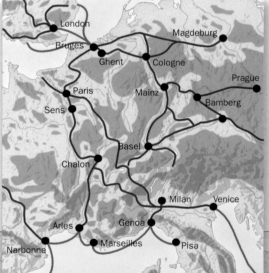

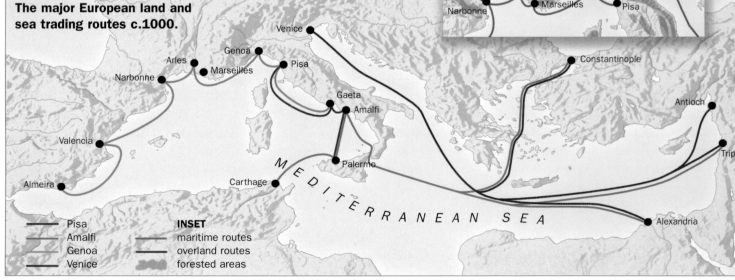

The major European land and sea trading routes c.1000.

—— Pisa	**INSET**	
—— Amalfi	—— maritime routes	
—— Genoa	—— overland routes	
—— Venice	forested areas	

In northern Europe, Flanders (now Belgium) became a production center for woolen cloth, which became a major trading commodity. From the early 12th century, Flemish merchants were protected by powerful feudal lords, and traded throughout England, France, and Germany. The Flemish towns of Bruges, Ghent, and Lille became flourishing marketplaces, and raw materials were shipped to Flemish mills from England in return for wine. By the mid-12th century Flanders and Italy were at the center of a commercial revival in Europe, but the geographical barrier of the Alps limited trade between them.

Slow but steady development

Trade and the administrative roles of townships helped to stimulate urban growth from the late 11th century onward. Outside the commercial centers mentioned above, towns were little more than a marketplace for local produce, although both secular and clerical rulers provided a market that supported skilled artisans like stonemasons and metalworkers. In turn these administrative centers and markets slowly developed into places where merchants could ply their more specialist wares.

In time mercantile districts grew in towns outside Flanders and Italy, and trade routes began to span the continent. By offering their feudal overlords financial revenue through taxation in return for protection and freedom to trade, merchants lined the coffers of the local nobility. This in turn stimulated patronage of the local artisans who built the nobles' castles and armed their retinues. In return, merchants and other urban dwellers were granted a charter freeing them from feudal obligations; in other words economic freedom. A bond was formed between merchant and feudal lord that is reflected in most of the city charters produced during this period. It would be a century before these towns and cities would feel the need to break their feudal bonds and establish their own political identity.

The Foundation of the Italian City-States

For much of the period from the late tenth to the early twelfth century, the Italian peninsula became a battleground between various warring factions. Norman adventurers fought for control of southern Italy and Sicily. With the Pope and the emperor engaged in an increasingly bitter battle for supremacy, Italian townspeople could expect little protection from their spiritual or temporal overlords. As a necessary alternative they developed their own means of protection.

Facing: *Siena was one of the growing Italian cities to reject outside rule and seek protection as a commune from local nobility.*

Below: *Italian noble families required strong fortifications to withstand imperial forces; Este castle.*

In Italy, urban life had not suffered the same decline as it had north of the Alps and many were able to benefit from the re-establishment of European trade in the 11th century. The merchants and artisans who produced the wealth of these cities resented the intrusion of feudal, imperial, and ecclesiastic overlords, and opted for an alternate system, where they united for mutual protection and advancement.

By 1080 the townspeople of Lucca and Pisa had rejected the overlordship of the emperor and his bishops and established "communes," which were protected by the regional nobility. This political movement spread beyond Tuscany and Lombardy during the 11th and 12th centuries, and similar communes appeared in France, the Low Countries, and parts of Germany. As these cities thrived and their internal governments developed, they evolved into the city-states that came to dominate Italy and other parts of Europe in the later Middle Ages.

Another form of mutual protection was the defensive League. The rich cities of the north Italian plain were coveted by a succession of German monarchs who needed funding for their near-continual wars with rebellious senior nobles. When Lombardy was captured by the Germans in 1162, the excesses of the troops led the population to rise in revolt, a rebellion supported by the Pope and the Norman King of Sicily.

In 1167 the rebels united into the Lombard

League, a confederation of a dozen cities, including Milan, Genoa, and Pavia. A similar League of Verona united the cities surrounding the tributary of the River Po, including Verona, Venice, and Padua. Frederick Barbarossa sent an army to crush the Lombards, but the imperial forces were defeated at Legnano (1176), forcing the Emperor to sign a truce with the League. In 1183 at the Peace of Constance the members of the Lombard League agreed to imperial taxation and protection in return for peace. In truth, the German nobles were the best form of protection the Italian cities had, whose rebellions kept the Emperor occupied north of the Alps. There were exceptions, and both the son and grandson of Frederick Barbarossa campaigned extensively in southern Italy.

A patchwork of states

During the pontificate of Innocent III (1198–1216) political power in Italy stabilized to some degree, with the Pope administering a large Papal State in central Italy, the kings of Sicily consolidating their control over southern Italy, and the emergent city-states of Lombardy and Tuscany left to develop under nominal imperial control.

Apart from invasion, another by-product of the feud between Pope and emperor was the creation of rival political camps in Italy. As in Germany, the adherents of both sides adopted the party names of Guelph (for the Church) and Ghibelline (for the emperor). The rivalry existed at all levels, and while some claimed moral advantages, calling the emperor a savior or a heretic (depending on the party line), others used the rivalry to pursue partisan agendas. In many Italian cities, the split followed family, city, or economic lines. While the Guelphs eventually triumphed in decisive military victories during the mid-13th century, the terms continued to be used for more local political feuds. In some communes, open street fighting between rival factions became commonplace, forcing many townspeople to look toward less democratic forms of civic leadership.

In some of these cities during the 12th century, civic power was granted to outside *podesta* (or city magistrates), in an attempt to counter internal political or family rivalries. This was not altogether successful, and first republican oligarchies, then individual families, struggled for civic dominance. These families—the Visconti in Milan, the Lambertazzi in Bologna and others—developed into the *signori*, or despots of the 13th century. By the early 13th century, while Venice, Genoa, Padua, and the Tuscan cities retained their rights of self-determination, most of the rest of the cities of northern Italy were under signorial domination.

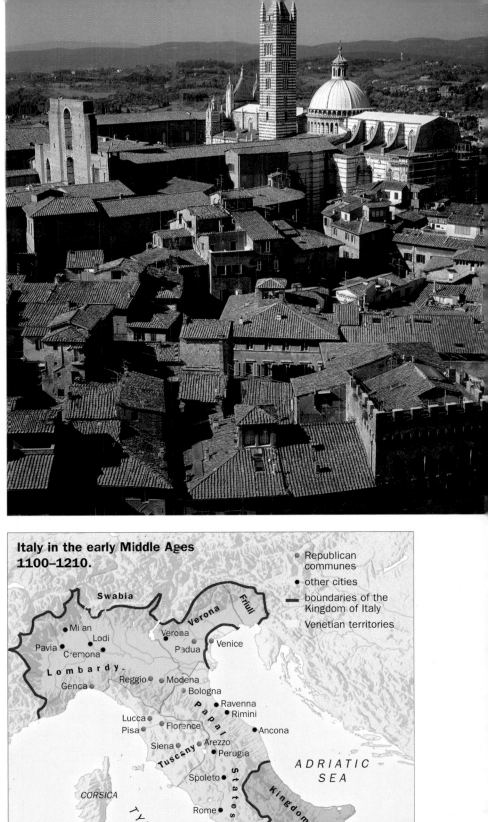

Italy in the early Middle Ages 1100–1210.

- Republican communes
- other cities
- boundaries of the Kingdom of Italy
- Venetian territories

FOCUS: LEADERS
Frederick I Barbarossa

Emperor Frederick I ruled as head of the Holy Roman Empire for almost 40 years from 1152; a reign that witnessed increased German influence within Europe and the establishment of a working feudal society within the Empire itself. His striking appearance and commanding presence were reflected in his appellation of "Barbarossa" (Redbeard). Despite being the Emperor who first added the word "Holy" to the title "Roman Emperor," his reign was marked by an increasingly bitter dispute between Church and State.

During the first half of the 12th century the rulers of the German states of central Europe were divided by arguments over inheritance, dynastic power struggles, and territorial ownership. One of these nobles was Frederick of Hohenstaufen, the Duke of Swabia in southern Germany, who became the heir to the personal lands of his uncle, Emperor Henry V (1106–25). When elections for Emperor were held on Henry's death, a rival to Frederick was appointed, and the Duke spent the next decade challenging the rule of Emperor Lothair II.

The future Emperor was born the son of a duke. His childhood was dominated by warfare and political struggle between his own house of Hohenstaufen and the Welf (Guelf) house headed by Emperor Lothair. When Lothair died, the princes and churchmen elected the young Frederick's uncle, who became Conrad III (1137–52). Dynastic rivalries continued, and Imperial authority diminished as the German nobility indulged in factional conflict. When Frederick succeeded to his father's dukedom in 1147, he set himself up as a

Right: *This 12th-century relief from the portal of Freising Cathedral, Germany, shows Emperor Frederick I, Barbarossa with Bishop Albrecht von Freising on the left.*

conciliator, establishing links in both dynastic camps, while re-establishing his ducal authority over the lesser nobility of Swabia. By the time of Conrad's death, the German princes were drained by these struggles, and elected Frederick as a candidate who offered the chance of unity and peace.

Machiavellian tactics

Duke Frederick became Emperor Frederick I in 1152, but his direct authority was limited to his own feudal lands. Any attempt to force his authority on the German princes would cause a resumption of dynastic conflict, and he was less powerful than his leading Welf rival, Henry the Lion, Duke of Saxony and Bavaria. He placated Duke Henry with gifts of territory while

1015	1022	1054	1059
First Italian commune established at Benevento	Synod of Pavia insists on celibacy in higher clergy	Split between Catholic and Orthodox Churches occurs	Role of College of Cardinals assured in Papal elections

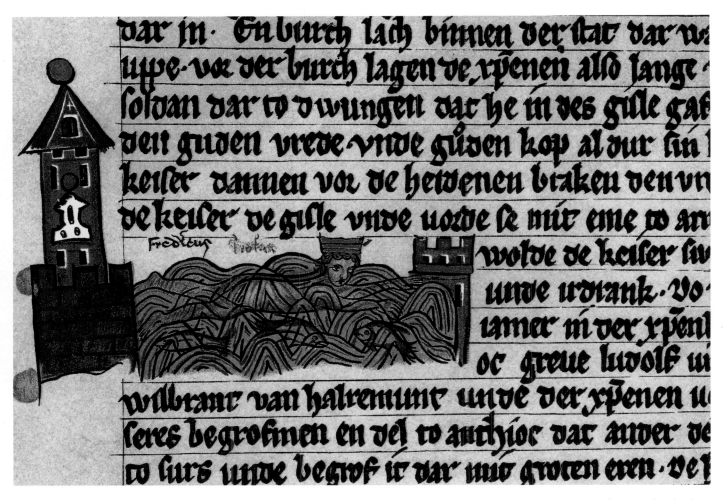

dar jn · En burch lach binnen der stat dar wa
uppe · vor der burch lagen de xpenen also lange ·
soldan dar to dwungen dar he in des gulle gaf
dett guden vrede · vnde guden kop al dut sin
keiser dannen vor de heidenen braken den vn
de keiser de gulle vnde vorde se mit eme to an
wolde de keiser su
unde urdrank · Do
iamer in der xpenl
oc greue lovolf u
wilbrant van halremunt unde der xpenen u
feres begrofmen en del to antchioc dar ander de
to surs unde begrof it dar mid groten eren · de]

strengthening the power of Henry's rivals to ensure a political balance. He then insisted that the leading German princes pay feudal homage to him, in return for their freedom to impose control over their feudal vassals. By reinforcing feudal obligations, he ensured some degree of stability at all lower levels in the feudal system, while emphasizing his own position at its head.

In 1156 he married Beatrice of Burgundy and took control of her lands. He then directed his attention to Lombardy in northern Italy, a territory that was nominally under imperial control, but which had been virtually autonomous for a century. Barbarossa's troops conquered Lombardy, and established feudal control over the countryside and political dominance over the self-governing communes that ran the cities. Pope Adrian IV became concerned about this increase in imperial power, and feared any emperor who might have designs on the Pope's Roman power-base. Adrian attempted to enforce a degree of feudal authority over Frederick, but his efforts were fruitless.

Adrian's successor was Pope Alexander III, a man opposed to any increase in imperial authority. In 1160 he excommunicated Frederick, and the Emperor responded by appointing an antipope. The rivalry continued for a decade until Alexander's support for the city communes helped encourage a revolt in Lombardy. After Frederick's army was defeated at Legnano (1176), the Emperor was forced to negotiate a truce with the Pope. The Emperor begged the Pope's forgiveness and the two made a public pronouncement of reconciliation in 1177.

Frederick devoted the remainder of his life to strengthening the feudal system within the Empire, modeling the German structure on French and English lines. He saw the crusading movement as a means to unify his German nobility in a common cause, and led a German contingent on the Third Crusade in 1190, only to drown during an Anatolian river crossing in what is now Turkey.

He left behind a strengthened empire built on solid feudal lines. His adoption of the term "Holy Empire" arose from his struggle for supremacy with the Pope. That it remained in use after his death is an indication of the increased power and prestige of the empire that Frederick Barbarossa saved, reinvented, and united during a critical period in German political development.

Above: *The death by drowning of Frederick Barbarossa from the Gotha Manuscript of the Saxon Chronicle, written in the second half of the 13th century.*

1065	1070	1071	1071	1075	1077	1081	1083
Benedictine manual of clerical music written	Diet of Augsburg	Constantine the African introduces Greek medicine to western Europe	Defeat of Greek army by Turks at Manzikert	*Dictus Papae* defines papal authority	Submission of Emperor Henry IV to the Pope at Canossa	Venetians negotiate trade privileges with the Byzantine Empire	Emperor Henry IV captures Rome

FOCUS: WARFARE
Feudal Warfare

Following the Norman conquests of the kingdoms of England and Sicily in the late 11th century, warfare in western Europe followed a pattern that remained relatively unchanged until the start of the 14th century. In almost every sphere of war the mounted knight dominated Europe's many battlefields, and the feudal structure of society was replicated in the composition and command structure of the contemporary army.

Below and facing: *The European feudal army in full battle array, laying siege to a large town.*

The composition of a Norman army (outlined on page 40) provided the basic model for all feudal armies for the next two centuries. The granting of land by a feudal superior was essentially for the purpose of supporting one or more armed soldiers for an agreed period. The numbers of troops and length of required service varied widely, and a vassal could fulfil his quota by hiring mercenaries instead of supplying his own men.

In Germany, a class of *ministerialis* or unfree knights were directly employed by some nobles purely to fulfill military obligations to feudal superiors. In some instances, feudal retinues could be kept in the field longer than the agreed period, or consist of more troops if the men were paid for their additional service. This led to paid and unpaid feudal contingents within the same army. In times of grave emergency the king or a leading noble could call an *arrière-ban*; a muster of all able-bodied men, irrespective of agreed quotas.

From the 12th century, a fee called *scutage* could be paid in lieu of required military service, and the money was then used to hire mercenaries. Mounted knights (or sergeants) and archers, usually crossbowmen, formed the principal corps of mercenaries. By the 13th century these mercenary (or stipendiary) troops formed a substantial part of a medieval army, hired individually or in bands. Mercenaries were generally more experienced than their feudal counterparts, and better equipped. By the end of the 13th century the proportion of knights in a feudal army was small, due to re-evaluations of knightly status, the increasing expense of equipment, and growing reliance on mercenaries.

Military strategy

Armies were usually divided into three *battles* (divisions); the vanguard, main body, and rearguard. On rare occasions a fourth division might be formed. The variations of deployment were considerable, with the three bodies in line (*en haye*), echeloned (*en échelon*), in column, or a combination of these, with one battle held in reserve. The general army commander led the main body or the reserve, while leading nobles commanded the other formations. Each battle was composed of a body of cavalry, a mass of infantry, and sometimes a skirmishing line of archers or crossbowmen.

The principal battle-winning tactic during this period was the charge of mounted and armored knights. These warriors and their armored horses have been likened to the modern-day tank. They charged in close-packed lines, each knight bearing a lance, and the impetus of their momentum and sheer weight ripped apart enemy formations. Cavalry advanced at a trot, only speeding to a gallop during the last 300 feet before contact. If neither side was broken from the charge, lances were discarded and the knights used hand-to-hand weapons such as swords, axes, and maces. This furious charge and the mounted melée that followed invariably proved the decisive period of the battle. With their knights routed, the infantry of a feudal army could rarely hold their ground.

In most battles the infantry was used

1084	1086	1094	1122	1123	1138	1149	1150
Carthusian Order founded	Domesday Book provides a survey of English land ownership	The first gondolas are recorded in Venice	Concordat of Worms increases secular power over the German Church	The First Lateran Council ratifies division of secular and spiritual power	Start of Hohenstaufen dynasty in Germany	The Second Crusade ends in failure	The University of Paris is founded

defensively, formed into large close-ranked blocks, and armed with spears or a variety of handheld weapons. When these troops were composed of a feudal levy of peasants, they were unlikely to perform well on the battlefield. In many cases, feudal quotas were made up of men who were experienced soldiers; well-armed and armored. In some instances, well-armed knights were dismounted and formed the front rank of infantry formations, in order to stiffen their resolve. During the closing decades of the 13th century, well-trained infantry spearmen appeared on the battlefields of Flanders and Scotland, capable of resisting determined mounted charges. These were the exception, and unless placed in a strong defensive position, infantry were unlikely to stand under intense missile fire or in the face of determined cavalry.

Missile fire became increasingly common during the feudal period, usually provided by crossbowmen but also from archers. Almost always mercenaries—and generally employed in small numbers—they had an increasingly influential role in warfare. By the start of the 14th century massed archers in English service came to dominate the European battlefield; an ascendancy that helped hasten the demise of the knight.

FOCUS: SOCIETY

Romanesque Architecture

By about AD 1000 increased security and prosperity in Europe was being expressed through a wave of construction, principally religious buildings. These towering edifices were the largest structures built in Europe since the fall of the Roman Empire, and owed much to classic Roman designs. The term "Romanesque" was coined to describe this miracle of medieval architecture.

Facing: *The Cathedral Santa Maria del Mar, Barcelona, already shows Gothic style in the crossing arches, but the diagonals are pure Romanesque.*

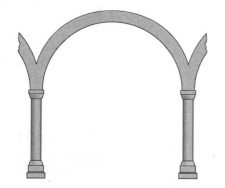

Above and right: *The Romanesque style developed from the Roman rounded arch. By crossing diagonal rounded arches, powerful barrel-vaults could be raised. In early Romanesque basilicas, the right-angled central arches were also round, but gradually assumed more pointed shapes.*

In AD 955 stonemasons began work on a new abbey at Cluny in France. No building larger than any of the modest-sized provincial Roman ruins had been erected for over 500 years. Cluny was to be a new beginning.

Following the ending of the Viking and Magyar raids of the previous century, a sense of security arose, encouraged by the relative stability of the feudal system. As towns sprang up and secular rulers prospered, new ambitious building projects were planned.

From the start of the 11th century this building trend intensified and created the wave of construction that would last throughout the Middle Ages. Although stone castles were being built almost everywhere, most construction was for religious purposes—cathedrals, abbeys, churches. One contemporary chronicler claimed that the land was covered in a "white robe of churches," such was the building frenzy.

These structures owed much to remaining Roman buildings and ruins, but their architects added their own adaptations to the older designs to create a unique form of architecture. This became known as "Romanesque," and the term was later applied to decorative arts produced within the same period—from about 950 to the mid-12th century. Although in northern Europe Romanesque architecture is largely associated with the Normans—the term "Norman" is sometimes used as a substitute for "Romanesque"—their influence in Italy promoted some of the earliest fine examples throughout the peninsula.

The classic form of the large late-Roman church is the *basilica*, essentially a long rectangular building consisting of a central *nave*, flanked by one or more *aisle*s. As with most Christian buildings, basilicas are aligned on an east-west axis. In these churches, the nave and the aisles are separated by a row of large columns, which support the roof over the nave. If there are two aisles on either side of the nave, a secondary line of columns separates the flanking aisles. In most cases the aisles are covered by a lower roof, while the nave's walls soar above them and are pierced by windows. This upper area, or *clerestory*, lets light into the building.

At the eastern end of the nave a semi-circular area—the *apse*—houses the altar. In some cases, the apse is distanced from the nave and the side aisles by a rectangular area called the *transept*, which runs at right angles to the nave and forms the shape of the cross. In many later churches, the transept exceeds the width of the main building to create a cruciform basilica. Durham Cathedral in northern England is a classic example of a Romanesque basilica.

Architectural innovation

A keynote of Roman engineering was the rounded arch, although rarely used in building construction (notable examples, which may have influenced Norman architects, are the Baths of Caracalla and the Basilica of Maxentius in Rome). Romanesque architects understood the principles of the arch and replaced simple

1154		1155	1163	1176
Henry II becomes the first Angevin king of England		Earliest recorded fire insurance (in Iceland)	Construction of Notre Dame Cathedral in Paris begins	Battle of Legnano; Emperor defeated by Lombard League

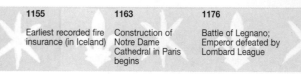

Roman flat roofs with a far grander, rounded barrel-shaped vaults of stone.

An arched roof creates its own problems. The nave walls must be immensely thick to support the lateral pressure of the arched roof and, ideally, there would be no clerestory windows to weaken the walls, making the church gloomy. To get around the design weakness, the nave columns were strengthened and then linked by transverse arches that ran along the vaulted nave like a series of ribs. Where the barrel-vaults of the nave and transept intersected, box-like groin-vaults added sufficient strength to the structure that clerestory windows could be added. This form of rib-vaulting would eventually lead to a later and lighter architectural form—the Gothic.

This basic design created a building that was still dark, but of a size, solidity, and grandeur previously unimaginable; veritable "fortresses for God." Later modifications included the increased use of groin-vaulting to allow for more windows, and an increased use of internal and external decoration. Unlike the sparse Romans, medieval architects used sculpture extensively, especially in the semi-circular *tympana* over the porch and in the pillars lining the nave. These religious sculptures—often quite simple—were deeply symbolic and added to the spiritual aura of the building. For the population, the lofty styles of new liturgical music would have made worship in these awe-inspiring buildings an awe-inspiring and deeply spiritual experience.

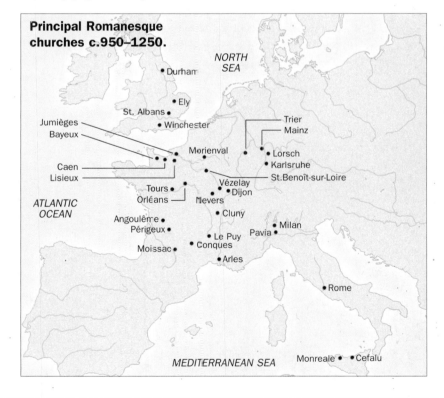

Principal Romanesque churches c.950–1250.

1177	1179	1179	1184	1187	1190-92	1194	1204
The Peace of Venice; reconciliation between Emperor and Pope	Construction starts on the Leaning Tower of Pisa	Third Lateran Council undertakes Church reform	The Waldensians are labeled as heretics	Defeat of crusading army leads to fall of Jerusalem to the Muslims	Third Crusade under Richard I; Cyprus captured	Emperor Henry VI conquers Norman kingdom of Sicily	Army of the Fourth Crusade sacks Constantinople

63

CHAPTER FOUR

God Wills It: The Crusades

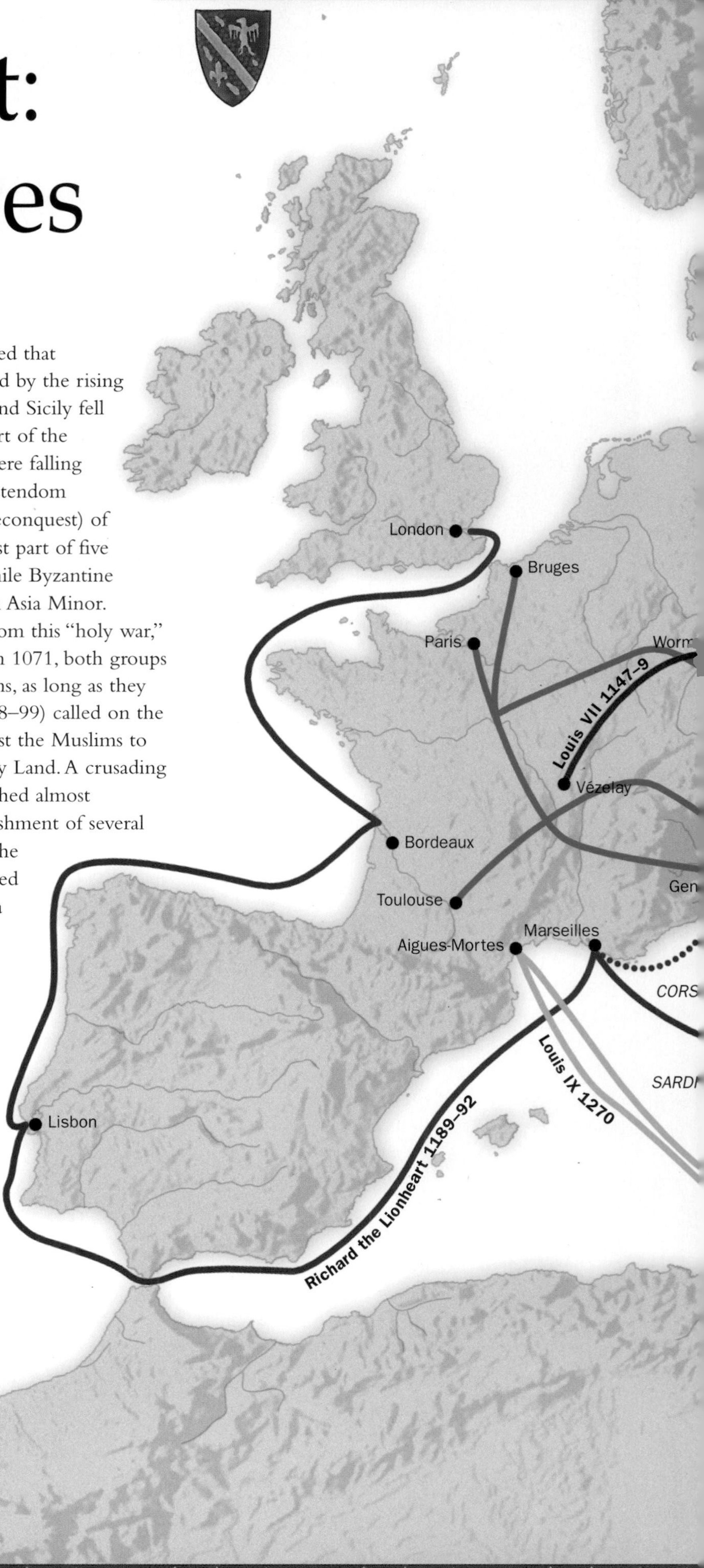

During the seventh and eighth centuries it seemed that Christian Europe was destined to be submerged by the rising Islamic tide. In the west, North Africa, Spain, and Sicily fell to the Moors, and Muslim armies penetrated to the heart of the Frankish kingdom. Further to the east the Byzantines were falling back under pressure from their Islamic opponents. Christendom survived, and by the mid-11th century the *reconquista* (reconquest) of Spain was underway, a campaign that would last the most part of five centuries. Norman adventurers campaigned in Sicily, while Byzantine armies tried to recapture some of their lost territories in Asia Minor.

Both the Church and the feudal nobility benefited from this "holy war," and when the Byzantines suffered a cataclysmic defeat in 1071, both groups were willing to come to the aid of their fellow Christians, as long as they benefited from the gesture. In 1095 Pope Urban II (1088–99) called on the Christians of western Europe to launch a Crusade against the Muslims to save Constantinople (Byzantium) and recapture the Holy Land. A crusading army was in the field within two years, and it accomplished almost everything its commanders desired, including the establishment of several new Latin or Christian states in the Middle East. Over the next two centuries these lands would be bitterly contested by Christians and Muslims, a battle that would provide a focus for religious zeal and personal bravery.

London

Bruges

Paris

Worm

Louis VII 1147–9

Vézelay

Bordeaux

Toulouse

Gen

Marseilles

Aigues-Mortes

CORS

SARDI

Lisbon

Richard the Lionheart 1189–92

Louis IX 1270

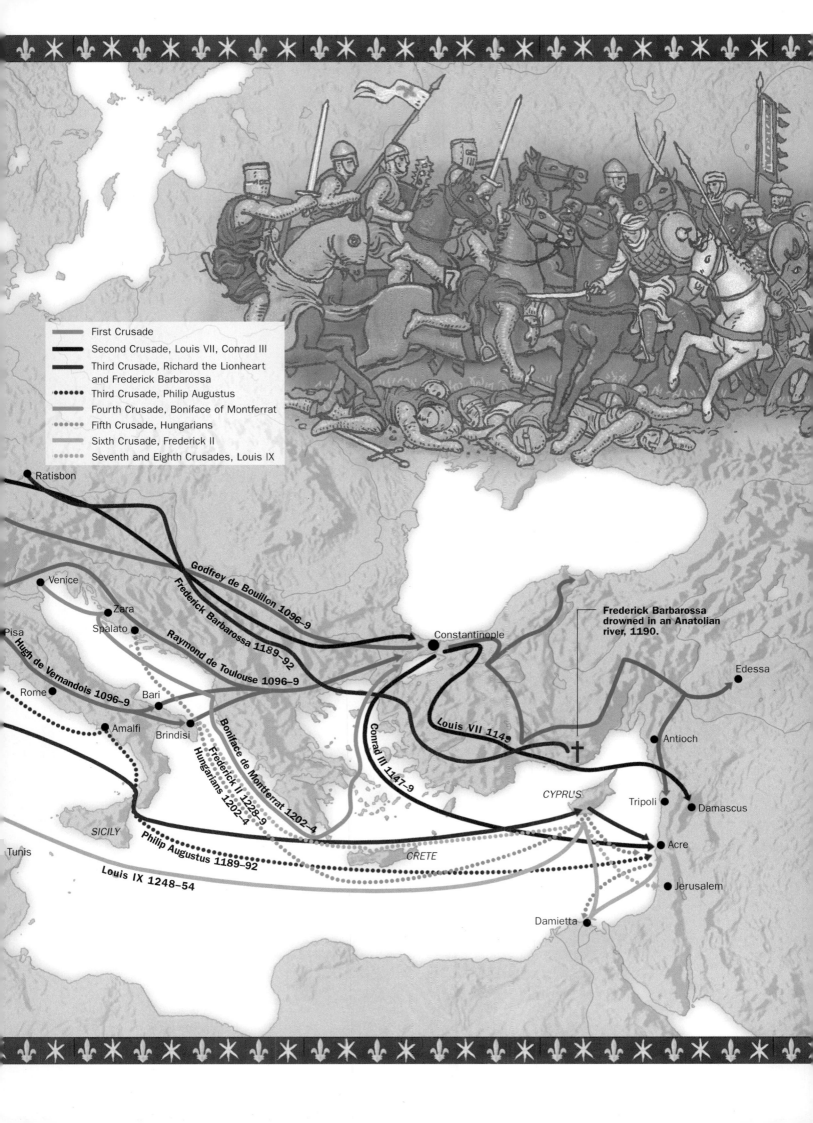

First Crusade
Second Crusade, Louis VII, Conrad III
Third Crusade, Richard the Lionheart and Frederick Barbarossa
Third Crusade, Philip Augustus
Fourth Crusade, Boniface of Montferrat
Fifth Crusade, Hungarians
Sixth Crusade, Frederick II
Seventh and Eighth Crusades, Louis IX

Ratisbon

Venice

Zara

Spalato

Pisa

Hugh de Vernandois 1096–9

Rome

Bari

Amalfi

Brindisi

SICILY

Tunis

Godfrey de Bouillon 1096–9

Frederick Barbarossa 1189–92

Raymond de Toulouse 1096–9

Boniface de Montferrat 1202–4

Frederick II 1228–9

Hungarians 1202–4

Philip Augustus 1189–92

Louis IX 1248–54

CRETE

Constantinople

Conrad III 1147–9

Louis VII 1149

CYPRUS

Frederick Barbarossa drowned in an Anatolian river, 1190.

Edessa

Antioch

Tripoli

Damascus

Acre

Jerusalem

Damietta

The Origins of the Crusading Movement

When the Byzantines asked the Pope for help in their fight with the Muslims, they unleashed a force that would change the landscape of the Middle East. When Pope Urban called for a crusade against the infidel, he received an enthusiastic response. These crusaders went on to carve out a new feudal Christian state in the Holy Land, ushering in centuries of religious conflict.

When the Byzantine Emperor Alexius Comnenus (1081–1118) asked for the support of the Roman Church in recovering its lands lost to the Muslims, he set in motion a chain of events that would bring down the Empire. That the request was even made indicates the desperate straits the Byzantines found themselves in. Conflict between the Greek

opportunities a holy war against the Muslims would provide. Crusaders would be fighting for the Church, and he also saw the opportunities that this precedent would set in establishing papal supremacy over the secular feudal powers of western Europe.

While the Emperor needed military help to recover his lost territories in Asia Minor, the Pope had different plans. He envisaged an attack through Constantinople to the Holy Land, where his crusaders could recapture the city of Jerusalem from the Infidel. On November 27, 1095, Pope Urban II preached to a council of secular and spiritual dignitaries at Claremont, France. He spoke convincingly, declaring that the Muslim control of Jerusalem was an affront to Christendom, and that any Crusader who died in this holy war would be rewarded in heaven.

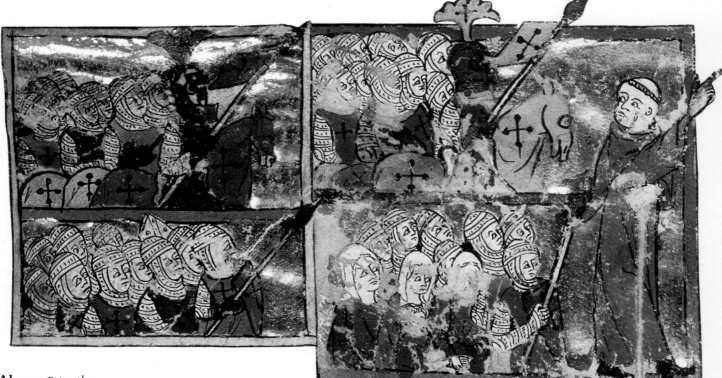

Above: *Peter the Hermit (Peter of Amiens) leads the First Crusade in 1096; from a 14th-century manuscript.*

patriarch and the Pope over leadership of the Christian Church had strained relations between Rome and Constantinople for the past two centuries. The two churches were now separated by a rift that appeared unbridgeable.

Pope Urban II (1088–99) saw the appeal for help as a chance to establish influence over the Byzantine Church and to take advantage of the

He called on the secular powers of Europe to stop their internecine fighting and unite under his holy banner. To avoid bickering between secular commanders he appointed Adhemar, the bishop of Le Puy, to lead the crusade. While the Pope toured France to gather support, other clerics took up the cause, and together they created a frenzy of crusading zeal.

Transcending class

Not all of those who took up the crusading challenge were from the higher echelons of feudal society. Thousands of peasants and members of the lesser nobility broke away from their feudal obligations and formed into several groups. Peter the Hermit and the knight Walter Sansavoir became the leaders of these bands, who crossed through France and Germany, gathering supporters as they went—and massacring Jews as a substitute for Muslims. Most of the groups that made up this Peasants' Crusade never reached Constantinople, but were massacred by Hungarians and Bulgars, who saw them as disorganized mobs of looters. Those who reached Constantinople were quickly ferried to Asia Minor, where the Muslims defeated them with ease.

The main crusade was ready to march by the summer of 1096. Its secular leaders included Robert, Duke of Normandy, Count Baldwin of Flanders, Raymond, Count of Toulouse, and Godfrey, Duke of Lorraine. While Godfrey marched overland, others traveled by sea from Italy, or along the Adriatic coast to Greece. The forces gathered at Constantinople, where an understandably distrustful Emperor fed and sheltered the 12,000 crusaders, before shipping them to Asia Minor. In May 1097 the crusaders laid siege to the Muslim city of Nicea, then marched toward the Holy Land.

The Byzantines followed the forces to reoccupy their lost territory. The Seljuk Turks were defeated at Dorylaeum (1097), and most of the crusaders had reached Antioch by late summer. While the main party laid siege to the city, Baldwin of Flanders detached his own force to claim a feudal domain for himself, centered around the Syrian city of Edessa.

The crusaders outside Antioch lacked proper siege equipment. It was proposed to storm the city, and the first leader inside its walls would claim the city as his own. The rash assault succeeded, and Bohemond of Sicily won the challenge. A Turkish relief army arrived and besieged the crusaders, but the Christians were heartened by the discovery of the Holy Lance, the spear allegedly used to wound Christ on the cross. Carrying the relic as a standard, they assaulted and routed the Turkish army.

While Bohemond (who now styled himself the Prince of Antioch) remained to rule his new city, the rest of the crusading army marched south toward Jerusalem. In June 1099 they laid siege to the holy city, and captured it after a month-long siege, which culminated in the storming of its walls. The Arab and Jewish inhabitants were massacred, and then a mass was held to celebrate the bloody victory. The crusaders now held most of the Mediterranean coast of the Middle East, from Antioch to Ascalon, southwest of Jerusalem, together with the inland territory of Edessa, which stretched as far as the River Tigris. This Christian enclave in the heart of the Muslim world would be a battleground for the next two centuries.

Above: *Book illustrations showing a crusade ship and the conquest of Nicae by crusaders on June 20, 1097, during the First Crusade.*

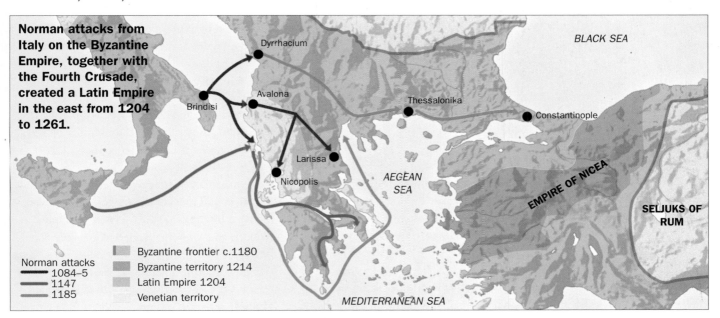

Norman attacks from Italy on the Byzantine Empire, together with the Fourth Crusade, created a Latin Empire in the east from 1204 to 1261.

Dyrrhacium

Avalona

Brindisi

Larissa

Nicopolis

Thessalonika

Constantinople

BLACK SEA

AEGEAN SEA

EMPIRE OF NICEA

SELJUKS OF RUM

MEDITERRANEAN SEA

Norman attacks
— 1084–5
— 1147
— 1185

Byzantine frontier c.1180
Byzantine territory 1214
Latin Empire 1204
Venetian territory

Outremer: The Crusader States

Following the capture of Jerusalem in 1099, the leaders of the First Crusade established their own feudal states in the Middle East. Surrounded by their Muslim enemies, they were vulnerable to attack, and subsequent crusades were needed to ensure their survival. By the 13th century these Christian outposts had become little more than a reminder of the ultimate failure of the crusading movement.

The secular leaders of the First Crusade were partly motivated by religious zeal, but they also saw the crusade as an opportunity to carve out their own feudal fiefdoms in the Middle East. Most of them had crossed swords with each other at some stage during the campaign, and already two had established their own feudal domains: Bohemond of Sicily's Principality of Antioch and Baldwin of Flanders' County of Edessa. The remainder elected the relatively popular Godfrey de Bouillon as their feudal overlord, naming him

Below: *Geoffrey de Bouillon, wearing the instruments of Christ's passion.*

"Defender of the Holy Sepulcher." His Kingdom of Jerusalem followed similar geographical boundaries to the modern states of Israel and Lebanon, extending to Bohemond's borders.

This kingdom was far from secure, however. Many of its cities were still in Muslim hands, and it was surrounded by enemies. Within weeks Godfrey was forced to defend his new territory against an Arab army, which he defeated at Ascalon (1099). When he died the following year, he was succeeded by his brother Baldwin de Bouillon, Count of Flanders and Edessa. The self-styled King Baldwin (1100–18) consolidated his hold over his territory while Raymond of Tolouse claimed the northern portion of the kingdom for himself, creating the County of Tripoli. Further to the north, "Prince" Bohemond of Antioch captured the Syrian city of Aleppo. The Turkish cities in the region fell one after the other, and when Tyre was captured in 1124, the crusaders controlled the entire coastline of the Holy Land.

Jerusalem, Tyre, and Acre formed the royal demesne, while the rest of the Kingdom of Jerusalem was distributed among the king's followers in return for their oath of fealty. This was a direct copy of the feudal system of western Europe, transplanted into a new land. The relationship between the three Crusader States and the Kingdom of Jerusalem was vague, and while the Prince of Antioch and the Counts of Edessa and Tripoli were vassals of the king, for the most part they operated as independent entities.

Weakening zeal

Edessa fell to the Turks in 1144, prompting the declaration of the Second Crusade. Led by the kings of France and Germany, it failed to recapture Edessa, and fizzled out. A series of weak monarchs during the late 12th century gave the Muslims the opportunity they needed to launch a counter-attack. A Muslim (or Saracen) army led by Saladin (1137–92), the Fatimid ruler of Syria and Egypt, met the crusaders at Hattin (1187). The badly led Christian army was decimated, leaving the Crusader States virtually defenseless. Jerusalem and most of its kingdom fell to Saladin, followed by the other Crusader States. Only Antioch and Tripoli remained in Christian hands.

Pope Clement III (1187–91) called for a Third Crusade, and this time the secular rulers responded with alacrity. Henry II of England, Philip II Augustus of France, and the Emperor

Frederick I Barbarossa, all raised troops, but internal disputes prevented all but Frederick from leaving Europe. The Germans crossed into Asia Minor and captured the Turkish Sultanate of Rum before marching on Antioch.

Frederick drowned in an Anatolian river in 1190, and his troops returned home from Antioch, but Henry II's son was ready to join the fray. Richard I the Lionheart (1189–99) sailed to the Holy Land in 1191 and captured Byzantine Cyprus on the way. He linked up with the army of King Philip, the surviving German crusaders, and the remnants of the Kingdom of Jerusalem's army, which was laying siege to Acre.

The city fell, but disagreements between the English and French monarchs reached a head, and Philip returned home. Richard led the remaining crusaders south toward Jerusalem, defeating Saladin at Arsouf (1191) and Jaffa (1192). But by this time his army was too weakened to capture Jerusalem, so Richard and his crusaders had to be content with consolidating the gains they had already made.

Richard left the Holy Land in 1192, and when Saladin died the following year, his successors changed their policy toward the Christians. Richard had negotiated a fragile peace, and the remaining Crusader States, now referred to collectively as *Outremer* (Overseas) were allowed to survive, at least for the moment. The Principality of Antioch and the County of Tripoli had re-established their old borders, but the Kingdom of Jerusalem was now confined to the area around Acre. These territories were no longer a threat to their Muslim neighbors, and when the Fourth Crusade ended in the ignominious sack of Constantinople in 1204, the crusading zeal that had dominated Europe for more than a century came to an end. While the Latin states of Outremer survived until 1291, they had become little more than the anachronistic remnants of a failed ideal.

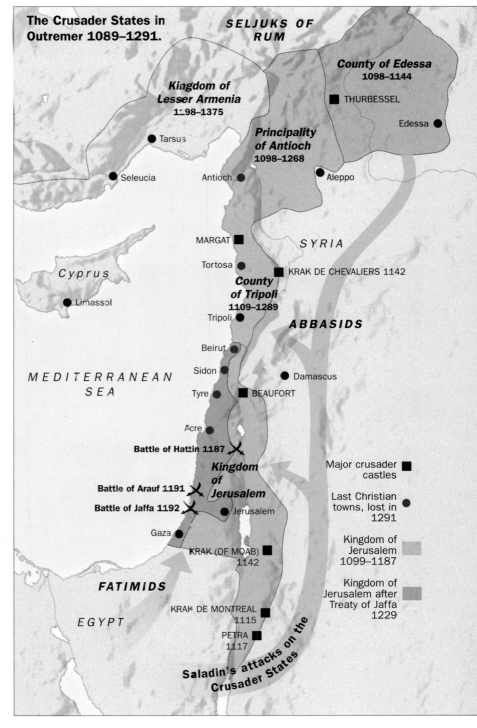

The Crusader States in Outremer 1089–1291.

SELJUKS OF RUM

Kingdom of Lesser Armenia 1198–1375

County of Edessa 1098–1144

THURBESSEL

Edessa

Tarsus

Principality of Antioch 1098–1268

Seleucia

Antioch

Aleppo

MARGAT

S Y R I A

Tortosa

KRAK DE CHEVALIERS 1142

County of Tripoli 1109–1289

Cyprus

Tripoli

ABBASIDS

Limassol

Beirut

Sidon

Damascus

MEDITERRANEAN SEA

Tyre

BEAUFORT

Acre

Battle of Hattin 1187

Kingdom of Jerusalem

Battle of Arauf 1191

Battle of Jaffa 1192

Jerusalem

Gaza

KRAK (OF MOAB) 1142

Major crusader castles

Last Christian towns, lost in 1291

Kingdom of Jerusalem 1099–1187

Kingdom of Jerusalem after Treaty of Jaffa 1229

KRAK DE MONTREAL 1115

FATIMIDS

PETRA 1117

EGYPT

Saladin's attacks on the Crusader States

The Knights of the Military Orders

When the First Crusade captured Jerusalem in 1099, the zeal sweeping through western Europe was at its peak. The Christian army defending the Crusader States was tiny compared to the surrounding Muslim forces. From the early 1100s, dedicated bands of crusaders were formed to protect pilgrims, defend overseas territories, and to fight the infidel. These were the religious military orders, or "Knights of Christ," who kept the crusading ideal alive.

These religiously motivated volunteers provided the best source of recruits for the Crusader States of the Middle East. They maintained a degree of independence from the Kingdom of Jerusalem, since the military orders they belonged to answered directly to the Pope. This degree of independence was tolerated within the feudal system of the Latin Crusader States because the Kingdom of Jerusalem and its satellite states had no option. They needed these military orders to help them defend their lands against the Muslims who surrounded them.

This reliance led directly to an increase in the importance of the military orders, and land,

Below: *The retaking of Jerusalem from the military orders by Saracen forces under the command of the Fatimid Saladin on October 3, 1187.*

castles, and special privileges were frequently granted to them. In 1244, the Knights Hospitaler alone held 29 castles in the Crusader States, and the orders held land and estates throughout Europe, donated by grateful royal or noble benefactors. Although there were numerous military orders of this kind, two major groups dominated: the Knights Templar and the Knights Hospitaler. In addition, the Teutonic Knights campaigned against the pagans they encountered along the eastern frontiers of Europe, while Spanish Military Orders were involved in the *reconquista* of Spain.

The Knights Templar

This was a purely military order, founded in 1115 in northern France. At first their role was to provide an escort for pilgrims traveling within the Holy Land, particularly on the route from Jerusalem to Jericho. Their brotherhood avowed chastity, poverty, and obedience, therefore they mirrored the doctrines espoused by the Cistercians. But an increasingly important role for the Templars was as bankers and money brokers—their honesty was beyond question.

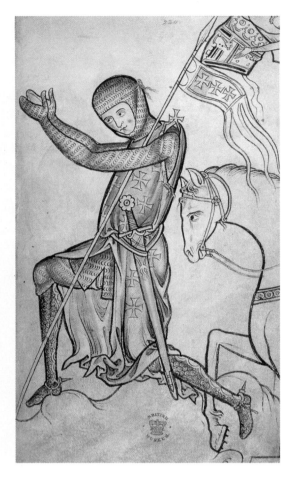

The Knights Hospitaler

By 1113 the Benedictine monastery hospital founded in Jerusalem after its capture had become the Order of the Hospital of St. John. Within seven years a chain of similar hospices extended throughout the Crusader States. Members of the order were known as the Knights of St. John, and after breaking with the Benedictines, they became the Knights Hospitaler.

During the mid-12th century they took control of several key crusader castles, including Krak des Chevaliers and also undertook limited military duties. It was only after the disaster at Hattin (1187) that they became a military order. In 1206 the order contained both brother knights and priests to run the hospitals. They soon rivaled the Templars as a military power, and friction between the two orders became commonplace, as each vied for supremacy. The decline of the Crusader States after the Third Crusade matched the decline of the order, and when Acre fell in 1291 the few surviving knights established a new base on Cyprus. From this point, the order became a naval power, basing itself in Rhodes after the capture of Cyprus from the Byzantines in 1310. The Hospitalers survived into the 16th century, when they moved to Malta, an island it controlled until 1798.

Left: *An English manuscript illumination from the late 12th century of a kneeling crusader, from the Westminster Abbey Psalter.*

Their founders were reputedly two knights who shared a horse to emphasize their poverty, and this image became the symbol of the order. Originally known as The Poor Knights, they were given the site of the Temple of Solomon in Jerusalem for their headquarters, which led to the adoption of their new name. They developed a reputation for fanaticism and courage in battle, often to the point of foolhardiness. By the late 12th century this strictly disciplined group had become a crucial part of the defense of the Crusader States.

The order was almost destroyed in the military debacle at Hattin (1187), and lost power and prestige during the subsequent decades. By the time the last territories of the Crusader States were lost in the late 13th century, their numbers had been reduced to a handful. By the early 14th century the order had no military function, but still held extensive lands in Europe. Inevitably, this aroused envy among the secular rulers of Europe. Bogus charges of heresy, homosexuality, and even Satanism were laid against the order, and the French courts denounced the Templars and seized their estates. The Pope issued a Bull denouncing the movement in 1307, and surviving Templars were arrested, imprisoned, tortured, and executed. Inevitably, the Templar lands were claimed by the secular powers.

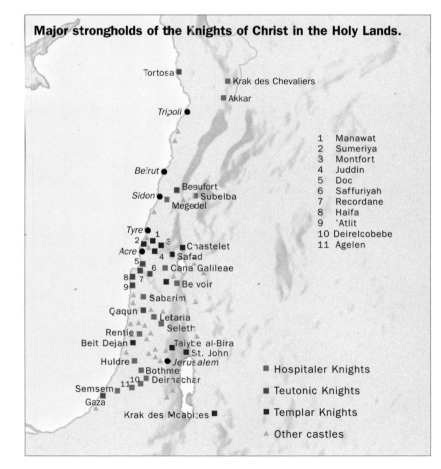

Major strongholds of the Knights of Christ in the Holy Lands.

Tortosa

Krak des Chevaliers

Akkar

Tripoli

1 Manawat
2 Sumeriya
3 Montfort
4 Juddin
5 Doc
6 Saffuriyah
7 Recordane
8 Haifa
9 'Atlit
10 Deirelcobebe
11 Agelen

Beirut

Beaufort
Sidon
Subelba
Megedel

Tyre
1
2 3
Acre
4 Chastelet
Safad
5
8 7 6 Cana Galileae
9
Be voir
Sabarim
Qaqun
Letaria
Seleth
Rentie
Beit Dejan
Taiyte al-Bira
Huldre
St. John
Bothme
Jerusalem
10 Deirnachar
Semsem 11
Gaza

Krak des Mcabites

■ Hospitaler Knights
■ Teutonic Knights
■ Templar Knights
▲ Other castles

Reconquista of Spain

In 1050 the Moors held all but the most northerly part of Spain. Over the next two centuries the Christian *reconquista* (reconquest) of the country would ebb and flow, but ultimately the Moors would be driven back to the extreme southern corner of Spain.

Below: *As the reconquista crusaders pushed further south, they captured many strongholds from the Moors who had built them. This is Castel Almodóvar del Río, 14 miles west of Cordoba on the Guadalquivir river, taken by Christians c.1236.*

The northern territories not held by the Moors were originally the last stronghold of the Visigoths, where their descendants founded the Kingdom of Asturias, later divided into León and Castille. Further to the east, the mountainous territory set up as a buffer zone by Charlemagne in the early ninth century (the Spanish March) had become the autonomous Kingdom of Navarre, the homeland of the Basques. The southern part of its territory included the province of Aragon, which broke away in 1035 and became a separate kingdom. Further to the east, the Catalan region of Barcelona remained a semi-independent state, centered around its port city. This thin strip of territory would form the springboard from which an invasion would be launched. The *reconquista* of Spain would take centuries, but, like the Moorish conquest of the eighth century, it appeared to be an inexorable advance.

In 1034 the Caliphate of Cordoba disintegrated in the face of quarrels between its regional chieftains. The Moorish kingdom was therefore divided into small states, each unwilling or unable to support their Muslim neighbors. This fragmentation gave the Christians in the north the opportunity to expand their territories. By the early 11th century, French "crusading" expeditions crossed the Pyrenees and campaigned south of Aragon. About 1070, King Alfonso VI of León and Castille (1065–1109) and King Sancho of Aragon and Navarre (1063–94) joined forces, and launched the *reconquista*.

When crusaders captured the former Moorish capital of Toledo in 1085, the Moors called on the North African Almoravids (or Berbers) for assistance. For a time the tide of conquest flowed the other way. This intensification also gave rise to the most celebrated hero of this period; Rodrigo Diaz de Vivar, or El Cid. El Cid was a semi-legendary figure whose exploits were romanticized in medieval literature. A vassal of King Alfonso, the nobleman fought for his king against the Moors, but also helped the Moors defeat the Count of Barcelona. Like many Spanish nobles with estates in Christian and Muslim territory, loyalty was a flexible word. His greatest achievement was the capture of Valencia (1094), but he was subsequently killed while defending the city against an attack by an Almoravid army (1099). While Valencia had to be temporarily abandoned, similar advances by Alfonso VII (1126–57) were also premature, and the dividing

line between Spaniard and Moor became stabilized to the south of Toledo and Tortosa.

The Kingdom of Portugal was the next Christian state to evolve. Previously a county of Castille, a marriage treaty between Alfonso VI and a French crusader established the region as a semi-independent state. Under Alfonso (1112–85) Portugal was enlarged with the help of English and Flemish crusaders, and its territory defended against both Spaniards and Moors. Pope Innocent II (1130–43) made Alfonso king and a papal vassal. Lisbon became the kingdom's new capital and, following the Battle of Ourique (1139), Portuguese control was extended southward to the estuary of the Guadiana River.

Reduced to Granada

During the early 12th century the Almohades defeated the Almoravids in North Africa and by 1150 they had moved into Spain to help defend the Moorish states. A crusade was called and it turned the tide. The Moors were decisively defeated at Las Nevas de Tolosa (1212). Until this point, a lack of unity among the Christians had weakened the *reconquista*. Under Ferdinand III of Leon and Castille (1230–52) the Christian alliance reformed, and both Cordoba and Valencia were captured between 1236–8. By the mid-13th century, Moorish territory had been reduced to the region of Granada in southern Spain, which they continued to hold until the late 15th century.

With the capture of the great Moorish ports of Seville, Cadiz, and Cartagena, the Spaniards gained access to Mediterranean trade. The re-establishment of commerce was safeguarded by the capture of the Balearic Islands by King James I of Aragon (1213–76). This maritime growth allowed the

Spanish to extend their power and, in 1282, Aragon claimed Sicily, laying the foundation for a Spanish involvement in Italy that would last into the 16th century. Late 13th-century Spain was a land scarred by war, where feudalism was restricted to the territories that had never been under Moorish control. Elsewhere, a form of slavery similar to that found in eastern Europe predominated. It would take the Spanish more than two centuries to consolidate the *reconquista* and to become accepted as a European power.

Above: *The Alhambra Palace—Granada, the last Moorish toehold in Spain, fell to Ferdinand and Isabella in 1492, the year Christopher Columbus crossed the Atlantic Ocean and discovered America.*

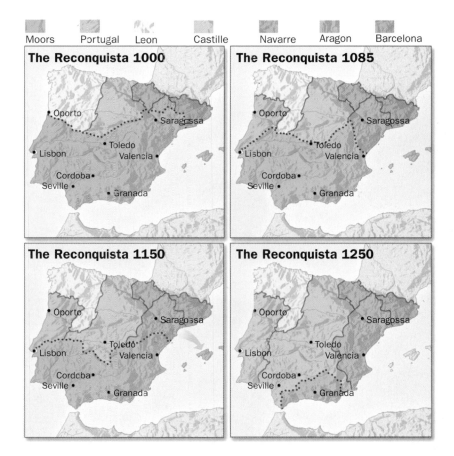

Moors   Portugal   Leon   Castille   Navarre   Aragon   Barcelona

The Reconquista 1000

The Reconquista 1085

The Reconquista 1150

The Reconquista 1250

Constantinople: Caught Between Rome and Mecca

In the mid-eighth century the Byzantine Empire gave the impression of being a powerful and stable state. The Muslim advance in the East had been checked and the Emperor still maintained his territorial claim to "Roman" Italy. Over the next three centuries, a succession of military and religious setbacks undermined the Empire, leaving it vulnerable to attack. The ultimate disaster at Manzikert (1071) cost the Empire its territories in Asia Minor, and invited the intervention of the crusaders of western Europe.

The Byzantine Empire found itself at the mercy of either its sworn enemy, the Islamic forces, **below**, *or its co-Christian defenders, who sacked the capital, Constantinople, for a second time in 1204,* **facing page**.

A series of successful rulers stabilized the frontiers of the Byzantine Empire in the eighth century. Emperor Leo III (717–41) halted the advance of Islam into Cilicia and Asia Minor, while Emperor Constantine V (741–75) prevented any further expansion of the Bulgars into the Byzantine provinces of Thesalonika and Macedonia. With their borders secured by the late eighth century, the emperors felt free to turn their attention to a religious dispute that was threatening to create an unbridgeable schism with the Papacy in Rome.

A controversy over iconoclasm fired the hostility of both the Greek and Roman Churches and aroused popular feeling. This Iconoclastic Controversy first appeared about 730, when Emperor Leo III tried to limit the spread of iconoclasm; what he saw as the excessive veneration of holy images by sections of the population, particularly by Orthodox monks.

The use of icons (or images) during the early development of Christianity was favored by Greek monks, who saw the power these images held over Christians and pagans alike. In 730 a council of the Greek Church formally condemned the veneration of icons. The persecution of *iconodules* by *iconoclasts* received official sanction, which alienated sections of both the Church and the secular community. Feelings ran high, and the Patriarch of Constantinople resigned in protest over the ruling. The Pope also supported the iconodules, a stance that led to the confiscation of the Papal lands in Italy, which the emperor had granted to the Church. Further Church Councils (those of Nicea and Constantinople) upheld the iconoclastic. The controversy continued into the ninth century, and in 843 iconoclasm was officially abolished within the Church. The cultural effects of this controversy were widespread. Not only did it lead to the destruction of thousands of works of religious art, it also widened the religious rift between Rome and Constantinople.

The two branches of the Christian Church continued to clash over theological differences, and over the control of the Church in Bulgaria and Moravia. By the early 11th century the Eastern Church had extended its influence into Russia and Serbia. The final schism took place in 1054, when the Patriarch and the Pope excommunicated each other during an argument over the ceremonial nature of the Eucharist.

A similar argument over the nature of The Holy Spirit led each group to accuse the other of heresy. The schism of 1054 proved to be permanent, but for the next century both parties tried to bridge the gap and reunite the Christian Church. From that point, the Orthodox Church and the Roman Church would go their separate ways. This growing divide led to increasing distrust between west and east, and also directly to the sack of Constantinople by crusaders in 1204.

Enemies on all sides

The schism with Rome was only one of the problems to beset the Byzantine Empire in the 11th century. A series of border disputes with the Bulgars, Russ, and Magyars saw a Bulgar kingdom develop at the expense of the western Byzantine provinces, threatening the stability of the Balkans. Vigorous campaigning by the Emperor Basil II (976–1025) subdued the Bulgars and re-established Byzantine control of the Balkan region.

Even more serious was the resurgent threat of Islam. The disintegration of the Abbasid Caliphate during the tenth century as a result of religious and political dispute marked the end of a unified Islam. Following the Fatimid rule of the early 11th century, Syria and Persia were taken over by the Seljuk Turks, the rising power of the Middle East. By 1067 they had conquered the Byzantine province of Armenia, and the Byzantine heartland of Anatolia (Asia Minor) was threatened with invasion. The Byzantine Emperor Romanus IV (1067–71) attempted to restore his eastern borders by recapturing Armenia. The two armies met at Manzikert (1071), the Byzantine army was decimated, and the Emperor captured. The disaster effectively marked the end of Byzantine military and imperial pretensions. Within two years most of the rich lands of Asia Minor were in Muslim hands, and the once-great Byzantine Empire was confined to Greece, parts of the Balkans, and the western coast of Asia Minor.

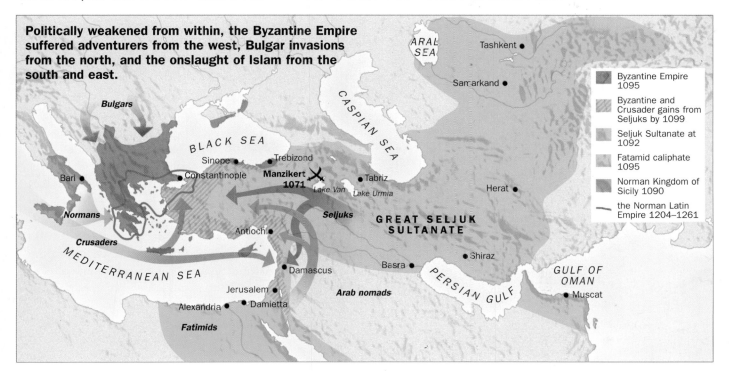

Politically weakened from within, the Byzantine Empire suffered adventurers from the west, Bulgar invasions from the north, and the onslaught of Islam from the south and east.

Byzantine Empire 1095

Byzantine and Crusader gains from Seljuks by 1099

Seljuk Sultanate at 1092

Fatamid caliphate 1095

Norman Kingdom of Sicily 1090

the Norman Latin Empire 1204–1261

FOCUS: LEADERS
Richard the Lionheart

The most popular image of the crusading era is the struggle between the two military giants of the age: Richard the Lionheart and Saladin. To both commanders, their campaigns in the crusades were interludes in their greater struggle to hold together their sprawling empires. While crusading in the Holy Land, Richard was unable to oversee his extensive Angevin possessions in France. His fellow crusader Philip Augustus of France made full use of Richard's absence.

Below: *In this miniature from a manuscript written by Peter of Eboli, probably in 1195, Richard the Lionheart is seen kissing the feet of Emperor Henry VI, while a servant holds his pilgrim's cloak in which he disguised himself while traveling incognito through Austria.*

In 1157 Queen Eleanor of England gave birth to her third child, a son named Richard. The boy was also the first to be fathered by King Henry II of England. Although born in England, Prince Richard never spoke the language, since French was the tongue of the Angevin (or Plantagenet) court. Henry II's lands included England and all of western France. Richard became the Duke of Aquitaine at 15, and promptly joined his brothers Henry and Geoffrey in a revolt against their father. This was Richard's first opportunity to display his military prowess and, although the revolt failed, his accomplishments were noted by his father, who forgave him his lack of loyalty.

A second conflict—this time between Richard and his brothers—ended when Prince Henry died of influenza in 1183. Richard was promptly nominated as Henry II's successor, but further family feuding led to war between Richard and his father, when Henry tried to give Aquitaine to his youngest son, Prince John. Henry II never revoked his declaration about his successor, and when he died July 1189, Richard became Richard I of England the Lionheart (1189–99).

Seeking foreign adventures

Immediately after Richard's coronation in Westminster Abbey, he made plans to leave his domains in the hands of deputies and go on a crusade, together with his old ally against Henry, King Philip II, Augustus of France (1180–1223). However, hostility developed between them when Richard married Berengaria of Navarre in 1191, rather than Philip's sister Alice, to whom he was betrothed. Richard also angered his regent, Prince John, by denying his brother the right to succeed him. On his way to the Holy Land, Richard landed at Cyprus, and conquered the island from the Byzantines after the local ruler tried to imprison his new wife.

Richard landed near Acre in mid-1191, and joined forces with Philip. The rift between the two kings extended to their followers, with the exiled King Guy of Jerusalem and the Knights Templar supporting Richard, while Guy's rivals and the Knights Hospitaler sided with Philip. This divided command succeeded in capturing Acre in July 1191, largely through Richard's inspiring leadership.

King Philip returned home a month later to conspire with Prince John against their joint enemy, leaving Richard free to continue his crusade. Richard's massacre of thousands of prisoners at Acre stiffened Islamic resistance, and the Saracen leader Saladin (1137–93) spent the next year in a campaign to deny Richard access to Jerusalem. Richard defeated Saladin at Arsuf (1191), which gave him control of Jaffa (1192), but Jerusalem proved to be too well defended. Dissention between the crusading leaders

1009	1071	1081
The Holy Sepulcher in Jerusalem is destroyed	Battle of Manzikert; Byzantines lose control of Anatolia	Constantinople threatened by the Seljuk Turks

hindered Richard's advance and the campaign against Jerusalem was abandoned. Alarmed by reports of Philip and John's activities back in Europe and frustrated by Outremer politics, Richard and Saladin signed a five-year truce in September 1192. Jerusalem would remain in Muslim hands, but Christian pilgrims were guaranteed access to the city.

As a crusader, the security of his lands were guaranteed by the Pope, but when Richard discovered that John and Philip were plotting behind his back, the English king sailed for Europe. He landed near Venice and traveled overland into Austria. Although disguised, he was recognized and captured by the Duke of Austria, who promptly sold his prisoner to the German Emperor, Henry VI, an ally of Philip's. Richard remained incarcerated until early 1194, when a ransom was arranged with the German princes, against the wishes of his rival monarchs. Richard

reached England in March 1194, where a second coronation reasserted his right to the throne. John was stripped of his powers, and Richard returned to France, where he launched a campaign against Philip.

The French king was no match for Richard on the battlefield. The inroads he had made into Angevin lands during Richard's absence were quickly lost, and Richard even threatened to conquer the Capetian heartland of the Île de France. Philip made peace, then resorted to intrigue, encouraging Richard's Angevin vassals to revolt. During the siege of a rebel castle at Chalus in Poitou, Richard was wounded by a crossbow bolt. He died of his wounds in April 1199, leaving his lands to his scheming younger brother, John. Within a decade, John would lose almost all of the territories so ably held by his father and brother.

Above: *The tomb effigy of Richard the Lionheart at Notre Dame de Fontrevraud, France.*

1095	1096	1098	1099	1137	1144	1145	1147
Pope Urban II proclaims the First Crusade at the Council of Clermont	The People's Crusade ends in disaster	The crusaders defeat the Muslims at Antioch	Jerusalem captured, and The Kingdom of Jerusalem is created	Antioch ceded to the Byzantines	The Duchy of Edessa falls to the Saracens	The Second Crusade is proclaimed	The Second Crusade ends in failure

FOCUS: WARFARE
Bastions of Faith: Crusading Castles

In order to protect their conquests, the crusaders built castles throughout the Crusader States of the Middle East. Many used principles of design based on the massive fortresses built by the Byzantines. These castles played a vital part in crusader strategy in the Middle East and influenced the actions of both crusader and Saracen armies.

Feudal power in Europe was anchored around the use of castles. When the Kingdom of Jerusalem was founded in 1100, it seemed natural that it would be governed using the feudal system the crusaders were used to, and feudal power would be enforced by the construction of fortresses. During the 12th century, 64 castles and fortified sites were built in the Kingdom of Jerusalem alone, from the northernmost at Beirut

to the Ile de Graye in the Gulf of Aqaba. Further north, similar castles dominated the territories of the County of Tripoli, the Principality of Antioch, and the County of Edessa. But the crusaders did not have a monopoly on fortification building. The Byzantine and Muslim fortresses they encountered were equally well constructed, and many of the defensive innovations of the crusader castles were adaptations of designs they first encountered in Byzantium.

Constantinople itself was the most extensive fortress of its time. The main Wall of Constantine was studded with a series of massive towers. A covered road behind it allowed for the movement of troops within the defenses, and behind that an inner wall with more towers provided a last line of defense. In front of the Wall of Constantine a low wall provided an outer defense, and in front of this ran a deep moat, usually filled with water and underwater stakes. Taken in their entirety, the defenses of Constantinople were considered impregnable. However, the Byzantine capital fell in 1204 because the attacking crusaders had naval superiority and landed on the lightly protected seaward side of the city. Impregnability was clearly relative.

The largest of the crusader castles were built on these Byzantine principles; massive inner walls protected by large round towers, and a lower outer wall with its own set of towers and moats. Defenders on the inner wall were able to fire over the top of the outer wall, providing protective fire for its defense. The greatest of the crusader castles in the Holy Land was Krak des Chevaliers, held by the Knights of St. John from 1142 to 1271, when it was besieged and captured by a Muslim army.

A similar design was used in the construction of the castles at Beaufort (Belfort), Latrun, and Safad. The crusaders also made extensive use of natural defenses. This could involve the fortification of a spur of land extending into the sea (such as at 'Atlit), or at a river junction (Sahyun), or the defenses could incorporate a natural rocky escarpment, such as the castle of Krak des Moabites in modern Jordan. Because of the shortage of wood, crusader castles lacked the numerous internal floors of European keeps, and consequently were lower structures. Another Byzantine feature the Crusaders adopted was the use of wide wall-walks, allowing for the placement of defensive artillery.

Reliance on the Orders

One of the constant problems facing the rulers of the Crusader States was lack of manpower. Most castles required a substantial garrison; consequently, when men were in short supply, these rulers handed over castles to the military orders. In 1136, Bethgibelin castle in Judea was handed over to the Knights Hospitaler. By the time the Kingdom of Jerusalem collapsed following the battle at Hattin (1187), the Order owned 25 castles, while the Knights Templar controlled 18 more. Crusader strategy inevitably centered around its castles. Their possessions were guarded by a network of castles and garrisons, augmented in time of war by mobile field armies. Lack of manpower meant that garrisons were denuded to create these field armies, and so a disaster on the battlefield left the castles virtually defenseless. After Hattin, most castles in the Kingdom of Jerusalem fell within three months, because their garrisons had been stripped to well below the levels needed for defense.

Following the collapse of the Crusader States, a fresh wave of castles were build in the islands of the Eastern Mediterranean and Aegean, the new front line in the war between Christians and Muslims. Inevitably, these coastal fortifications relied on control of the seas to secure their supply lines. In an ironic twist, the maritime supremacy the crusaders used to capture Constantinople in 1204 was turned against them. During the 15th century, when the Ottoman Turks became the dominant seapower in the western Mediterranean, these coastal castles fell as easily as the impregnable Byzantine capital had done.

*Krak des Chevaliers (in modern day Syria) is probably the most imposing of the crusader castles. A natural part of its defenses is the towering glacis (pictured to the left of the photograph **facing**), which denies assault on two sides. The outer curtain walls (pictured in the engraving **above**) are not crusader, but were added later by Muslim conquerors.*

1171	1176	1187	1189	1190	1191	1192	1202
Saladin gains control of Egypt and establishes Sunni orthodox rule	Saladin conquers Syria	Battle of Hattin, Collapse of Crusader States	Third Crusade proclaimed	Frederick Barbarossa drowned in river in Anatolia	Richard I captures Cyprus and Acre	Crusaders return home without recapturing Jerusalem	Fourth Crusade proclaimed

FOCUS: SOCIETY
Persecution of the Jews in the Middle Ages

The spirit that revitalized the Roman Church in the 11th century and gave rise to the crusading movement also led to attacks on members of other religious creeds. External enemies included the Muslims of the Mediterranean, the Orthodox Greeks of Byzantium, and the pagans of eastern Europe. Within Europe's borders the same forces were turned against the Jewish population.

Above: *Burning Jewish "heretics" at the stake, from a colored woodcut by Michael Wolgemut, c.1493.*

During the five centuries following the collapse of the Western Roman Empire, the Jews of Europe enjoyed a certain degree of security. Long after other mercantile groups had ceased to function, Jewish merchants and bankers continued to provide some degree of service for the warlords who ruled the continent. The Carolingian Franks extended their protection to Jewish communities in the hope that this would lead to the revival of trade within their domains.

Following the Arab conquest of the southern Mediterranean in the seventh and eighth centuries, Jewish merchants were able to maintain trading links that were blocked to their Christian rivals. Jewish traders exported timber, slaves, and furs from Europe and brought silks, spices, and other Oriental luxuries back to the courts of the Frankish kingdoms. This trading position was particularly prominent in Spain, where the Jewish community was protected by the Moors.

Moorish Spain had no discriminatory policy against its Christian and Jewish population, and Jewish historians have looked upon the early medieval period in Spain as a "golden age," free from persecution. While Jewish merchants traded extensively throughout the Mediterranean under Iberian Moorish protection, the Jewish communities of southern Spain prospered. Writers, scientists, and philosophers all thrived in this Iberian community, but, like any society of the period, wealth and privilege was highly stratified, and most Spanish Jews saw little financial benefit from their open access to Arab trade. This golden period ended in the mid-11th century. As the Christian *Reconquista* made inroads into Moorish territory, North African Muslims were called in to help, and they brought with them a less tolerant form of Islamic rule. Persecution by Islamic militants led many Jews to seek refuge in Christian territory. By the 15th century, pressure from militant Christians left the Jewish community with nowhere to escape. While tens of thousands converted to Christianity, others retained their faith and were rewarded with expulsion from Spain in 1492, immediately after the final conquest of Moorish Granada.

Increasingly volatile

In northern Europe, the privileged position held by Jewish merchants was eroded by increased persecution and the re-emergence of widespread

1204	1204	1208	1212	1215	1216	1219	1228
Constantinople captured and sacked by crusaders	The Latin Empire of Nicea founded in western Anatolia	Campaign against the Albigensian Heretics	The Children's Crusade	The Fifth Lateran Council obliges all Christians to perform an annual confession	Fifth Crusade promoted by Innocent III	The crusaders briefly capture Egypt and Acre	Sixth Crusade led by the Emperor Frederick II

80

commerce from the 11th century. Anti-Semitism permeated all levels of Church and society, even including some of the secular writers and religious leaders regarded as the most enlightened of their time, figures such as Chaucer, St. Anselm, and St. Bernard.

With increasing urban growth and an expansion of trade, the older Jewish trading networks were no longer required by Europe's secular rulers. Even as special trading privileges were being revoked, clerics began to condemn the Jewish community, inciting Christian militants to acts of persecution and violence. The small Jewish population in Germany was decimated by the movement known as the "Peoples' Crusade" in 1096–7, and it introduced the mass slaughter of Jewish communities that marked the crusading era as a particularly black time for European Jewry.

When the crusaders reached Jerusalem, the Jewish community that had thrived under the Muslims was massacred and its survivors expelled. In Europe, the financial benefits of Jewish persecution were obvious. With the help of the Church, condemnation of the Jews incited the

populace and provided the excuse needed to expel the Jewish communities and seize their property. All debts to Jews were immediately canceled, and the booty was divided between the secular powers, the Church, and the angry mob.

In 1182 Philip II Augustus of France promoted a scheme whereby debtors paid the Crown a percent fee, and in return their debts to Jewish usurers were canceled. He also banished Jews from France for a decade. Philip IV The Fair expelled the French Jews three times, confiscating property and canceling debts on each occasion. In England, Jews who crossed the English Channel in the wake of the Normans formed a mercantile and banking community that prospered, despite heavy royal taxation. This changed in the 13th century, when a pogrom in York was inspired by the declaration of the Third Crusade. Edward I expelled the Jewish population from England in 1290, seizing their property in an effort to raise ready money for his military campaigns. Many of those expelled from Spain, France, England, and Germany moved east, to the relatively secure states of Poland and Russia. This security would prove to be short-lived.

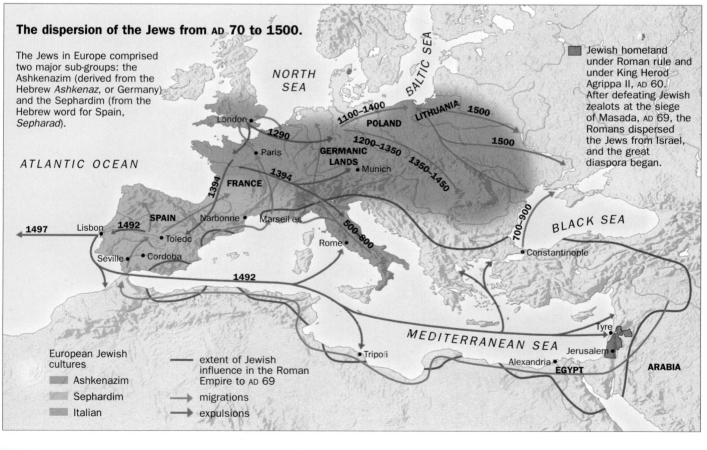

The dispersion of the Jews from AD 70 to 1500.

The Jews in Europe comprised two major sub-groups: the Ashkenazim (derived from the Hebrew *Ashkenaz*, or Germany) and the Sephardim (from the Hebrew word for Spain, *Sepharad*).

Jewish homeland under Roman rule and under King Herod Agrippa II, AD 60. After defeating Jewish zealots at the siege of Masada, AD 69, the Romans dispersed the Jews from Israel, and the great diaspora began.

European Jewish cultures
- Ashkenazim
- Sephardim
- Italian

— extent of Jewish influence in the Roman Empire to AD 69
→ migrations
→ expulsions

1249	1250	1256	1261	1291	1300	1302	1302
Seventh Crusade takes place in Egypt	The French King Louis IX is captured by the Muslims	The Mongols attack Persia and Syria	Constantinople recaptured by the Byzantines	The last crusader bastion of Acre is captured by the Muslims	European population s approximately 73 million	Territorial expansion of Muscovy begins	Expulsion of Crusaders from the Holy Land

CHAPTER FIVE

Europe in the mid-12th century

NORWAY

SWEDISH TERRITORIES

Christiania

Uppsala

SCOTLAND

Edinburgh

NORTH SEA

DENMARK

BALTIC SEA

IRELAND

Dublin

Irish

Welsh

ANGEVIN ENGLAND

London

Schleswig

Danzig

Prussia

Hamburg

POMERANIA

POLAND

SAXONY

Bruges

THURINGIA

ATLANTIC OCEAN

Bayeux

Rouen

Paris

LORRAINE

Mainz

Worms

Prague

BOHEMIA

ANGEVIN FRANCE

FRENCH ROYAL DOMAIN

HOLY ROMAN EMPIRE

Vienna

BAY OF BISCAY

SWABIA

Buda ● ● Pest

HUNGARY

LEON

Léon

Bordeaux

Lyons

BURGUNDY

Milan

Venice

CROATIA

PORTUGAL

CASTILLE

NAVARRE

Toulouse

COUNTY OF TOULOUSE

Genoa

Pisa

Zara

BOSNIA

ARAGON

Marseilles

ADRIATIC SEA

SERBIA

Lisbon

Toledo

CORSICA to Pisa

PAPAL STATE

Rome

Dyrrachium

CALIPHATE OF CORDOBA

BALEARIC ISLANDS

MINORCA

SARDINIA to Pisa

TYRRHENIAN SEA

Bari

Cordoba

IBIZA

MAJORCA

Granada

Tangiers

Ceuta

KINGDOM OF SICILY

Palermo

Tunis

SICILY

ALMOHAD CALIPHATE

MALTA

MEDITERRANEAN

The Flowering of Europe

The 12th century came to be seen as something of a renaissance. While in previous centuries it seemed unlikely that European civilization would survive, by the 11th century a degree of political and social stability had been achieved. This stability had numerous effects in the 13th century, the most important being the re-establishment of commerce throughout Europe and the reintroduction of monetary economy. More income for feudal kings and leading nobles allowed them to extend patronage to ecclesiastical institutions.

The establishment of new religious houses led to increased emphasis on learning, while direct patronage included the widespread construction of new cathedrals and churches, designed to reflect the latest architectural innovations. A more educated ecclesiastic and secular elite created a demand for literature, and while churches produced splendidly illustrated religious works, chivalry and romanticism were popular themes for temporal audiences.

In the medieval period, stability was a relative term. While much of western Europe enjoyed the fruits of peace, commerce, and improved agricultural techniques, other regions were repeatedly fought over in a series of dynastic disputes and in conflicts between kings and their nobles. The principal battlegrounds centered around the growing number of castles, which guarded the borders of provinces or housed rebellious barons. In eastern Europe the situation was even more volatile, and a fragmented patchwork of principalities was unable to offer any real defense against determined invaders.

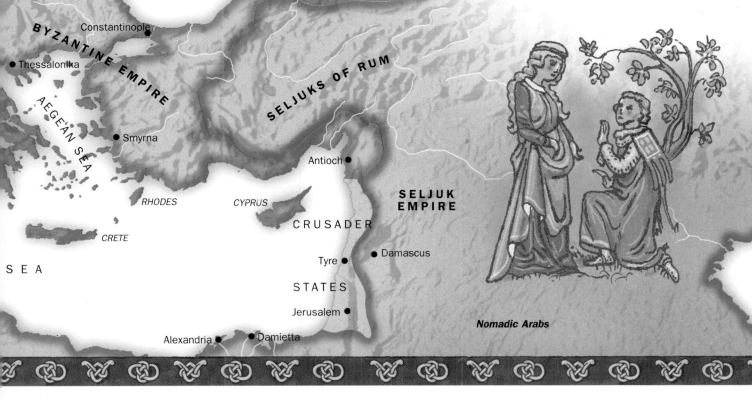

LITHUANIA

Riga

RUSSIA

Cumans

Alans

BLACK SEA

BULGARIA

Trebizond

BYZANTINE EMPIRE

Constantinople

Thessalonika

AEGEAN SEA

Smyrna

SELJUKS OF RUM

Antioch

RHODES

CYPRUS

SELJUK EMPIRE

CRUSADER

CRETE

Tyre

Damascus

SEA

STATES

Jerusalem

Nomadic Arabs

Alexandria

Damietta

The Development of European Commerce

During the 11th century there was a slow improvement in the medieval economy, based on a resumption of trade throughout most of Europe; the first real commerce since the collapse of the Roman Empire. As market centers began to trade with each other, the ports of the Mediterranean and Baltic experienced a shipping boom.

Below: *Dietmar von Aist (1139–1171) buys his lady some finery, from an illustration in the Manesse Codex of Zurich c.1310.*

The decline in trade that accompanied the barbarian invasions toward the end of the Western Roman Empire reached a low point during the ninth century AD. Maritime commerce was at a standstill, although Arab merchants continued to operate in the Mediterranean. In the Baltic and the Low Countries, Vikings destroyed whatever commercial centers survived, and Magyar raids cut off overland communication with the Orient. The one saving grace was the survival of the Byzantine Empire and, from the tenth century onward, Venetian merchants shipped small quantities of wine and grain to Constantinople.

From the late tenth century, mariners from Genoa and Pisa shipped cloth from Lombardy to French and Spanish ports, and in 1016 Italian galley squadrons cleared the region of Muslim pirates. Later that century, Norman adventurers extended Frankish influence into southern Italy and Sicily, and Genoese expeditions captured Corsica and Sardinia.

The First Crusade in 1096 helped open Middle Eastern markets to Venetian and Genoese ships, and by the start of the 12th century a maritime trade route was established between Italy and the Latin Crusader States in the Holy Land. Italian maritime communities established in Levantine ports such as Antioch ensured a monopoly of trade. This provided limited access to the great trading cities of the east: Baghdad, Damascus, and Alexandria. While sugar, silks, and spices arrived in Italian ports, European cloth, grain, and timber were transported to the Middle East. The Levantine ports also provided a conduit for the transport of Slavic slaves from the Black Sea to Egypt and Syria.

Securing trade

A simultaneous revival of trade took place in northern Europe. From the late tenth century, production of cloth resumed at Flanders; by 1050 it flourished. Wool was imported from England to supply the growing demand for raw materials, and wine was shipped over the Channel through Norman ports such as Rouen. The demand created by the Norman Conquest triggered a boom in the wine-producing regions of Bordeaux and the Loire.

Similar developments were taking place along the Baltic coast. The port of Lübeck became the focus for trade in grain and timber, and the Hanseatic League was formed to regulate this commerce and protect the German ports from political and economic encroachment.

While northern Italy and Flanders were both booming commercial centers by the 12th century, there was little contact between them. Transportation via rivers such as the Rhône, Rhine, Seine, and Loire was not safe, since the feudal system did nothing to protect travelers.

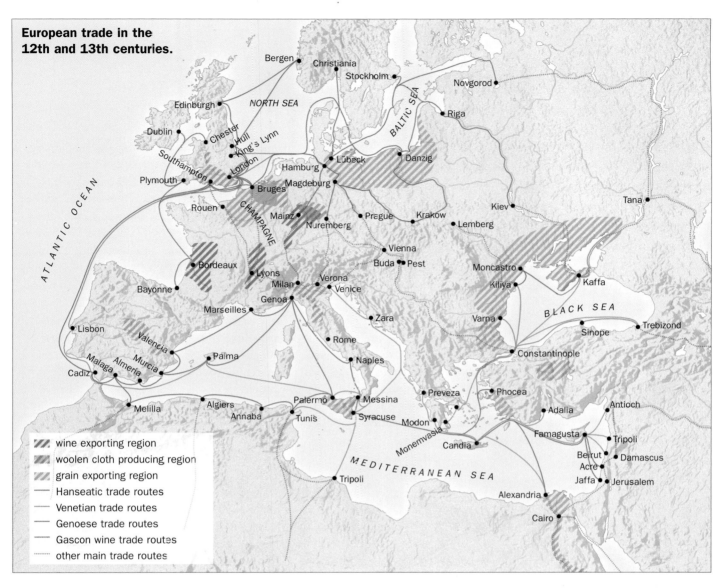

European trade in the 12th and 13th centuries.

wine exporting region
woolen cloth producing region
grain exporting region
— Hanseatic trade routes
— Venetian trade routes
— Genoese trade routes
— Gascon wine trade routes
······ other main trade routes

True European trade would remain restricted until the safety of its merchants could be guaranteed.

During the early 12th century the Counts of Champagne realized that their lands were ideally placed to extract considerable income from the patronage of merchants. The result was the Champagne Fairs, a series of markets in the region's principal towns. The fairs were well-regulated, currency exchanges were monitored, and grievances were investigated. More important, the feudal backers ensured the security of merchants traveling between the Champagne Fairs. These markets allowed northern and southern European merchants to meet, and the medieval economy blossomed as a result.

The fairs continued for more than two centuries, and when other temporal lords saw the benefits of markets, they organized similar events in their own domains. By the end of the 12th century, hundreds of general and specialized markets operated throughout Europe. These produced revenue for the communities, provided access to hitherto unavailable goods, and ensured a demand for hard currency. Commerce had become a vital part of medieval life.

Below: *A view of Genoa—rival of Venice—showing a galley and a sailing ship in the harbor, the jetties and dockside warehouses. From Hartmann Schedel's Chronicle, 1493.*

85

Centers of Learning

During the 12th century a fundamental shift revolutionized monastic life in Europe. Traditional and conservative monastic communities began to discover they had a duty to provide centers of learning, and saw education as a means to establish themselves amid the feudal and secular world that surrounded them. In the process they opened a debate that could make or break the medieval Church and paved the way for future religious discord.

During the previous half millennium since the collapse of the Western Roman Empire the Christian monks who maintained the religion amid a sea of chaos tended to retreat into secure enclaves. The nature of monastic life was to turn away from the confusion of the outside world, and monks absorbed themselves in daily routines of devotion and duty. Reformers began to question this introspective role. Instead, they argued that, like the rest of the Church, monasteries had a duty to reach out to the secular world.

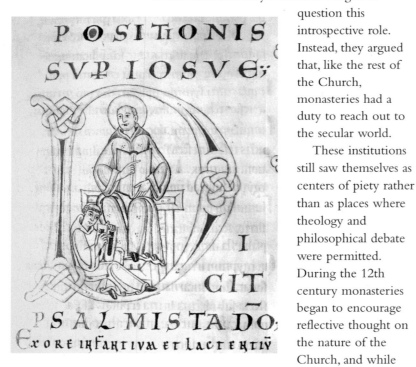

These institutions still saw themselves as centers of piety rather than as places where theology and philosophical debate were permitted. During the 12th century monasteries began to encourage reflective thought on the nature of the Church, and while Cathedral schools trained young priests, monasteries provided places where theological problems were examined. Together with the development of schools outside the monastic system, these havens of study would help the Church to understand the world that surrounded them.

During the 11th and 12th centuries, leading clerical scholars became resident in cathedral cities, so that these centers became havens of learning as well as of clerical administration and worship. An emphasis was placed on teaching the

Above: *A young monk at his learning, sitting at the feet of his tutor, from an illuminated manuscript of the 12th–13th centuries.*

liberal arts, particularly philosophy and literary study, and certain cathedral schools developed a specialization in particular fields. For example, in France Orléans became a center for the study of law, Chartres for literary study, and Paris for philosophy and theology. Education for children was run by the clerics and served little function other than the training of potential priests and the religious education of the sons of the feudal elite. Further education was seen as pointless for secular students. However, in a few instances schooling in monasteries and cathedrals paved the way for secular students to establish themselves in professions outside the Church, principally as lawyers or doctors. These were the exception, and the majority of students were destined for positions within the Church.

A new philosophy

Law was administered by feudal lords, but the Church provided the lawyers who maintained and developed the law upon which feudal justice was based. Monastic and cathedral schools taught Church law and Roman law, which provided the framework on which the secular legal structure of Europe was based. The study of logic, rhetoric, and debate helped to develop the administrative and communicative skills of the clerical students, but it also created the tools with which the same minds could ponder the leading religious issues of the day. The Church faced several basic philosophical and theological problems, which provided these freshly trained minds with intellectual challenges. The clerical debates that ensued during the 12th century would have a profound influence on the future development of the medieval Church.

Religious thinkers such as St. Anselm and Peter Abelard had already argued for the existence of God on philosophical grounds during the late 11th and early 12th centuries. Another philosophical challenge was the theory of the "Universals," which questioned whether individuals could be grouped together into larger collective bodies, such as peoples or nations. Similar debates led to questions over the nature of the sacraments, the relationship between Church and consecrated monarchs, marriage, mass, and penance.

In effect, during the 12th century the Christian Church developed the means to examine itself, and the skills to apply religious

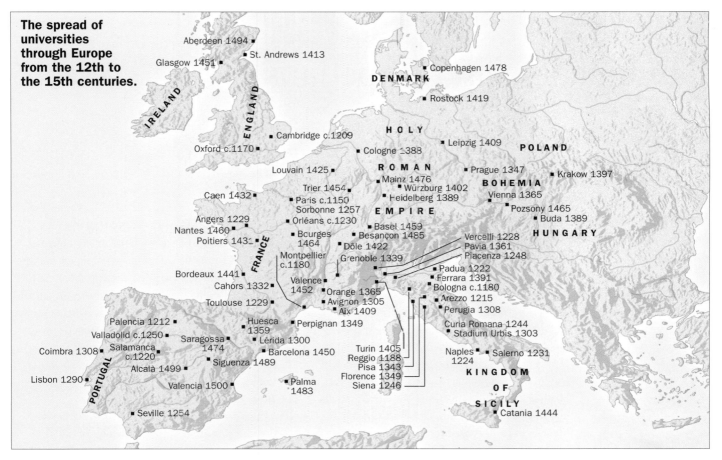

The spread of
universities
through Europe
from the 12th to
the 15th centuries.

Aberdeen 1494
Glasgow 1451   St. Andrews 1413
IRELAND   ENGLAND
Copenhagen 1478
DENMARK
Rostock 1419
HOLY
Cambridge c.1209   Leipzig 1409   POLAND
Oxford c.1170   Cologne 1388
ROMAN   Prague 1347   Krakow 1397
Louvain 1425   Mainz 1476   BOHEMIA
Trier 1454   Würzburg 1402   Vienna 1365
Caen 1432   Paris c.1150   Heidelberg 1389
Sorbonne 1257   EMPIRE   Pozsony 1465
Angers 1229   Orléans c.1230   Buda 1389
Nantes 1460   Bourges   Basel 1459   HUNGARY
Poitiers 1431   1464   Besançon 1485
FRANCE   Dôle 1422   Vercelli 1228
Montpellier   Grenoble 1339   Pavia 1361
Bordeaux 1441   c.1180   Piacenza 1248
Cahors 1332   Valence   Padua 1222
Toulouse 1229   1452   Orange 1365   Ferrara 1391
Avignon 1305   Bologna c.1180
Aix 1409   Arezzo 1215
Palencia 1212   Huesca   Perpignan 1349   Perugia 1308
Valladolid c.1250   1359   Curia Romana 1244
Saragossa   Lérida 1300   Stadium Urbis 1303
Coimbra 1308   1474   Barcelona 1450   Turin 1405
Salamanca   Siguenza 1489   Reggio 1188   Naples   Salerno 1231
c.1220   Pisa 1343   1224
Alcalá 1499   Florence 1349   KINGDOM
Lisbon 1290   Siena 1246   OF
Valencia 1500   Palma   SICILY
PORTUGAL   1483
Seville 1254   Catania 1444

doctrine to all aspects of secular life. As only the clerics were trained in philosophical and theological debate, nobody was in a position to question their findings. The danger lay in the possibility that agreement would prove impossible, and a theological divide would weaken the Church rather than make it stronger.

Left: *Outside of the monasteries, schooling in feudal Europe was scarce, but as urban centers grew, the newly emerging merchant class sent their children to schools, usually run by priests or lay monks.*

Plantagenets and Capetians

By the time of William the Conqueror's death, his Anglo-Norman dynasty was firmly in control of England, Normandy, and neighboring French provinces. While the holder of these territories remained the vassal of the King of France, French royal power was too weak to enforce feudal control. A century of political and military maneuvering followed.

On his father's death, Robert, eldest son of William the Conqueror, inherited the Duchy of Normandy; younger brother William Rufus (1087–1100) was King of England until a suspicious hunting accident in 1100. Younger brother Henry I (1100–35) claimed the crown, but was plagued by baronial revolt and the succession of his offspring.

When his only son William was lost in a shipwreck, Henry forced his barons to acknowledge his daughter Matilda as the heir. On his death Matilda claimed the throne, but the Anglo-Norman nobles backed her rival, Stephen of Blois. King Stephen I (1135–54) was forced into a civil war that only concluded when he

agreed that Matilda's son, Henry Plantagenet, should succeed him. Matilda's husband, Geoffrey of Anjou, had captured Normandy and control of the duchy was passed to their son.

The Capetian kings of France had their own battles. Under Philip I (1060–1108) the royal demesne around Paris was marginally enlarged, but he was unable to control the French nobility. His successor was Louis VI, the Fat (1108–37), who used military might to dominate his feudal vassals in the Ile-de-France. Attempts to control his leading nobles were hindered by a series of costly wars against Henry I and his allies along the western borders. The weaker French king forced a stalemate by encouraging rebellion among Henry's nobles.

Louis made slow inroads into ducal power, installing his own Count of Flanders and enforcing his right to call upon troops to fight threatened invasions by Henry I of England and Henry V of Germany. By the time of his death he had safeguarded the Ile-de-France and gone some way to enforcing his authority upon the nobles.

Rebellion

Louis's work was continued by his son, Louis VII (1137–80), who expanded his influence by marrying Eleanor of Aquitaine. The union was plagued by scandal and produced no male heir. Within months of its annulment in 1152, Eleanor married Henry of Anjou, who promptly became Henry II of England (1154–89). Eleanor's territories passed from the Capetians to the Plantagenets, doubling the size of Henry's empire.

Henry was also powerful enough to exert some control over the Aquitaine nobility. Although the loss of the Aquitaine to the Capetians was not a disaster, its acquisition by their arch-rival was a monumental political setback. For the next 30 years, Henry and Louis were to fight an almost unremitting war. Louis married the sister of the Count of Blois, and the subsequent marriage of his daughter to the Count ensured the loyalty of a

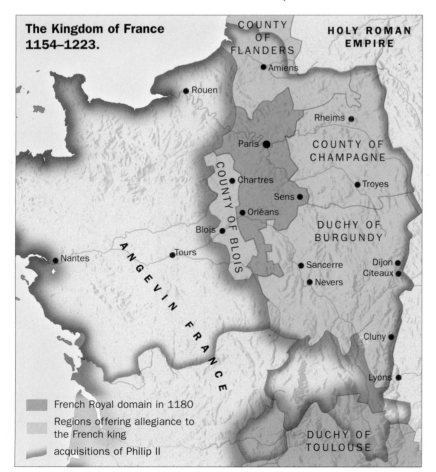

The Kingdom of France 1154–1223.

COUNTY OF FLANDERS

HOLY ROMAN EMPIRE

Amiens

Rouen

Rheims

Paris

COUNTY OF CHAMPAGNE

Chartres

Troyes

Sens

Orléans

DUCHY OF BURGUNDY

Blois

Tours

Nantes

Sancerre

Dijon
Citeaux

Nevers

Cluny

Lyons

ANGEVIN FRANCE

COUNTY OF BLOIS

French Royal domain in 1180
Regions offering allegiance to the French king
acquisitions of Philip II

DUCHY OF TOULOUSE

Left: *King Henry II of England disputes with the Archbishop of Canterbury, Sir Thomas à Becket.*

crucial province that guarded the southern flank of the Capetian demesne.

King Louis was succeeded by Philip II Augustus (1180–1223), a skilled politician who conspired with Henry II's sons to ferment a rebellion within the Angevin Empire. Philip also established control over the rebellious French provinces of Flanders, Burgundy, and Champagne. Soon after, when Henry was succeeded by Richard I, the Lionheart (1189–99), both monarchs departed for the crusades, but while Philip returned within a year, Richard was held captive in Germany until 1194.

Philip attacked Angevin territory and made significant gains, until Richard—now ransomed—returned and quickly recaptured his lands. Philip sued for peace, but when Richard was killed during a siege in 1199, the Angevin crown passed to Richard's weak brother, John I (1199–1216). Philip defeated John in battle in 1204, then recaptured almost all of the Angevin possessions north of the Loire. Although the French were temporarily triumphant, rivalry between the two houses would continue.

Left: *King Henry II hunting a stag.*

Eastern Europe before the Mongols

Beyond the reach of the Roman Church lay vast eastern territories, whose nature was largely unknown in medieval Europe. While Christendom saw the peoples of the east as barbarians, the truth was very different.

Russia emerged as a political unit during the tenth century. It was home to Slavic people concentrated in what would become Novgorod and Kiev, although it retained traces of earlier Persian races. But during the ninth century, Viking traders, or *Russ*, began using rivers to travel between the Baltic and Constantinople.

In 911 Prince Oleg of the Russ settled in Kiev and subjugated the surrounding Slavic tribes. In the late tenth century the Russ captured Novgorod and carved out a Russian state. By the 11th century Russia was made up of a number of semi-autonomous city-states, dominated by Novgorod and Kiev.

The region was plagued by near-constant warfare against the Bulgars and Byzantines, but during the latter part of the century the Russ adopted Byzantine "Orthodox" Christianity. Under the reign of Yaroslav the Wise (c.1019–54) Russian culture and the arts were encouraged

Right: *A cavalry skirmish between Russians and Bulgars in the tenth century, from a Slavonian manuscript.*

and cathedrals were built. Kiev became Russia's metropolitan center and religion gave impetus for further campaigns against non-Christians.

Following Yaroslav's death, Kiev's dominance diminished as his successors proved unable to prevent provincial nobles and city-states from devolving. This disunity continued into the 13th century, when the lack of central control made it easy for the Mongols to capture most of the Russian State.

Further to the west, migratory Germanic tribes established permanent settlements between the Vistula and Oder Rivers during the ninth century. This grouping was soon dominated by the Wislanie tribe, centered around Cracow, and the Polanie to the north, who, by the late tenth century, dominated the whole region, which became known as Poland (from the Slavonic *pole*, meaning plain or field). The Polish Duke Miezko (963–92) was recognized by King Otto I of Germany, who converted him to Christianity. The first Roman church was established in Miezko's capital of Gneizno.

Weathering the invasions

Miezko was succeeded by his son, Duke Boleslaw I the Brave (992–1025), who expanded the Polish state to incorporate Silesia and further lands to the east and north, including Pomerania. Just before his death in 1025, Boleslaw crowned himself King of Poland.

Internal revolt plagued the Polish state for much of the next century, and relations between the Poles and the Germans deteriorated, largely as a result of German encroachments into Polish territory. Under Boleslaw III the Widemouthed (1102–39) Poland was stabilized under central authority, but this disintegrated in the face of later hereditary struggles. Over the next two centuries Poland was divided into Greater Poland and Little Poland.

Further to the south the Magyar invaders of the tenth century settled in the Hungary region, bounded by the Carpathian Mountains in the east and Germanic Austria to the west. In the 11th century the Magyars adopted Roman Catholicism, and under King Stephen I of Hungary (1000–38), they established permanent settlements along the River Danube.

The 11th century settled into a cycle of stability followed by civil war, and the weak monarchy of Stephen II (1116–31) turned Hungary into a pawn, fought over by Byzantine and Germanic armies. Hungary was part of the Byzantine Empire for much of the 12th century and only regained its independence in 1180,

following the death of Emperor Manuel I Comnenus.

Unlike the rest of eastern Europe, Hungary started the 13th century as a relatively stable state, practicing a form of feudalism that combined Byzantine and German elements. In 1221 the Hungarian nobles forced the adoption of the Golden Bull, establishing a limited monarchy and a form of parliamentary administration.

Although Hungary was the most organized eastern European state, it was unable to prevent conquest by the Mongols in the mid-13th century, when half the population was massacred. However, Hungary survived to rebuild its shattered dominions.

Above: *Olga, the widow of Igor, prince of Kiev (c.877–945), orders the execution of envoys who have arrived by boat. From a 15th-century Russian chronicle.*

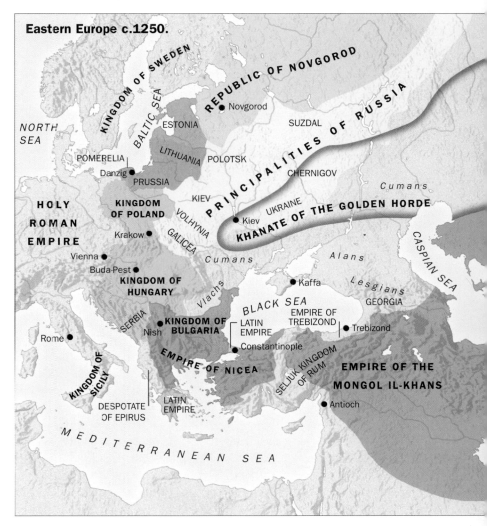

Eastern Europe c.1250.

Medieval Vernacular Literature

Before the 12th century, almost all manuscripts were written in Latin and followed heavily stylized Church guidelines. A benefit of more educated clergy was the development of vernacular writing, breaking the staid constraints of earlier works and bringing new, popular forms of prose.

Facing: *English literature in the vernacular would find its finest expression (and greatest popularity) in the work of Geoffrey Chaucer (c.1345–1400) with his* Canterbury Tales.

In the early medieval period, literacy was almost exclusively confined to clerics, many of whom were reluctant to produce anything based on classical (and therefore pre-Christian) styles. The increase in monastic learning during the 12th century changed attitudes and the more literate clergy from the great educational establishments began producing Latin prose and poetry in styles related to Greek and Roman texts. Previously, medieval writing had followed a heavily formulaic style established by the Church, using set phrases (tropes) to describe almost everything.

The next development was the writing of prose and poetry in vernacular languages. Although there was a slowly growing body of literate secular nobility, they had no desire to read vernacular works. Instead, a limited number of these French, German, and Spanish works were written so that they could be read aloud, thereby reaching an audience beyond the literate.

English was a special case, having existed as a written language from at least the ninth century and used for the production of legal documents and occasional pieces of poetry. While many earlier vernacular poems were never recorded, the increase in demand for vernacular stories ensured the survival of tenth century English poems such as *Beowulf*. If they had never been written down, they would probably have been lost forever. Other less well-known examples of the genre include the Saxon elegies, such as *The Wanderer* and *Wulf and Eadwager*, or heroic epics, such as *The Battle of Maldon*.

Similar examples of heroic vernacular poetry were produced in France, where the *Song of*

Above: *Chaucer even inspired other authors to sequels, such as John of Lydgate (c.1370–c.1451), whose* Story of Thebes *was intended as an additional* Canterbury Tale.

Roland was extremely popular. An account of heroic events from the age of Charlemagne, it found a market in the growing attachment to heroic, chivalric, and romantic notions among contemporary aristocratic society.

Epic adventure and romance

In some cases, vernacular literature developed from the retelling of classical, mythological, and Celtic stories, often adapting earlier styles to suit contemporary characters. Examples include the Arthurian legends shrouded in Celtic mythology, or the romantic verses describing Charlemagne by Einhardt, which have vague parallels in classical histories, such as the works of Plutarch. The Arthurian legends are of particular importance; they first appeared in Geoffrey of Monmouth's *The History of the Kings of Britain* (1136) and re-emerged in a more romantic form in the late 14th century as *Sir Gawain and the Green Knight*.

From the mid-12th century onward, romantic themes were an important part of vernacular prose, and contemporary chivalric values—the conflict between love and loyalty being of primary importance—became recurring themes in a fresh literary movement. Romanticism was particularly common in Germany and Italy, and, like earlier vernacular works, it was meant to be recited to appreciative, chivalric audiences.

Many of these vernacular romantic works have become regarded as cornerstones of Europe's various national literatures. It has been argued that romanticism marked a shift in demand from heroic epics to heroic romances. Within a short span, epics such as the French *Song of Roland* and Spanish *El Cid* were replaced in popularity by romantic and mythological works, such as *The Nibelungenlied* (c.1200), Wolfram von Eschenbach's *Parzival* (1210) and Chrétien de Troyes' *Narratives*. Less elegant pieces were written, probably for less discriminating audiences, including animal fables like *Renard the Fox*, allegorical tales, and even humorous anecdotes, such as Notker the Stammerer's stories about Charlemagne.

Whatever the subject, medieval literature was written by clerical authors working for secular patrons. They reflected the interests of their audiences, but also represented a change in the Church's attitude. These works survive today as a means to understand both writer and listener.

FOCUS: SOCIETY

Gothic Architecture

In 1132 an abbot began overseeing the construction of an abbey church at Saint-Denis, Paris. Encompassing the latest architectural innovations, this light, soaring new building began the Gothic style of architecture.

Facing, both:

Lincoln Cathedral, built between 1192 and 1280, represents a perfect form of early Gothic church-building, but with the English predilection for great length and a double transept. It illustrates the Gothic ideal of the soaring height to heaven and the visual sweep toward the altar.

The term "Gothic" was never used in the feudal period; it was coined by supporters of the new classical revival style introduced during the Italian Renaissance of the 15th century. They opposed the Gothic architecture revival, which ultimately disappeared in the cultural landslide of the Renaissance.

In the mid-12th century the French court was prospering: in its heartland, centered around Paris and the Ile-de-France, secular patrons commissioned new religious buildings. Fresh architectural ideas allowed them to ignore the constraints of Romanesque buildings. This was a period when the spread of learning and the development of universities encouraged theologians and secular patrons to question existing values and experiment with new ideas—at least within the limited framework allowed by the Church.

The two basic architectural innovations that gave expression to this cultural movement were the ribbed vault and pointed arch. A Romanesque vault was ribbed from side to side, dividing a vaulted roof into a number of square or rectangular bays. Initially, two semi-circular ribs joined all four corners of a bay, creating a square of ribs. Later, two diagonal ribs formed a cross between the corners. This sturdy framework allowed the triangular sections between the ribs to be constructed of far lighter stonework than Romanesque square vaults.

Diagonal ribs broke the clean lines of Romanesque vaults and rose higher than other arches, so to some minds they lacked a certain esthetic quality. The solution was a pointed arch; if the vault roof (clerestory) was more pointed, the reinforcing arches supporting the pillars could be raised to the same height as the diagonal ribs, like the spokes of an umbrella. New ribs were raised far higher than the heavy square they replaced, creating a light, lofty appearance. This transferred some of the strain on the piers from the horizontal axis to the vertical, allowing designers to reduce the size of the support columns while raising the height of the vault.

Freeing the form

As an insurance, it was important to provide extra reinforcement to the piers at the point where they supported the pointed ribs. The final Gothic innovation was the flying buttress; a heavy stone pier built outside the cathedral. Arches spread from these, over the low roofs of the cathedral aisles to reinforce the piers of the nave at the maximum point of stress. Secondary arches sometimes supported the walls of the aisles.

With the weight of the building resting on a highly engineered structure of ribs, piers, and buttresses, a whole host of design opportunities presented themselves. Walls were no longer load-

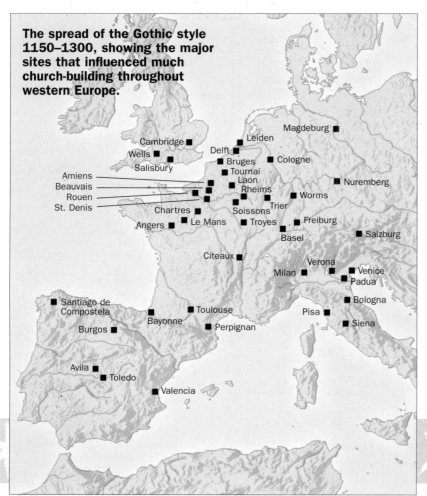

The spread of the Gothic style 1150–1300, showing the major sites that influenced much church-building throughout western Europe.

Magdeburg
Cambridge
Leiden
Wells
Delft
Bruges · Cologne
Salisbury · Tournai
Amiens · Laon
Beauvais · Rheims · Nuremberg
Rouen · Worms
St. Denis · Trier
Chartres · Soissons
Angers · Le Mans · Troyes · Freiburg
Basel · Salzburg
Citeaux
Verona
Milan · Venice
Padua
Bologna
Santiago de Compostela
Toulouse · Pisa
Bayonne · Siena
Burgos · Perpignan
Avila
Toledo
Valencia

1110	1113	1115
The First Miracle Play is performed	St. Nicholas Church built in Novgorod	St. Bernard establishes a monastery at Clervaux

bearing, so could be pierced with high windows. This led to the introduction of stained-glass windows, filling cathedrals with magnificently colored light. Inner tiers of arcades, clerestory windows, balustrades, triforium, and other forms of dressing could be added, according to the budget and desire of patron and architect. The result was a magnificent, light, airy structure, filled with a soaring sense of grace, where spiritualism was allowed free rein.

The terms "Early Gothic" and "High Gothic" were coined to divide the various forms of this architectural development. High Gothic style also came to be associated with a more flamboyant use of decoration; statuary, tracery, fan designs on vaulting, and ornamental stonework. The elegance of "functional" Gothic lines was reflected in a whole artistic movement, extending from the decorative arts through painting to calligraphy.

To the medieval mind, the elegance of the Gothic form and the light it created were linked to medieval belief, and its mathematical basis expressed the harmony of the universe. It also demonstrated a flowering of scientific and artistic ability that paved the way for the Renaissance.

FOCUS: LEADERS
The Lion in Winter: Henry II

When Henry Plantagenet acceded to the English throne, he was already Duke of Normandy and Count of Anjou through inheritance. Despite constant struggle with four rival forces, he added territories until his Angevin Empire stretched from Scotland to Spain.

Below: *Seen in restful pose in Notre Dame de Fontrevaud, Maine-et-Loire, this painted stone sculpture of Eleanor of Aquitaine and King Henry II belies their usually stormy relationship.*

Stephen I of England (1135–54) was perhaps the weakest Norman successor of William the Conqueror. His reign was dominated by a civil war between baronial factions loyal to him and those of his cousin, Matilda, daughter of Henry I. Royal power diminished and his barons effectively controlled the Anglo-Norman kingdom. On his death he was succeeded by Henry Plantagenet who created a feudal powerbase that covered most of northwest France.

Eleanor of Aquitaine (1122–1204) was one of the most remarkable women to emerge from the medieval period. She was the eldest of the two daughters of Duke William of Aquitaine and his wife Ainor, who had been mistress to the duke's father. When her father died in 1137, the beautiful teenage Eleanor inherited Aquitaine, as well as the neighboring provinces of Gascony, Poitou, and Auvergne, making her the most eligible woman in Europe.

In July 1137 she married King Louis VII of France (1137–80), but the relationship was a stormy one. In 1152 Louis divorced Eleanor, but within months she married Henry of Anjou, soon to become King Henry II. As Queen of England, Eleanor bore Henry seven children, but when mother and offspring began to plot against him, she was imprisoned. Although she provided Henry II with vast territories, she was a thorn in his side and was only released on Henry's death.

Technically, Henry owned his French territories as a vassal of King Louis, but since he spent much of his reign fighting the French king, this fealty was rarely honored. In England, royal power was restored through tight control over his

barons and the introduction of extensive bureaucratic, legal, and financial institutions, laying the foundations for a powerful civil service.

A troublesome priest

Although the innovation of the royal courts—which superseded regional judicial assemblies—was intended to curb the power of his nobles, the effect was to reform justice within the Angevin Empire. Rebellions were brutally repressed and baronial strongholds demolished if Henry thought them a threat.

He also placed increasing emphasis on *scutage* as a means of obtaining funds to hire troops, allowing resources in one part of his Empire to help control another region. Henry used warfare as a means to control his unruly nobles, and kept them busy fighting the Scots in the 1150s and the Irish during the 1170s, which also created new feudal territories for loyal supporters.

When Henry II tried to increase royal control over the Church, he came into conflict with Thomas à Becket, the Archbishop of Canterbury. Before becoming head of the English Church in 1162, Becket had served as Henry's chancellor, but he opposed the king's Constitutions of Clarendon (1164), which strengthened Henry's

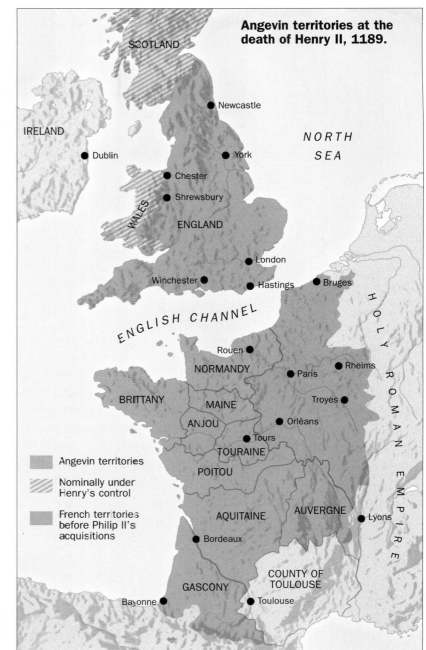

Angevin territories at the death of Henry II, 1189.

SCOTLAND

IRELAND

Dublin

Newcastle

NORTH SEA

York

Chester

Shrewsbury

WALES

ENGLAND

London

Winchester • • Hastings • Bruges

ENGLISH CHANNEL

HOLY ROMAN EMPIRE

Rouen

NORMANDY

Rheims

Paris

BRITTANY

MAINE

Troyes

ANJOU

Orléans

Tours

TOURAINE

☐ Angevin territories

POITOU

▨ Nominally under Henry's control

☐ French territories before Philip II's acquisitions

AQUITAINE

AUVERGNE

Lyons

Bordeaux

COUNTY OF TOULOUSE

GASCONY

Toulouse

Bayonne

control over clergy appointments. Becket was exiled but reinstated in 1170, when the confrontation continued. When Henry wished to be "rid of such a troublesome priest," four knights rode to Canterbury and killed Becket in front of the cathedral altar. The murder aroused such indignation that Henry was forced to publicly confess penance at Becket's shrine, and make a humiliating peace with the Pope in 1172.

During the last years of his reign Henry II was plagued by rebellions, usually instigated by his wife, sons, or the new French king, Philip I Augustus (1180–1223). On his death in July 1189 Henry's Angevin Empire was passed on intact to his sons, Richard I the Lionheart (1189–99) and John I (1199–1216).

1136	1137	1140	1145
Geoffrey of Monmouth's *History of the Kings of Britain* is written	Outbreak of civil war in England	Abelard condemned by St. Bernard	Chartres Cathedral built on Gothic lines

FOCUS: WARFARE

Castles and Siegecraft

Although castles in the 12th century were largely unchanged from Norman stone keeps of the preceding century, modifications were made to counteract increasingly effective siege equipment. Castle design and siege techniques matched pace until the invention of gunpowder.

Castles built for Henry II of England (1154–89) and Louis VII of France (1137–80) countered the fundamental dangers of rectangular structures: being undermined or battered at their vulnerable corners. Orford and Conisborough castles in England (both built c.1170) were polygonal, with three flanking towers strengthening each exposed side, while Pembroke in Wales (c.1200) had a completely round keep.

During the 13th century curtain walls became popular, where a high surrounding wall with towers (bastions) at regular intervals provided perimeter defense. Like keeps, curtain wall bastions evolved from square to round structures.

The next development was to eliminate the inner keep, creating a pure curtain-wall castle. One of the perimeter walls was often much larger than the rest and performed the same domestic functions as the keeps of earlier castles.

During the 13th century, greater emphasis was placed on domestic quarters—a reflection of the growing affluence of the feudal aristocracy—and new defensive elements were introduced, such as water-filled moats around curtain walls.

Developments in castle-building reflected the perceived threat to the defenders. In peaceful areas, older designs were used for some time, while the latest defensive principles were adopted in regions such as the Holy Land, northwestern France, and the Scottish and Welsh borders.

Military experience abroad gave engineers the opportunity to examine different approaches. The Crusader castle at Krak-des-Chevaliers (c.1205) added a second curtain with towers around an inner wall; this element was included in castles built for Edward I of England (1272–1307), such as Beaumaris in Wales (c.1295).

Castles like these were the best that could be

Below: *In the siege of Jerusalem in 1190 Frederick Barbarossa's army employed tall towers and bridges to enfilade the enemy positions. From an engraving of 1740.*

1147	1147	1153	1162	1167	1167	1168	1170
Work begins on Lisbon Cathedral	First mention of Moscow in historic documents	Death of St.Bernard	Frederick Barbarossa sacks Milan	Council of Cathar heretics formed in southern France	Foundation of Oxford University	The romantic verse *Lancelot* is written	Waldo preaches value of poverty in Lyons, founding the Waldensians

produced to foil assaults by determined besieging forces equipped with siege engines. It would take almost a century for engineers to develop a method of protecting medieval castle walls from siege artillery.

Adopting Roman methods

Siege engineers owed their methods of attacking and capturing a castle to those recorded in classical Roman sources. Medieval siege engines did little more than mirror earlier Roman designs for the catapult (or mangonel), which was the basic siege weapon. A boulder was placed in a cup at the end of an arm slotted into a wound rope; when released the boulder was hurled in an arc. A later modification was the trebuchet, where winches and counterweights employed gravity to fire boulders. These weapons could also be used to launch incendiary missiles. Recent reconstructions have demonstrated the power and accuracy of the catapult and trebuchet.

Castle gates were battered down using a ram or giant screw, whose crew were protected inside a hut-like wooden structure. One final method of attack was by mining: a tunnel was dug under a tower or wall, using wooden supports. When the supports were fired, the timbers and mine collapsed and so did the castle foundations above.

After a breach was made, or if there was insufficient time for an extensive siege, a commander ordered an assault on the castle walls. While archers or crossbowmen gave covering fire (usually from behind large *pavis* shields), storming parties ran forward with ladders and scaled the walls. Alternatives to ladders included siege towers that, when wheeled against the walls, allowed the attackers to sally out at the top.

During the siege of Acre (1189), towers were even mounted on rafts to attack harbor defenses.

When the attackers gained a foothold, weight of numbers usually told—and the besiegers usually had superior numbers. To save unnecessary bloodshed, it became increasingly common to surrender as soon as the besiegers breached the inner castle wall, a nicety that was repeated during the highly ritualized sieges of the 18th century.

Below: *In the background of this battle scene from a 15th-century French manuscript is a castle with motte and bailey, and on the river bank in front of the castle, a fortified manor house.*

On several occasions, apparently impregnable walls fell to the unchivalrous technique of bribery and treachery from within, when a traitor among the defenders opened a sally port, or even the front gate, to the besiegers.

1170	1180	1180	1186	1189	1190	1261	1270
Thomas à Becket murdered in Canterbury Cathedral	Hungary gains its independence	First recorded windmill in western Europe	*Reynard the Fox* is written	The First Florin is minted in Florence	The Teutonic Order is founded	Constantinople is recaptured by the Byzantines	Approximate date of the first mechanical clocks

CHAPTER SIX

Feudal Europe in the 13th Century

The political upheavals of the 12th century were followed by a period of relative peace in Europe, which allowed the peasantry the opportunity to develop their holdings under the protection of their feudal masters. The feudal system used throughout most of western Europe continued to evolve, adapting to the spread of commerce and urban centers. At the same time the monarchs and senior nobles of France and England vied with each other for political control, placing further strain on the upper echelons of feudal society.

By the end of the 13th century, these feudal monarchies had emerged triumphant in their struggle with the nobility, creating the basis for the powerful central authorities of the next century. The growth of towns ensured greater wealth for European monarchs, and Europe was linked in a network of trade. Warfare was largely restricted to the crusading expeditions, although the target of these missions increasingly became fellow Christians in the Byzantine Empire, rather than Muslims. These developments created tensions and laid the framework for the disasters that would befall western Europe during the 14th century.

Faroe Islands

Shetland Islands

Orkney Islands

SCOTLAND

Edinburgh

NORTH SEA

IRELAND

Dublin

WALES

ENGLAND

York

Lincoln

Oxford

London

Bruges

Colog

Winchester

Canterbury

Ghent

Caen

Rouen

Paris

Reims

FRANCE

Orléans

Basel

Poitiers

Dijon

BAY OF BISCAY

Bordeaux

Geneva

Bayonne

Toulouse

Avignon

Ger

León

NAVARRE

Marseilles

PORTUGAL

CASTILE

ARAGON

Corsica

Lisbon

Barcelona

Toledo

Cordoba

Valencia

Palma

Lagos

Seville

BALEARICS

Sardinia

Malaga

Granada

Almeria

Madeira

Tangiers

Ceuta

Algiers

Melilla

ATLANTIC OCEAN

Annaba

Tur

AFRICA

Canary Islands

NORWAY

Christiania

SWEDEN

Stockholm

Calmar

ESTONIA

Novgorod

Copenhagen

BALTIC SEA

Riga

RUSSIA

DENMARK

Lübeck

Danzig

TEUTONIC ORDER

LITHUANIA

AXONY

Hamburg

Berlin

HOLY

Magdeburg

Poznan

POLAND

Kiev

ROMAN

Nuremberg

Prague

EMPIRE

Vienna

Augsburg

MONGOL EMPIRE

SEA OF AZOV

Buda

Pest

HUNGARY

Kaffa

an

venice

Moncastro

Zara

ADRIATIC SEA

Belgrade

Kiliya

Bologna

Florence

Pisa

SERBIA

Nis

Varna

BLACK SEA

Sinope

Trebizond

Assisi

BULGARIA

Rome

Bari

Constantinople

Naples

KINGDOM OF SICILY

Palermo

Messina

Syracuse

LATIN EMPIRE OF CONSTANTINOPLE

Nicea

SELJUK SULTANATE OF RUM

MONGOL ILKHANATE

EMPIRE OF NICEA

Athens

Smyrna

Antioch

Aleppo

Famagusta

Rhodes

Tripoli

Cyprus

Candia

Beirut

Damascus

Crete

Acre

MEDITERRANEAN SEA

King v. Baron: Feudal France and England

Although most of Europe adopted the feudal system, its development was centered in France and England. This was set against a backdrop of almost continual political and military conflict between the French and English crowns, an antagonism that led to the devastation of the Hundred Years War.

Below: *The saintly King Louis IX of France passes judgment when the Abbot of St. Nicholas-au-Bois accuses a knight of wrongly hanging three young men. From a French illustration of 1330.*

In the 13th century, the power of the monarchies grew throughout Europe. This increasing influence was largely because of the institutional adoption of the feudal system, and was particularly marked in France and England. Philip II Augustus (1180–1223) of France was a strong king who was able to enlarge his royal power, and his Capetian successors continued the trend by expanding the royal demesne. Marriage alliances added Toulouse and the Champagne region to the royal lands, but the practice of giving *appanages* (land gifts) to minor royal

was a marked increase in the revenue to the crown: taxed income from the burgeoning French towns. Philip II and his successors used this income to pay for an improved administrative system, thereby ensuring increased wealth from accurate taxation. The French crown was growing rich, and under the reign of perhaps the greatest French medieval monarch, Louis IX (1226–70), its territories extended from the English Channel to the Mediterranean Sea.

King Louis—later canonized as St. Louis—was a deeply pious man, respected by his people. He made peace with Henry III of England, who still held Gascony, in return for the Plantagenet king abandoning his claim to all other French provinces. He reformed the taxation system, making it more just, while enforcing laws that supported the rights of his feudal vassals. He clearly saw feudalism as a system that should benefit all parties; those higher up its ladder offering their protection to those beneath them.

Philip III (1270–85) and Philip IV the Fair (1285–1314) continued the policies advocated by St. Louis, and royal authority was used to curb the excesses of the lesser nobility. The *Parlement* of Paris became the premier court in France, while the same city housed an increasingly effective and burgeoning civil service. These two organizations developed a policy whereby the raising of feudal dues was gradually replaced by a system of general taxation by the crown, at least in the territories directly controlled by the Crown.

Facing: *The less saintly King John of England is forced by his barons to sign the Magna Carta at Runnymede on June 15, 1215.*

offspring limited the effect of this centralization. While they increased the power of the Capetian dynasty, *appanages* reduced the king's direct control. Warfare aided French expansion, as Philip captured Normandy from the English King John (1199–1216). Attacks against the Albigensian heretics also extended French royal control to the Pyrenees.

Linked to this extension of Capetian power

Philip IV also introduced the Estates General, which involved the Church and the nobles in secular government. By the start of the 14th century, France was a wealthy state, where central royal control was becoming all-powerful. This success naturally attracted the attention of France's neighbors, particularly the English, who still dreamed of regaining their lost Angevin territories in France.

The basis of English law

Although royal authority in England was also enhanced during the 13th century, it did so in a different way, and the trend was strongly opposed by the English nobility. Richard the Lionheart (1189–99)—perpetually fighting abroad—was mostly an absentee monarch, which left his nobles with freer hands to make mischief. On the other hand, his brother John I (1199–1216), although a poor military leader who lost Normandy to the French, proved proficient at increasing royal revenues. He did so by taking the increasing revenues from his nobles that they received from the growing towns within their fiefs. Antagonized, the English nobility revolted in 1215 and forced the beleaguered John to sign the Article of the Barons, a document which became known as the *Magna Carta*.

The *Magna Carta* ensured fair terms for the Church and the nobility, and an equitable system of justice and taxation, controlled by parliament and not the king. In effect it created a limited monarchy, where the king was forced to consult his nobles to a degree that was unimagined in France. It has also been seen as the forerunner of parliamentary democracy in Britain, a notion that led to Civil War in 1642.

John's son Henry III (1216–76) was a weak monarch, unable to prevent a major revolt of his nobles in 1258 when he tried to repudiate the provisions of the *Magna Carta*. The king was defeated and captured by the rebels led by Simon de Montfort, whose dreams of restoring the feudal status quo was undermined by quarreling between the nobles. Instead, Henry's son Edward raised an army and utterly defeated the rebels. An

astute monarch and formidable soldier, Edward III (1272–1307) combined rebuilding the royal power base with a policy of military conquest, employed partly as a means of keeping his nobles occupied.

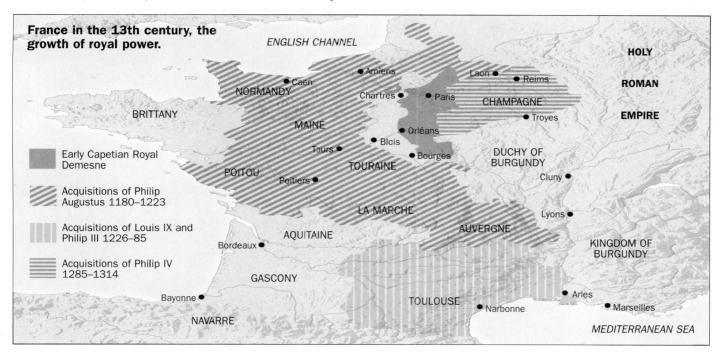

France in the 13th century, the growth of royal power.

ENGLISH CHANNEL

HOLY ROMAN EMPIRE

NORMANDY
BRITTANY
MAINE
POITOU
TOURAINE
LA MARCHE
AQUITAINE
AUVERGNE
GASCONY
TOULOUSE
NAVARRE

Caen • • Amiens
Laon • • Reims
Chartres • • Paris
CHAMPAGNE
• Troyes
• Orléans
Tours • • Blois
• Bourges
DUCHY OF BURGUNDY
Poitiers • • Cluny
Lyons •
Bordeaux •
KINGDOM OF BURGUNDY
• Arles
• Narbonne • Marseilles
Bayonne •

MEDITERRANEAN SEA

Early Capetian Royal Demesne

Acquisitions of Philip Augustus 1180–1223

Acquisitions of Louis IX and Philip III 1226–85

Acquisitions of Philip IV 1285–1314

The Revival of a Money Economy

The revival of commerce and the growth of towns created a need for coinage. The profits from taxation and feudal dues were increasingly paid in coins from the 12th century, and myriad different currencies were used throughout medieval Europe. In turn, this created a need for reliable financial institutions.

There was little gold to be had in Europe, which meant that this precious metal was rarely used for coinage until the 14th century, when overseas trade led to an accumulation of it in Europe. The vast majority of the money circulating in medieval Europe was made of silver. Silver had been used for coinage in Europe from the mid-11th century, following the discovery of rich silver mines in Saxony. Eastern Germany continued to be a reliable source for silver, although other mines were opened in the Alps and Tuscany. A shortage of silver in the 14th and 15th centuries led to a corresponding dearth of coinage.

The basic silver coin in circulation since Carolingian times was the *denarius* (originally the basic unit of the Imperial Roman monetary system). Twelve *denarii* made a *solidus* (shilling); and 20 *soldii* became a *libra* (pound). The system was retained in use in Britain until the late 20th century. During the 13th century, the *grossus*

Right: *A French mint at work. Merchants sit in comfort discussing their deals, while below them, two minters can be seen hammering out new coinage. From* De l'Institution et Administration de la Chose Politique, *1520.*

denarius (groat) was introduced, worth several pennies, and in Germany, a silver *mark* was worth 13 *soldii* and four *denarii*. Unlike modern currencies, the larger denominations (pounds and shillings) existed solely for the purposes of accounting and were not represented by coins of these values. The denarius was the standard coin in common circulation, although its value varied widely due to the variety of different types of denarii in circulation.

Every monarch and many great feudal lords minted their own currency, establishing their own standards of coin weight, silver purity, and value. Whenever one of these feudal rulers needed extra money, the temptation was strong to debase their own coinage by producing their provincial currency from poorer quality metal. Philip VI (1328–50) debased the French coinage to help finance his war with England. Debts were paid with these "black" coins, then the currency was "revalued" so that income from taxes was paid in "good" money. The effect was to undermine the stability of the French economy, particularly when Philip repeated the trick annually for a decade.

The regional and provincial currencies included the English pound sterling and the French Paris pound, together with those of several other French cities. Following a Norman decree, the pound sterling (and its attendant divisions of shillings and pence) became the standard form of currency throughout the English kingdom, but elsewhere, including the English possessions in France, numerous other currencies remained in circulation. In the 13th century King Louis IX of France issued a decree that the Paris pound would be accepted throughout his dominions, but regional coins remained in circulation for at least another century. As pennies became worth less and less, the larger denominations (marks and groats) became increasingly popular, and gold coins entered circulation in the 13th century in Germany (the *augustale*) and in England (the gold penny). The most widely circulated gold coins in the medieval world were the *Florin* of Florence and the Venetian *ducat*.

The first banks

Although the Church regarded commercial transactions and moneylending as forms of avarice, they soon began to take advantage of the money economy. From the 12th century currency exchange was dealt with by the religious military orders of the Templars and the Hospitalers. Both organizations held estates

Above: *Merchant using a counting board; from the title page of* Arithmeticae Practicae, *1544.*

throughout Europe, and these acted as clearing houses for transactions between different states or provinces.

Given the military strength of these orders, their buildings were relatively safe from being robbed, and the piety of the members of the order meant that their honesty was above reproach. The orders even conducted transactions with the Saracens in the Holy Land, paying the ransom for Christian prisoners captured during the crusades. Through their offices, it was possible to pay large sums of money into one estate, and have an equal sum issued from a different estate in another kingdom. In this respect, they functioned as the forerunners of banks, issuing letters of credit and supervising deposits, withdrawals, and cash transfers.

By the 13th century, moneylenders and merchants were beginning to establish themselves in this continental banking enterprise. Philip VI of France borrowed heavily from foreign and domestic moneylenders, and the resulting interest proved a serious drain on French resources. Although the large revenues produced by cities allowed feudal overlords to decrease their reliance on feudal vassals, it also created the problem of debt, demanded significant changes to bureaucratic administration to work, and reinforced a reliance on sources of monetary income.

The Decline of the Byzantine Empire

The Byzantine Empire was devastated by its loss of land and prestige following the Battle of Manzikert in 1071. The Empire survived and even rallied during the 12th century, but an even greater disaster would bring it to its knees.

Below: *Otto II (955–983) and his wife Theophano are blessed by Christ in this carved-wood Byzantine relief, now in the Musée National de l'Hôtel de Cluny, Paris.*

The decade following the disaster at Manzikert was marked by a loss of territory to the Seljuk Turks, civil war within the Empire's borders, and a resultant loss of central control. Alexius Comnenus emerged from the chaos as the leader of the most powerful Byzantine faction, and he became Emperor in 1081. He hastily made peace with the Seljuks, and repulsed Norman incursions into Greece. The reduced borders of the country were now more stable, and he was able to turn his attention to internal matters. Reforms of the bureaucracy, taxation, and regional government were all aimed at lessening the chances of further division through factional or regional conflict.

Emperor Comnenus' next venture was regarded as a triumph at the time, but it brought with it the seeds of the destruction of the Empire. An appeal for European help in fighting the Turks led to the First Crusade, in 1096. The crusaders were escorted through Byzantine territory, then unleashed themselves on the Seljuks. As the crusaders advanced through Anatolia toward Syria and the Holy Land, Comnenus and his army followed in their wake, recovering most of their lost coastal territories. When Comnenus died in 1118, the Byzantine Empire appeared to have regained much of its former status.

During the 12th century Byzantine emperors maintained an uneasy relationship with the crusaders, and their Latin state in Syria. Under John Comnenus the Byzantines made further inroads into Turkish Anatolia, especially when the attention of the Muslims was diverted by the Second and Third Crusades. Open warfare erupted during the latter half of the century, and central Anatolia was devastated by constant fighting, the conflict ending in stalemate by the end of the century. By 1195, when Alexius III was crowned Emperor, all seemed relatively stable. In reality, the whole edifice of the Byzantine Empire would be brought to its knees in less than a decade.

Betrayed by fellow Christians

The start of the 13th century found the Empire in disarray, split by a fresh wave of internal disputes and external attack. In 1199 Pope Innocent III had called for another crusade, but this time the German Emperor and the Venetians argued for an assault against their fellow Christians in the east rather than against the Muslims. Economic and political motives weighed strongly on the decision and, under the guise of reuniting the Church, the crusaders sailed for Constantinople in 1203. After a brief assault the Emperor fled, and the Byzantine nobles crowned the western puppet Alexius IV the new emperor. The unpopular monarch was eventually deposed in 1204, and the crusaders took their revenge by attacking and looting the city.

The loss of Constantinople was a mortal blow to Byzantium. While the crusaders set up yet another Latin province in the Middle East, the now isolated provinces of the empire reorganized and provincial governors in Greece, Anatolia, and the Crimea vied with each other for control of the empire's remnants. After several decades of fighting, a Byzantine army recaptured Constantinople in 1261, and a new Byzantine imperial dynasty was founded by Michael Paleologus, the leader of the winning faction. His dynasty retained control of the empire until the city finally fell to the Ottoman Turks in 1453.

This new Byzantine Empire was a mere shadow of its former self, relegated to the level of a minor power in the Mediterranean. The loss of territory, wealth, and military manpower as a result of the Fourth Crusade was too much to

recover from, and economic and political decay led to the slow erosion of the remaining Byzantine territories over the next two centuries.

Almost as significant as the political repercussions of the fall of Constantinople was the effect the loss had on the Byzantines themselves. Before the Fourth Crusade they regarded themselves as Romans, the last true descendants of the people who had once ruled the known world. After 1204 they regarded themselves as Greeks, especially since the early 13th century saw the loss of most of the empire's territories in Anatolia. From then on, the feudal states of western Europe would form the undisputed top tier of nations on the continent.

Above: *Once the greatest church in Christendom outside Rome, Santa Sofia's glorious mosaics were hidden by Muslim text when the Turks took Constantinople.*

FOCUS: SOCIETY

The Knight in Medieval Society

Knights appeared during the tenth century and evolved into the warrior we associate with the medieval period, with a highly developed code of honor and service. Knights played a vital role in the development of the feudal system.

In European society early knights were a separate social class between commoners and the nobles, and they were—as we might say today—upwardly mobile. Military service was a way to gain advancement in society, and the first knights were heavy cavalrymen, recruited by

Right: *Life for the medieval knight was not always battle. This book illustration shows Wernher von Teufen (documented 1219–1223) with his lady on a falcom hunt.*

Frankish noblemen from among the ranks of the peasantry. The same applied to most of knights in Norman service. Although regarded as a step above the irregular levy of foot soldiers, Norman cavalry were not strictly knights, but simply armed, mounted retainers. Their status only changed during the Norman expansion into southern Italy and Sicily.

By the time of the First Crusade, the knight had become almost synonymous with Christianity, and the code of chivalry was a natural extension. During the 12th century knights gained in prestige, and their deeds were glorified in romantic legend. Through being granted fiefs by their feudal lords, many knights became landholders in their own right, and passed this to the elder son through inheritance. Younger sons either took service with other knights of ranking or entered the Church; there was no option of going into trade.

The chivalric code that enfolded the medieval knight was fully developed by the 13th century. Linked to the induction of recruits, the young men swore allegiance to their feudal superiors and loyalty to a code of conduct. This placed an emphasis on military prowess, devotion to God and feudal superiors, bravery, and virtue. In return the medieval knight was guaranteed a secure place within the hierarchy of the feudal system. His military duties involved a certain period of service each year, and he was expected to be prepared at all times in case he was called upon. This involved attending in person, equipped with an increasingly lavish kit of horse, armor, and weapons—although wealthier knights were often required to bring along a retinue of foot soldiers or cavalry with them as well. The knight as an armed retainer had developed into a lower-ranking version of nobles

1200	1200	1203	1209	1210	1213	1215	1218
Foundation of Cambridge University	*Carmina Burana* written	Wolfram von Eschenback writes *Parzival*	Francis of Assisi founds the Franciscan Order	Gottfried von Strassburg writes *Tristan und Isolde*	King John of England agrees to make England a Papal fief	King John of England puts his seal on the *Magna Carta*	Genghis Khan conquers Persia

themselves. With sufficient revenues from his fiefs, a knight could avoid direct military service by paying a tax called *scutage* (from the Latin *scutum*, a shield), which his lord used for the hire of more experienced mercenary knights. This comfortable arrangement benefited everyone. Mercenaries were referred to as "unfree" in contrast to those knights attending their overlord as part of their proper feudal duty, who were known as "free" knights.

The practice of giving homage, fealty, and fighting men to an overlord was never as highly developed in Germany, northern Italy, or Spain as it was in France and England. The concept of knighthood was therefore less highly defined in these areas, at least until the 13th century. By this time, military duty was restricted to set periods of six or eight weeks; service beyond that was sometimes required, but the knights were paid for their time. This complex system was confused by *scutage* and the concept of "free" or "unfree" knights.

The importance of honor

In a period when education was ecclesiastic, the sons of knights were brought up according to the code of chivalry and, as children, they were sent to serve other knights or feudal superiors as pages. At 14 they became squires, and at 21 they were knighted, thereby perpetuating the system.

Since skill and prowess in battle was the ultimate aim, in a well organized household the military training pages and squires underwent was intensive. When there were no battles to be fought—and often when there were—the jousting tournament was a celebration and a test of a knight's skill. Tournaments became a feature of medieval life and something knights practiced throughout their lives. The events provided an opportunity for superiors to assess the fitness and suitability of the jousters for future tasks, honed the knight's fighting abilities, and showed off a knight's courage before the whole retinue—

including admiring ladies.

The third part of a knight's chivalric code was bound by religious devotion, virtue, and impeccable behavior toward women. Failure to

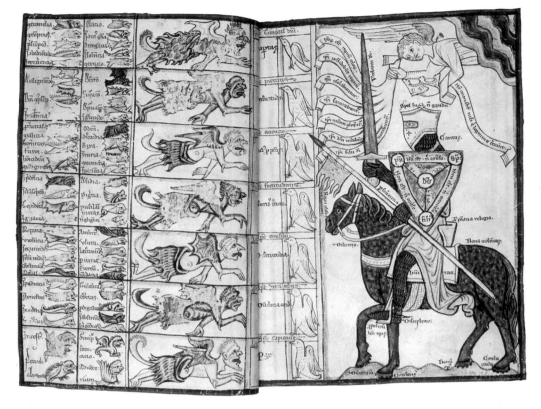

adhere to the code could lead to public humiliation and loss of social status. The power of these chivalric ideals are demonstrated by their influence on today's society.

When new military tactical doctrines emerged from the 14th century onward, the knight's influence on both the battlefield and within society began to wane.

Above: *A Christian knight fights vice and heresy in the form of devils. From a 13th-century manuscript illumination.*

Below: *A jousting tournament.*

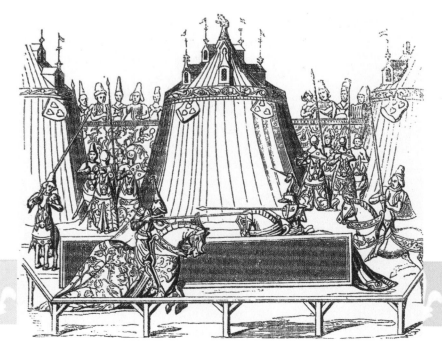

1218	1224	1226
The Danes adopt the first national flag in Europe	Foundation of Naples University	Death of St. Francis of Assis

FOCUS: WARFARE
Medieval Armor

The armor worn by a knight was expensive, and was therefore seen as a status symbol. While the richest knights kept up with the latest developments, others lagged behind, wearing obsolete equipment. Throughout the medieval period, the trend was toward greater and heavier protection, culminating in the full plate armor of the 15th century.

Right: *Model figure of a knight, late 13th century. He is clad in mail from head to foot, with a "pair of plates" beneath his gown.*

The arms and armor used by Norman knights during their conquests of England and Sicily was outlined on page 41. The *hauberk*, or mail shirt continued to be the main form of protection for wealthy soldiers throughout the 12th century. A *coif* or mail hood was usually worn over the head and attached to the shirt to provide protection for the neck. By the end of the century, mail gloves were also worn. Less well-off soldiers wore either no armor, or a *gambeson*, a form of quilted cloth jacket, which was occasionally also worn by knights under their hauberk for extra protection.

The conical helmets shown in the Bayeux Tapestry continued to be used, but toward the end of the century they developed into cylindrical, flat-topped helmets, and by the late 12th century a semi-circular face-plate was added, pierced with eye slits and breathing holes. Poorer knights or foot soldiers adopted a "kettle-hat," a round, wide-brimmed helmet reminiscent of that worn by British soldiers in the World Wars. The large kite-shields of the Bayeux Tapestry evolved during the 12th century into smaller, flat-topped "heater-shields," with larger shields carried by foot soldiers and smaller versions by cavalrymen.

The hauberk and coif continued to be worn by mounted knights, but by 1250 the coif was usually worn as a separate attachment. The head was also protected by a cloth "arming cap," which helped to support the weight of the increasingly heavy helmets worn by knights and men-at-arms. By the mid-13th century these flat or dome-topped helmets completely encircled the face and neck. This hid the identity of the wearer, which led to the general adoption of heraldic devices painted on shields, or sewn on cloth surcoats worn over the armor for identification. The protection offered by the hauberk was sometimes augmented by a more solid form of body armor. A surcoat with sewn-in metal plates or a sewn-plate corset known as a *curie* (or *cuir*) became increasingly popular as the century progressed. The neck and legs of a mounted knight were particularly vulnerable in battle, so scale or metal-stripped defenses were buckled on for

1227	1228	1229	1230	1233	1236	1237	1241
Death of Genghis Khan	Construction begins on the basilica at Assisi	The Spanish conquer the Balearic Islands from the Moors	First outbreak of leprosy in Europe	The Pope orders the creation of the Inquisition	Mongols invade Russia	St. Gotthard Pass opened up to traders	Mongols defeat the Hungarians and Poles at Mohi and Leignitz

extra protection. For foot soldiers or poorer knights, the gambeson continued to be worn, along with round skullcaps or kettle-helms.

An era of bloodshed

Because the 14th century was dominated by conflict there were significant developments in personal protection. The hauberk was no longer considered proof against archery, so metal plates were added to the mail, initially as leg or arm defenses which were strapped on around the limbs. Later, a form of padded or leather armor incorporating sewn-in metal plates known as a "pair of plates" was added over the hauberk itself. By this stage foot defenses were worn, mail stockings covered in overlapping metal plates, that allowed a reasonable degree of mobility. The neck continued to be protected by a "collar-of-plates," which became increasingly common among foot soldiers, who were otherwise only protected by a gambeson and helmet. The gambeson also became armored, and a version incorporating sewn-in armor plates was known as a "jack-of-plates."

Helmets also developed during the century, influenced by experimentation and fashion. The large "great helm" of the previous century continued in use, but was gradually adapted into a lighter and more practical form of head protection. The part of the helm covering the face could be hinged up when the wearer was not in combat. A development of the skull-cap, known as the *bascinet*, had a pointed crest, and this lighter helmet continued in use into the 15th century. Horse armor was also introduced during this period, first in the form of mail, while later a protective head-plate was added, known as a *chanfron*.

Above: *Heavily armored knights jousting with lances. From a 16th-century German woodcut.*

By 1400, armor was highly developed, but so too were the weapons used on the battlefield. The 15th and early 16th century saw the final development of the fully protected knight, allowing a last period of dominance on the battlefield before firearms and artillery would make the mounted man-at-arms obsolete.

Left: *Two helmets with pointed visors and breathing holes.*

1249	1250	1252	1266	1271	1277	1285	1290
Roger Bacon first records gunpowder in Europe	Building of St. Thomas Cathedral in Leipzig marks the start of High Gothic	Minting of gold coins begins in Europe	The Battle of Benevento is climax of dynastic struggle for Italy	Marco Polo journeys to China	Roger Bacon is imprisoned for heresy	The romantic poem *Lohengrin* is written	Spectacles are invented

115

The Black Death

In 1347 Europe was visited by the worst human disaster in its long history. The Black Death ravaged the continent for three years, killing up to a third of the inhabitants and creating a fatalistic view that precipitated a crisis in the medieval world. It would take Europe another four centuries to become as populous as it had been before the scourge.

The 14th century was a period when warfare, religious division, and social injustice were endemic. These were all man-made problems, and man-made solutions could be brought to bear to solve them. The Black Death, however, was another matter, and there was nothing mankind could do to combat it.

In the fall of 1347 seamen returning from Kaffa on the Black Sea, and suffering from a strange disease, arrived in Sicily aboard Genoese ships. Most died within a week of their arrival and shipborne rats spread the disease throughout the port of Messina. Within months the epidemic had spread to the mainland of Italy, and from there it spread rapidly throughout Europe and continued unabated for three terrible years. The disease originated in China and spread to the Black Sea along the caravan routes that crossed Asia.

The Black Death was bubonic plague, a disease spread from rats to humans by parasitic fleas. In a society where hygiene was an unknown word, the disease spread with ease. The initial symptoms are high temperatures, aching limbs, and lymph node swellings or buboes. It is now considered likely that the Black Death was a highly infectious bubonic variant known as pneumonic plague, where the plague bacillus attacks the lungs with effects similar to those of pneumonia. This form of bubonic plague is invariably fatal. Other symptoms include internal bleeding, boils, and fever. In medieval times, death usually came after three to five days. A profound melancholia accompanied the disease, a depression that would eventually influence the very fabric of medieval culture.

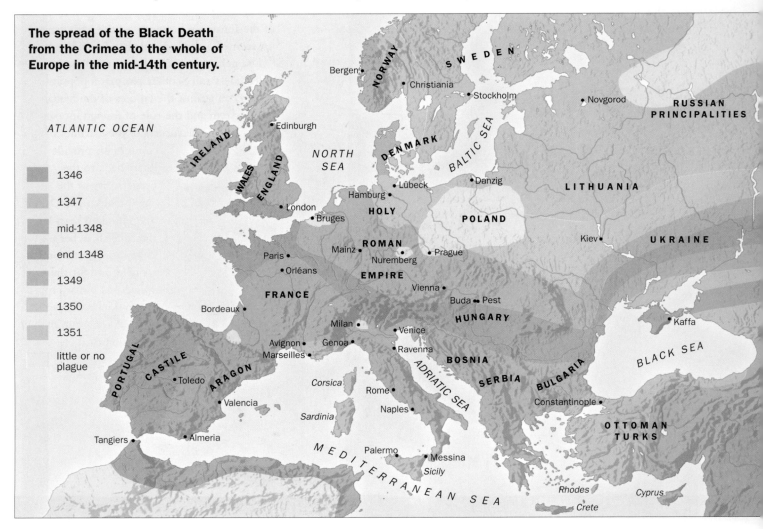

The spread of the Black Death from the Crimea to the whole of Europe in the mid-14th century.

- 1346
- 1347
- mid-1348
- end 1348
- 1349
- 1350
- 1351
- little or no plague

Left: *The Flagellants at Doornik in 1349, from* The Chronicle of Aegidius Limuisis. *Also known as The Brothers of the Cross, this religious fraternity sprang up in the Netherlands towns, especially Doornik, and its influence spread rapidly from there. They did penance for the sins of the world by scourging themselves of the plague.*

The plague spreads

The spread of the Black Death was extremely rapid. A French physician, Simon de Covino said that it seemed as if one victim "could infect the whole world." Italy was ravaged during 1347, and by the end of the year it had reached southern France through the port of Marseilles. During 1348 it swept through France, reaching the British Isles by the fall. By 1349 it reached Scotland, Poland, and Denmark, and by the following year it was decimating the populations of Russia and Scandinavia. By 1350 the plague had spent itself, although recurring minor bouts continued to afflict the continent for the next four centuries.

Although some towns and villages escaped, the effects were catastrophic. Even in lightly affected areas the mortality rate was between 15–20 percent, and in the worst hit regions well over 50 percent succumbed—in all, about 20 million people. In some urban centers the effects led to a complete collapse of the economy, and as the dead became too numerous to be given a Christian burial, corpses lay in the streets, accelerating the spread of the disease. In the countryside, peasants dropped dead in the fields and travelers at the roadside.

As usual in times of crisis, innocent scapegoats were held responsible for the calamity. The Jews were inevitably accused and massacres of Jewish communities in Germany were commonplace despite the clear evidence

that they suffered from the Black Death as much as everyone else. As the priesthood was decimated, many developed their own extreme religious views, and groups such as the self-punishing Flagellants sprang up across the continent despite the condemnation of both Church and State. To the medieval mind, the Wrath of God had visited them or they had been abandoned by God; the end of the world had arrived.

Death became interwoven into European art, architecture, and religion for the rest of the medieval period, an inescapable constant in a changing society. The plague also raised theological questions about divine will, which would continue to trouble Christians until the Reformation. The people of medieval Europe were left to pick up the pieces of their civilization, and to question their place in a world that could be almost obliterated for no apparent reason.

Below: *Burial of plague victims in Tournai in 1349, from a Flemish book illustration of 1352.*

Testing Faith: Humiliation of the Papacy

During the previous centuries various Popes had clashed with the secular heads of Europe and emerged victorious. A chain of circumstances, accusations, and confrontation during the early 14th century conspired to humiliate the Church. By 1350 the Pope was little more than a puppet of the French king. Ironically, confidence in the Church was shaken at a time when Europeans most needed strong spiritual leadership.

Below: *In their dealings with princes, the Popes' power lay in the holy right handed to them by St. Peter to crown kings and legitimize their reigns. By the time Henry IV of England was crowned, this ceremony had passed to lowlier clerics, and even the Pope's approval was being questioned.*

When Pope Nicholas IV (1288–92) died, the College of Cardinals was largely composed of two rival Italian families, the Orsinis and the Colonnas. After months of disagreement they agreed to elect a neutral candidate, a Neopolitan hermit who duly became Pope Celestine V in 1294. Naples was ruled by Charles of Anjou, who only permitted the holy man to travel to Rome if he elected a new set of French and Neopolitan cardinals. Celestine proved too saintly to cope with the intrigues of the Vatican, and he was forced to resign within a few months. The Italian cardinal who led the opposition to Celestine became Pope Boniface VIII (1294–1303).

Boniface engineered charges against rival Italian houses, especially the house of Colonna. The confiscated lands were given to members of his own Gaetani family, earning him the enmity of most of the Roman aristocracy. This unpopularity at home was then matched by tensions abroad. When King Philip IV of France (1272–1307) tried to tax the French clergy, Pope Boniface refused to let them pay. Philip

responded by preventing papal revenues raised in France from leaving his borders. Faced with a substantial loss of income, Boniface caved in.

The next conflict came in 1301, when the Pope refused to condone Philip's legal prosecution of a French bishop. The case had been fabricated, and Boniface sided with the cleric. He issued a Bull that asserted the independence of the clergy from secular authority. Philip was furious and summoned his parliament, the Estates General. Threats were exchanged between Pope and ruler, especially after Boniface promulgated the *Unam Sanctam*, a Bull that outlined the case for papal supremacy over secular leaders. Philip laid outrageous charges against the Pope, drawn up by the royal investigator William de Nogaret. Armed with the charges, Nogaret traveled to Rome in 1303 and, accompanied by the Colonna family and an urban mob, he seized Pope Boniface. This dramatic action was Nogaret's way of preventing the Pope from excommunicating his royal master. Although the resulting outcry forced Nogaret to release his prisoner, Boniface died immediately after his release, in circumstances which have never been fully explained.

His successor, Pope Benedict IX (1303–4) cleared the French king of any blame, but died before Nogaret could be punished. The French-dominated College of Cardinals elected the Archbishop of Bordeaux as the new Pope, who became Clement V (1305–14). Clement broke with tradition and was consecrated in Avignon rather than in Rome. This French town became the new seat of the papacy, although it was nominally a town held for the Holy Roman Emperor. Clement created 28 new Cardinals, of whom 25 were Frenchmen. The papacy had now become firmly linked with France.

The secular question

Clement's reign was dominated by the resumption of Nogret's charges against Boniface, and in Philip's persecution of the Knights Templar, again on trumped-up charges. Clement was succeeded by Pope John XXII (1316–34), who became embroiled in another clash over secular authority. Arguments over the succession to the Imperial throne rumbled on throughout the early 14th century, but the Germans refused to accept papal interference in the selection process. Eventually, in 1338, the German princes decreed that papal approval was not necessary in the consecration of the German Emperor. This was the issue over which Frederick Barbarossa and Pope Innocent III had clashed about 140 years earlier. The papacy had finally lost its battle to control the secular heads of Europe, and papal prestige was at a new low.

To compound the misery, a growing number of critics began to question the official papal stance on several important theological issues. In particular, the Franciscan Order came into conflict with John XXII over the issue of poverty. The Franciscan emphasis on Christ's poverty was at odds with an increasingly money-conscious papacy, and the debate raged until 1323, when the Pope deemed the Franciscan stance heretical. While most Franciscans retracted from their position, others fled for the safety of the German Empire, and the protection of Emperor Lewis III (1314–47). The Franciscans were supported by several respected theologians, including John of Paris (who argued in favor of the independence of secular rulers from papal authority), and William of Ockham (who questioned blindly accepting "truths of faith.") These writers helped to undermine papal authority and began a crucial argument over its true role in an increasingly secular world. Whether the Pope would listen to his critics was another matter.

Below: *The Fortress of Faith, an allegorical manuscript illustration of the 15th century depicting a castle of faith, defended by the Pope, bishops, and clerics, besieged by unbelievers and heretics.*

Papacy in Crisis: The Great Schism

The College of Cardinals became increasingly powerful during the 14th century, and soon after the papacy returned to the Vatican in Rome in 1377 they elected a new Italian Pope. When he threatened them with reforms, they declared his election invalid and appointed a successor. The first Pope refused to go, and for almost 40 years the Church was split by the schism, while most of Europe divided its loyalty between the contenders.

The French city of Avignon remained the home of the Roman Church for much of the 14th century, from 1305 until 1377. The six popes who succeeded Clement V (1305–14) were all Frenchmen, who cited unrest in Italy as the reason for their continued absence from Rome. The Avignon Popes created a magnificent papal palace, supported by a powerful ecclesiastical administration. This clerical bureaucracy's primary task was to replace revenues lost when the papacy abandoned its Italian holdings. During this period the Church came under criticism for its practice of appointing its own ecclesiastical officials, and for the selling of indulgences. Appointments made directly by the Pope ensured loyal office-holders and an assured stream of revenue to Avignon. It also led to widespread absenteeism, where a single cleric could hold several bishoprics, and draw revenue from them. While the sale of indulgences began as a donation to the Church as a gesture of good works, it developed into a cynical transaction for hard cash.

In 1377 Pope Gregory XI (1370–78) moved the papacy and its administration back to Rome, but when he died the following year, the Roman mob (supported by Italian noble families) tried to prevent any return to Avignon by his successor. Fearing for their lives, the College of Cardinals appointed the Italian Archbishop of Bari as their new Pontiff, who became Urban VI (1378–9). The French cardinals thought they could control the new Pope, but they had misjudged him. He vowed to reform the Church, and to appoint enough Italian cardinals to place the French clique in a minority. For years the position of the cardinals had been secure, and since Popes were continually elected from the College itself, papal protection was assured. The Italian Pope threatened to overturn this monopoly of power.

In August 1378 the College withdrew to the Roman hills and issued a manifesto, which

Below: *Le Palais des Papes in Avignon, France.*

declared the papal election invalid due to provocation by the Roman mob. Six weeks later they elected a new Pope, this time a Frenchman and former cardinal, who became Clement VII (1378–94). He and the cardinals returned to Avignon, while Pope Urban remained in Rome, supported by most of the Italian Church. He created a fresh body of cardinals, and on his death these clerics elected another Italian pope, Boniface IX (1389-1404). The loyalty of European rulers and the provincial Church was divided, largely along pro-French or pro-Imperialist lines. While France, Scotland, Spain, and Naples supported the Pope in Avignon, England, the Holy Roman Empire, the Scandinavian states, and most of Italy supported the Pope in Rome. This division became known by historians as the Great Schism.

Agreement through consensus

This situation was clearly intolerable, and from 1394 it was proposed that both Popes should abdicate, clearing the way for a single elected Pontiff. Neither Pope would resign, and their clerical and secular support weakened as the situation dragged on. A breakthrough came in 1408, when a majority of the cardinals from both camps met in Pisa. During the Council of Pisa it was declared that both Popes were to be deposed due to the crimes of schism of the Church. The Council elected a new Pontiff, who became Alexander V (1409–15). As the two other Popes refused to accept the Council's ruling, the effect was to create three popes: in Rome, Pisa, and Avignon.

Finally, a new assembly met in 1414. This body, the Council of Constance, involved most of the senior European clergy. John XXIII

(1410–15), the Pisan pope, failed to win popular support, prompting the Council to redefine its authority in the *Haec Sancta* decree, which emphasized the hegemony of representative authority within the Catholic Church. Pope John was deposed in May 1415, and Pope Gregory XII (1406–15) of Rome resigned two months later when his supporters abandoned him. This left Pope Benedict XIII (1394–1423) in Avignon. Although deposed and branded a heretic, Benedict continued to lay claim to his title until his death. The Council duly elected the Italian cardinal Otto Colonna as its sole leader, who adopted the title Pope Martin V (1417–31). Although reunited, the Roman Church was seriously weakened by the Great Schism, and the resulting loss of faith in papal leadership helped sow the seeds of religious revolt.

Above: *Otto Colonna is elected by the Council of Constance as Pope Martin V on November 11, 1417.*

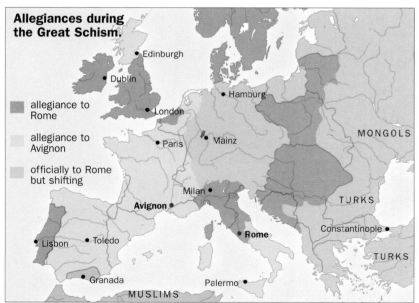

Allegiances during the Great Schism.

- ■ allegiance to Rome
- ■ allegiance to Avignon
- ■ officially to Rome but shifting

Edinburgh
Dublin
Hamburg
London
Paris
Mainz
MONGOLS
Milan
TURKS
Avignon
Constantinople
Rome
Lisbon
Toledo
TURKS
Granada
Palermo
MUSLIMS

The Scottish Wars of Independence

In 1296 Edward I of England invaded the independent kingdom of Scotland, beginning two decades of occupation, warfare, and brutality. Edward, who styled himself as "the Hammer of the Scots," misjudged the nationalist fervor in the small country. Scottish leaders, such as William Wallace and Robert the Bruce, waged a classic guerrilla war against the English, and their actions culminated in a battle that would save their country from English domination for centuries to come.

In 1286 King Alexander III of Scotland (1249–86) died in a riding accident. His children had all died before him, and it was arranged that his granddaughter, Margaret of Norway, would succeed him. His death marked the end of centuries of relative peace in Scotland,

where the former Celtic kingdom had developed into a small but unified feudal state. Margaret died on her journey to Scotland and the throne lay vacant. It proved impossible to choose a successor from the numerous contenders, so the Scots turned to King Edward I of England (1272–1307) to resolve the dispute.

Edward extracted an oath of fealty from all contenders, then chose John Balliol (1292–96), hoping he would remain loyal to the English crown. Balliol rebelled against Edward's humiliating treatment and the English king marched his army north into Scotland. Edward stormed the border town of Berwick (1296), then routed Balliol's army at Dunbar (1296). Scotland was occupied and Balliol was forced to abdicate. Edward I returned home, leaving garrisons in most principal towns and castles.

By the following spring, much of Scotland was in a state of insurrection. An English garrison at Lanark was destroyed by William de Wallace, the son of a local knight, and Wallace rapidly developed into the leader of a small guerrilla army. By the end of the year he posed a serious threat, and the Earl of Surrey was sent north with an army to crush him. Wallace demonstrated his military skill by defeating the English at Stirling Bridge (1297), prompting the abandonment of most of the English garrisons.

Edward was furious, and assembled an army at York. In 1298 it advanced as far as Edinburgh, where supply problems prevented any further advance. Wallace advanced to meet Edward, and in the ensuing battle at Falkirk (1298) Welsh archers destroyed the Scottish force. Wallace went into hiding and the English garrisons returned. For the next seven years Wallace waged a guerrilla war, until his capture in 1305. He was tried for treason, then hanged, drawn, and quartered, and his head mounted on a spike over London Bridge.

Robert the Bruce

In March 1306 Robert the Bruce, Earl of Carrick, was crowned King Robert I of Scotland (1306–29). His intention was to rally Scottish resistance, but his small force was scattered at Methven (1306), forcing Bruce and his rebels to hide in the Highlands and in Orkney. He returned to southwest Scotland in 1307 as a fugitive with a price on his head and with his family in an English dungeon. Bruce gathered another guerrilla

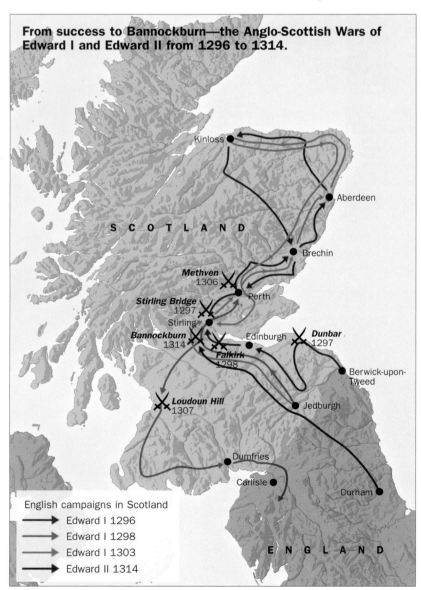

From success to Bannockburn—the Anglo-Scottish Wars of Edward I and Edward II from 1296 to 1314.

Kinloss
Aberdeen
SCOTLAND
Brechin
Methven 1306
Perth
Stirling Bridge 1297
Stirling
Bannockburn 1314
Edinburgh
Dunbar 1297
Falkirk 1298
Loudoun Hill 1307
Jedburgh
Berwick-upon-Tweed
Dumfries
Carlisle
Durham
ENGLAND

English campaigns in Scotland
→ Edward I 1296
→ Edward I 1298
→ Edward I 1303
→ Edward II 1314

army and campaigned in southern Scotland. Edward I marched north to crush this "pretender," but he died at Carlisle, leaving his kingdom to his weak son Edward II (1307–27).

Unlike his father, Edward II was no military commander, and left the war in the hands of subordinates. For the next two years Bruce captured most of the English garrisons north of the River Tay, and in 1309 he recaptured the province of Fife. This proved too much for Edward II, who marched north at the head of a new army. Bruce used scorched earth tactics to deny the invaders food and shelter, and the English retreated to Berwick. During the next three years Bruce's army captured almost all of the remaining English castles in Scotland, and even raided into northern England, reaching as far south as Durham. By 1314, only Stirling Castle remained in English hands.

Edward II gathered the largest army of its time and marched to the relief of Stirling in the summer of 1314. He advanced through the south of Scotland without meeting any opposition until he found the Scottish army blocking his path, two miles south of Stirling. Edward's army outnumbered that of Bruce by approximately three to one, although exact numbers are unknown. While the Scots relied on spearmen, grouped into blocks called *shiltrons*, the English relied on the power of the armored knight. The result was the Battle of Bannockburn (1314). The charge of the English knights was contained by the spearmen, who then reduced the English host until most were killed. Bannockburn was the most humiliating English defeat since Hastings (1066). While border raids continued for another decade, the English were unable to mount another invasion, and a truce was signed in 1328. The guerrilla warfare of Wallace and Bruce, combined with open battle at the right moment, had secured Scotland's independence, which it would retain until 1707.

Above: *Stirling sat at the center of the Scottish Wars, and its castle changed hands several times over the years. Three of the most famous battles took place in the castle's proximity: Stirling Bridge, Falkirk, and Bannockburn.*

Europe Divided: The Hundred Years War

The conflict known as the Hundred Years War was not one war but several. The war began as a feudal dispute between two monarchs. It decimated the feudal nobility of both England and France, and occasionally threatened to spread beyond the ravaged battlegrounds of northwestern France. It also introduced new technologies to medieval warfare, and achieved a French State that was unified behind its king.

T he collapse of the Angevin Empire in the early 13th century left the English kings with Gascony, a coastal region of southwestern France, as its only continental province. In theory the English kings paid homage for their lands to the Capetian monarchs, but were rarely asked to do so. Edward III of England (1327–77) paid homage to Philip VI of France (1328–50), but French lawyers claimed the ceremony was not conducted properly. Tensions were already high between the two nations over French support for the Scots, arguments over Flemish trade, and piracy. When Philip declared that Gascony was to

Below: *The Battle of Crécy took place on August 26, 1346, between the forces of King Edward III and King Philip VI of France. Among the dead lies King Jean de Luxembourg, king of Bohemia.*

be confiscated in 1337, Edward declared war. For four years the opposing armies did little but posture and drain their national treasuries, but when both kings supported rival claimants to the Duchy, open warfare erupted in Brittany in 1341. This minor war of succession continued intermittently for 23 years.

In 1346 Philip's army marched into Gascony and began to reduce the castles in the province. Edward sailed with a relief army, but contrary winds forced him to land in Normandy. Seizing the moment, he sacked Caen and its hinterland, and when Philip marched to intercept him, he retreated to the coast. Edward's navy was no longer there, so the English were forced to march northeast along the coast toward the safety of Flanders.

The French overtook them north of the River Somme, forcing Edward to fight a battle at Crécy (1346). The French launched a series of mounted charges, all of which were slaughtered by English archery. This was a great victory, and allowed Edward to capture a secure bridgehead on the Channel coast at Calais (1347) before returning to England. Edward spared most of the population, but expelled them, filling the town with English settlers and a powerful garrison. Calais remained in English hands for another two centuries.

The Black Prince

When Philip died in 1350, he was succeeded by his son John II the Good (1350–64), a chivalric but uninspiring king. A feud with King Charles of Navarre drove the Franco-Spanish monarch into an alliance with Edward. English troops garrisoned Charles's Norman castles in 1354 and threatened John's royal demesne in the Île de France. In 1355 the English launched two raids into France; one from Calais led by Edward III, and the second from Gascony led by his son Edward, Prince of Wales, who the French nicknamed the Black Prince because of his black armor. While John was kept occupied protecting Paris, the Black Prince led his troops on a fast-moving raid (*chevauchée*) through southeastern France, looting and pillaging what they could.

Both campaigns failed to produce a decisive battle, but in early 1356 another two-pronged attack was planned. An English force landed in Brittany, linked up with the garrisons there, and marched to Normandy. Another force led by the

Black Prince moved north from Gascony to meet it. The first force retreated to Brittany when John marched into Normandy to confront it, leaving the Black Prince unsupported in the middle of France. Prince Edward seemed unconcerned and pillaged the Loire Valley before starting to return to Bordeaux. The English were encumbered with their loot, however, and King John's army overtook them in September 1356, near the village of Poitiers.

Once more the French attacked and the English defended, but this time most of the French nobles dismounted and advanced on foot. Again, the French attack was uncoordinated. The first division was beaten in a bloody melee, and when the French were routed, they took their second division with them. John led his reserves

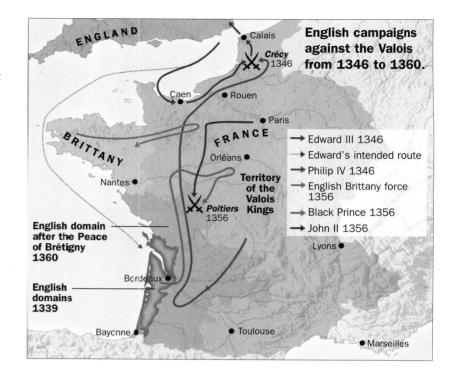

English campaigns against the Valois from 1346 to 1360.

→ Edward III 1346
┄┄► Edward's intended route
→ Philip IV 1346
→ English Brittany force 1356
→ Black Prince 1356
→ John II 1356

English domain after the Peace of Brétigny 1360

English domains 1339

into the attack, and was defeated and captured. Prince Edward returned to England with his plunder, the French king his prisoner.

The Dauphin (Prince) took control of France and negotiated for his father's release. Under the terms of the treaty of Brétigny, John agreed to surrender Aquitaine and Poitou to Edward III and pay a ransom, and in return Edward

renounced all claims to the French throne. Although the treaty brought the first phase of the war to a close, neither side was prepared to give up the struggle. The ransom was never fully paid, and when the king's second son (who remained a hostage) escaped from Calais, the chivalric King John surrendered himself to the English, and he died as a prisoner in London.

Above: *A battle of the Hundred Years War, as depicted in* The Chronicles of Jean Froissart.

Flanders: The Troubled Marketplace

The County of Flanders exerted a strategic and economic influence out of all proportion to its size throughout the medieval period. This was particularly true from the 12th century onward, when it became the leading commercial center in northern Europe. It was also the first region to suffer from the economic malaise that gripped the continent in the wake of the Black Death.

Flanders was first mentioned in 843, during the reign of Charles the Bald (842–77). In the Carolingian era the province was concentrated around the administrative center of Bruges, but by the year 1000 Flanders encompassed the region from the Schelde estuary to the settlement of Lille, extending west to the North Sea coast. From 1000 the region became known for the production of woolen textiles, and urban centers developed on both sides of the Rhine estuary. Bruges became a leading trading center and the seat of the Count of Flanders, while neighboring towns such as Ghent and Ypres also expanded. Similar developments took place in the neighboring provinces of Brabant, Holland, and Zutphen, and by the 12th century the revival of commerce produced growth in

Tournai, Lille, and Arras. Over the next three centuries the Flemings sold their cloth throughout northern Europe. Much of the wool was imported from England, and political and economic links were forged that would have serious ramifications after 1340.

By the late 13th century these manufacturing towns had become the busiest commercial centers in northern Europe, although the rate of urban growth had slowed. While the towns north of Antwerp became linked with the German Hanseatic League from the late 13th century, those further south maintained their political links with France, for better or worse. While the term Flanders had traditionally been applied to the entire Low Country area, from the 14th century the term became associated exclusively with the southern section, with its Walloon or Flemish-speaking population.

A nation's struggle to survive

The 14th century proved a traumatic time for the Flemish. A revolt against the heavy-handed taxation of Philip IV (1285–1314) led to armed conflict with France. The Flemish rebel artisans of Bruges defeated the French at Courtrai (1302), ensuring that French control over their urban life was kept at bay. This populist rising against external authority was mirrored in Scotland around the same period (*see page 128*). The decline of Flanders as a commercial center came as a result of war and plague. English support for the rebel cause in Flanders added to the tensions that resulted in the outbreak of the Hundred Years War. While the rebellion undermined the authority of both the Capetian king and the Count of Flanders, it emphasized the region's reliance on English support.

During the Hundred Years War the province was considered strategically important by both France and England. After 1360 the English maintained a garrison at Calais and controlled the small county of Ponthieu, on the border of the Flemish satellite province of Artois. Two of the most significant battles of the war were fought in this region; Crécy (1346) and Agincourt (1415). Flanders was one of the most valuable feudal fiefs in France, despite the urban Flemish opposition to French taxation. In 1367, Margaret, the daughter of Louis, Count of

Flanders, was married to Philip, the son of John II of France (1350–64). Already the master of Burgundy, Philip became Philip the Bold (1367–1404), the 25-year-old first Valois Duke of Burgundy. From this time until 1477, Flanders would remain in the Burgundian orbit, independent from both France and England. Instead of providing a battlefield for the English and French, the region became one for a three-cornered fight between the Burgundians, the French, and rebel Flemings.

This continual warfare or threat of conflict seriously disrupted Flemish trade during the century. The Black Death swept through Flanders between 1348–50, culling half of the population. The economic effects were considerable; with less people available to buy cloth, the demand for Flemish produce slumped. Cities like Bruges never recovered, while others, such as Antwerp (and Amsterdam to the north) prospered, as they were less seriously affected.

An oversupply of produce and a shortage of markets also led to a stratification of the merchant guilds, which dominated the Flemish cities. Profitable commerce devolved into the hands of a few entrepreneurial merchant families or guilds, while others faced ruin. This led to an urban revolt in Ghent in 1381, which was crushed by the Burgundian authorities. From the 1350s, the English developed their own wool industry and the economy of Flanders slumped even further. By the end of the calamitous century, Flanders was an economic backwater, and the neighboring states of England and Holland became the rising economic regions of northern Europe.

Opposite: *Bruges, largely unspoiled today, was among the first Flemish mercantile towns to defy the French as an urban center, and it became the seat of the Count of Flanders.*

Below: *The first Valois Duke of Burgundy, Philip the Bold, through marriage to the daughter of the Count of Flanders, took control of the region, removing it from English influence. Detail from his tomb in Brabant.*

Venice and Mediterranean Trade

From the 11th century, the island city-state of Venice developed into a significant trading power. Following its involvement in the crusades, Venice dominated trade in the eastern Mediterranean throughout the medieval period, and emerged as one of the richest cities in Europe; a political power in her own right.

Below: *A Venetian merchant does business with a textile seller; on the left money changes hands, while on the right the cloth is being examined. From a 1412 illustration on the travels of Marco Polo.*

During the early medieval period the island settlement of Venice on the northern coast of the Adriatic Sea grew into a thriving port. The city was nominally part of the Byzantine Empire, but remained virtually independent, protected by a ring of lagoons, marshes, and sea from the warfare that ravaged the rest of Italy. By the start of the tenth century Venetian trading vessels sailed the length of the Aegean Sea and provided a maritime link between the Byzantine Empire and western Europe. The lagoons had always produced salt and fish for export, but by 1050

irritation of the Roman Church.

By 1100 Venice had become a powerful force; an ally of the Byzantine Empire rather than a subject province. The city-state was a republic ruled by the Great Council, presided over by a doge (a Venetian dialect derivation of the Latin *dux*, or leader, from which also comes the feudal word *duke*), who was elected for life but answerable to the Council for his actions. The Council was essentially an oligarchy, selected from the rich aristocratic families of the city, and its members supervised all forms of city administration, trade agreements, and the judiciary. The Council also approved all trade treaties between Venice and her neighbors. At the start of the 12th century, Venice maintained trading agreements with the Byzantines, the Holy Roman Empire, most of the Muslim states of North Africa, and the neighboring Italian cities.

The city was unique in western Europe in that it was never subject to feudal control. With

Venetian artisans were producing glass, iron, and building ships, making the city-state one of the most dynamic industrial centers in northern Italy. Vessels also began trading with the Muslim states of the eastern Mediterranean, much to the

almost no agricultural base on which to base a feudal economy, Venice developed solely as a society built around maritime trade. Venice had refused to offer support to the First Crusade, for fear that it would disrupt her African trade. By

the time the crusaders captured Jerusalem and established their own Latin States in the Middle East, Venice was forced to support the crusading movement. Like most decisions made by the Council, this was based on economic necessity. The rival maritime cities of Genoa and Pisa had been quick to support the crusaders, and were now reaping the financial benefits. Venice could no longer afford to maintain a policy of relative neutrality simply in order to safeguard her Muslim trading interests. In 1099 a Venetian fleet sailed to join the crusaders, but an argument with the Pisans led to a sea battle that the Venetians won. Pisa agreed to stay out of the eastern Mediterranean, which ensured Venetian control of the crusading market, but also aroused the enmity of her rival Italian maritime powers.

Profiting from the crusades

Venice offered help in exchange for exclusive trading rights with the ports of the Kingdom of Jerusalem. After destroying the Egyptian fleet in 1123, their maritime control of the eastern Mediterranean was absolute. For the next 80 years Venice provided naval support for the crusaders, and benefited financially from their monopoly of Levantine trade. Her ships ferried pilgrims to and from the Holy Land, transported troops and supplies and, above all, carried the oriental cargoes that reached the ports of

Antioch, Tyre, Acre, and Haifa.

The only impediment to Venetian trade was the Byzantine revocation of their trading agreements. This was resolved in 1204, when the crusaders captured Constantinople, assisted by a powerful Venetian fleet. The Venetians then conquered and occupied many of the Byzantine ports of the Aegean and Adriatic, ensuring their dominance of the eastern Mediterranean trade until the 15th century.

An economic decline after 1400 was coupled with Ottoman Turkish expansion in Asia Minor, and by the late 15th century the Muslims occupied most of Greece and the Balkans. Starved of her lucrative eastern trade, Venice sought out new markets in Russia, the western Mediterranean, and the Atlantic.

During the 14th and 15th centuries Venice was the most prosperous city in Europe, boasting trading links with most of the known world. Her interests were protected by a powerful fleet of war galleys, and her financial and mercantile institutions were among the most respected in Europe. By the early 15th century the Venetian Republic controlled a substantial portion of the northern Italian mainland and the Dalmatian coast, making her a new power in Italy. From that point on they would be unable to exist solely as a maritime trading power, but would be linked to the political development of the rest of Italy.

Above: *The prosperous city-state of Venice at about the time Marco Polo set off on his trek along the Silk Road to Kublai Khan's China.*

FOCUS: LEADERS
Medieval Kingship

The development of the feudal system placed a greater emphasis on the nature of medieval kingship. For much of the period, a king was not so much at the top of feudal society but rather the strongest member of the feudal nobility. During the 14th century the feudal basis for kingship was gradually replaced by one that emphasized his supreme power, set above the nobility, parliamentary bodies, and even the Church.

Below: *The coronation of King Henry II of Castile (1369–1379) at Burgos, from a 15th-century manuscript illustration.*

In classic feudal form, the vassals of a king held their land as feudal subjects of the Crown. In reality, true power was based on political, economic, and military strength, and the most successful feudal monarchs were those who could exercise effective power over their leading nobles. Under this system, the increase of royal power was a slow process, involving the gradual expansion of the royal demesne through marriage, treaty, legal claim, and conquest. In order to control the nobility, a medieval king needed great military strength and financial resources from his own royal demesne, so that he could dominate any one of his leading nobles, or a combination of several of them. The larger the demesne, the greater the economic and military resources the king could draw on.

Since feudal fiefs were hereditary, lands were usually passed on intact to successors, and the process of expansion continued. A monarch was unable to influence this process beyond the finite limits of feudal or Roman law. In many cases, the estates of the king's leading nobles were substantial, and operated as semi-autonomous regions within the kingdom's nominal boundaries. When called upon to fight, an earl or a count pressed his own feudal subjects to join him at his king's side—men whose loyalty was to their overlord rather than to their king.

Without military and economic might, the feudal monarch was all but impotent. In France

Left: *The French King receives the English envoys. Medieval kings varied a great deal in their qualities of statesmanship, and an ambassador's task was rarely an easy one. Frequently, they suffered the standard treatment for bearers of bad tidings, and were imprisoned or even executed.*

and England, a succession of Angevins, Capetians, Plantagenets, and Valois expanded royal land and power, and benefited from a hereditary monarchy. In Germany, the monarch was elected from the ranks of the nobility, and although this usually evolved along hereditary lines, this was not always the case, which partly explains why central royal power increased in western Europe during the 14th century and decreased in Germany.

German monarchy

The election of a king in Germany was conducted by the leading nobles, representatives of the urban communities and prominent churchmen. Although hereditary concerns were a leading consideration (particularly under the Luxembourg, Wittelsbach, and Hapsburg kings after 1273), the nominated hereditary successor had to ensure his powerbase among the elective body. This created a delicate political situation, which effectively hindered the centralization of power because lands, offices, and titles were required to be dispersed in order to ensure the loyalty of the electorate.

Minority claimants faced another problem. In feudal Europe, a minor was either passed over for a more distant hereditary claimant, or the country was ruled in his or her name by a regent, usually a leading noble. This inevitably led to a loss of royal power. Women claimants were usually bypassed unless they were supported by a powerful spouse. In the few cases where hereditary succession

could not be readily determined and the nobility were unable to select one of their peers (such as in late 13th century Scotland), outside assistance was required, either from a neighboring powerful monarch or the Pope.

The coronation of a monarch became an increasingly symbolic process during the medieval period. Holy relics, special crowns, or national symbols imbued the process with special significance. The king was anointed with holy oil during the coronation ceremony by the Pope or the most senior cleric, which symbolized a degree of divine power. In time, this led to the emphasis on the "divine right" of kings to govern, as they were "anointed by God" (or his representatives on Earth). An oath of office stressed the feudal as well as the spiritual commitment of the king, while his legal oaths were designed to emphasize his judicial authority.

The king was the senior legal authority in the kingdom, supported by a legal and bureaucratic system to ensure his control over the affairs of his realm. The English notion of a limited monarchy and of parliamentary involvement in government were still radical notions in the 14th century; a by-product of a series of unsuitable monarchs. This set a precedent and, while royal power was becoming more centralized, the basis for a less feudal system of government was already in place. Disputes over the power and function of late medieval monarchs would become increasingly common during the 15th century.

1302	1303	1305	1305	1314	1326	1331–35	1334
The Flemish cities rebel against French authority	The Pope is seized by political enemies in Rome	Giotto paints his frescoes in Padua	The papacy is moved from Rome to Avignon	Battle of Bannockburn assures Scottish independence	The Florentine army is the first to use cannon	The Serbian empire dominates the Balkans	Construction is started on the Papal Palace in Avignon

FOCUS: WARFARE

The English Longbow

In 1300 warfare in western Europe was dominated by the knight. In the 15th century the English adopted the Welsh longbow, and the archer soon came to dominate the battlefields of the Hundred Years War. These English longbowmen were common soldiers, and their ability to cut down the cream of feudal France had social and political consequences beyond the field of battle.

At the start of the 14th century, warfare in western Europe followed certain well-established patterns. Armies were invariably composed of a corps of infantry, mounted knights, men-at-arms, and mercenaries—usually crossbowmen or archers. Already it was rare to find an army based exclusively on feudal lines because the *scutage* tax introduced during the previous century had made it common for nobles or knights to form their own military units, and to sell their services to their superiors.

At first, such mercenary bands were comprised of knights and a handful of foot soldiers in support roles, but gradually it paid to be able to provide a fuller service, and mercenary units began to comprise a cross-section of a feudal army. Companies of professional mercenaries were commonly found, particularly in French, German, and Italian service.

During the Battle of Falkirk (1298), King Edward I of England (1272–1307) defeated the Scottish spear formations by using archers, who unleashed showers of arrows at their target, which was then scattered by a massed cavalry charge. Edward I used Welsh archers for these purposes; men whose ability with the bow had already been demonstrated to Edward's cost during his Welsh campaigns of 1277–82. The Welsh used longer bows than other archers, which gave rise to the weapons' name. A typical longbow was about six feet long, cut from yew, elm ash, or wychelm, and fitted with cowhorn tips and a linen drawstring. This weapon was copied by the English and, from the 14th century, it came to be associated almost exclusively with English archers.

The English also introduced it into the wider sphere of Anglo-French warfare. Until that time, the two forms of firepower on the battlefield came from the traditional bow or the crossbow. The former was simply a smaller version of the longbow; easier to use but lacking the range and penetration of the longer weapon. The crossbow was far more common. In the 14th century it was fitted with a stirrup to help span the crossbow, and a trigger to release the bolt (or *quarrel*). The crossbow had great range and penetration, but was slow to reload. The great advantage of the longbow was that it combined the advantages of a crossbow with a far higher rate of fire.

The secret behind the use of the longbow was training. While anyone could be taught to shoot a crossbow, the use of a longbow required strength and skill. To shoot an arrow the archer gripped the center of the bow in his left

Below: *The Battle of Agincourt, October 26, 1415, from a French book illustration of 1484.*

1337	1338	1346-51	1347	1347	1348	1350	c.1350
Start of the Hundred Years War between France and England	Germans decide the Pope is not required to consecrate German Emperors	Approximately 24 million die in the Black Death	Calais captured by the English	Arrival of the Black Death in Italy	Jewish persecution rife in Germany	Black Death ends, after ravaging almost all of Europe	Marine premium insurance begins in Genoa

Left: *This 14th-century book illustration shows King John II of France leading his reserve knights in the doomed attack against English longbowmen at the Battle of Poitiers.*

hand and drew the string with his right until it was fully extended. However, it was not a case of aiming and firing; the archer had to fire upward to get range, and the arrows fell like rain from the sky onto their targets. From the first decades of the 14th century, archery training became a compulsory part of English village life, and men would be trained to use the weapon from childhood. The three-foot-long arrow was tipped with a variety of heads, including ones designed to penetrate armor. The longbow's maximum range was about 400 yards, and a trained archer could loose his entire quota of 24 arrows within two minutes.

Proven in battle

The devastating superiority of the longbow was most comprehensively demonstrated during the Hundred Years War. At the battles of Crécy (1346), Poitiers (1358), and Agincourt (1415), French attacks were halted by massed archery from longbows. At Crécy the arrow storm virtually annihilated the mounted French knights, and accounts of the sky being "black with arrows" was probably no exaggeration.

The French had no answer to the longbow, and its strategic impact after 1415 was to make them wary of fighting set-piece battles. While the French turned to "Fabian" tactics and siege warfare, they also came to embrace the new technology of gunpowder, which would eventually eclipse the longbowman's dominance of the battlefield. The use of the longbow had social as well as military consequences. While national pride was becoming a recognizable emotion during the century, so too was a degree of social equality—at least on the battlefield. English archers were recruited from the yeomanry (free peasants), and these commoners had the tools to kill the mounted chivalric elite of society. At a time when social unrest was growing, this set a dangerous precedent for the future.

1356	1356	1360	1367	1369	1369	1375	1377
Charles IV issues a Golden Bull ending papal role in imperial elections	French decisively defeated at the Battle of Poitiers	Treaty of Brétigny leads to a temporary peace between France and England	Philip the Good founds the dynasty of the Valois Dukes of Burgundy	Construction begins on the fortress of the Bastille, in Paris	The Hundred Years War is renewed	John Barbour writes *The Bruce*, a eulogy to the Scottish national hero	The papacy returns to Avignon

CHAPTER EIGHT

Europe Comes of Age

The 15th century was a period of profound change in western Europe. While some of the traumas of warfare, disease, and economic stagnation from the previous century continued after 1400, they failed to create the perpetual misery that had characterized the 14th century. France and England were still locked in the dynastic conflict known as the Hundred Years War, but the character of the conflict was changing. A growing sense of national identity made it increasingly difficult for the English to justify keeping large provinces in France. While France herself was becoming an increasingly centralized kingdom, its province of Burgundy broke away to create her own place in European politics. For most of the century it seemed as if a new and powerful state would emerge in Europe between France and Germany. In the end, the Duchy of Burgundy disintegrated even more rapidly than it had appeared.

Following her defeat in the war with France, England was split by dynastic and factional fighting, in marked contrast to the increasing unity of the French State. Similarly, while the Holy Roman Empire was collapsing as a political entity and her influence in Italy was waning, religious tensions in Germany were to have a major impact on the Roman Church, and on the relations between the Church and the secular heads of Europe. Further to the south, the Italian city-states began to excel in commerce and banking. This new style of economic development made the city-states sufficiently wealthy to support a growing band of artists and thinkers who would bring about the Italian Renaissance.

ATLANTIC OCEAN

Brest

BRITTANY

Rennes

MAINE

Nantes

ANJO

Angers

POITOU

Tours

BAY OF BISCAY

La Rochelle

Poitiers

Castillon
.1453

Bordeaux

Limoges

LIMOUSIN

Bayonne

GASCONY

AQUITAINE

NAVARRE

ARMAGNAC

Cahors

AUVERGNE

Toulouse

LANGUEDOC

Avignon

Narbonne

Arles

PROVENCE

Aix

Marseilles

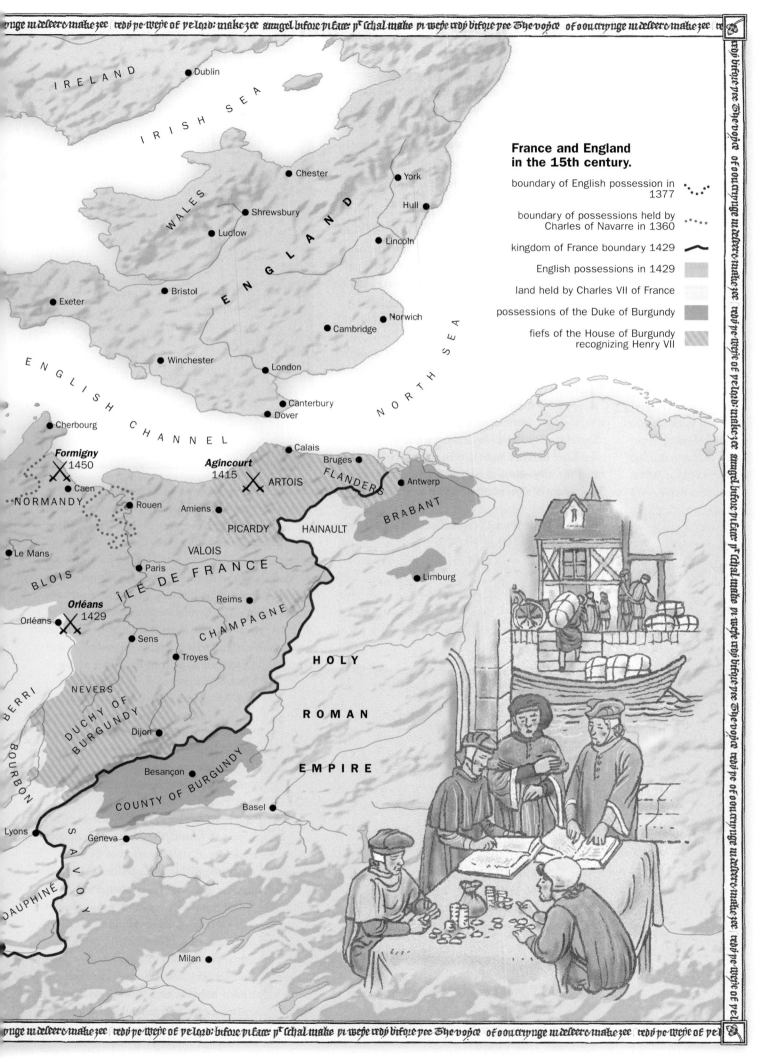

France and England
in the 15th century.

boundary of English possession in 1377

boundary of possessions held by Charles of Navarre in 1360

kingdom of France boundary 1429

English possessions in 1429

land held by Charles VII of France

possessions of the Duke of Burgundy

fiefs of the House of Burgundy recognizing Henry VII

IRELAND

Dublin

IRISH SEA

Chester

York

Hull

WALES

ENGLAND

Shrewsbury

Ludlow

Lincoln

Bristol

Exeter

Norwich

Cambridge

Winchester

London

NORTH SEA

Canterbury

Dover

ENGLISH CHANNEL

Cherbourg

Calais

Formigny 1450

Bruges

Agincourt 1415

ARTOIS

Antwerp

FLANDERS

Caen

NORMANDY

Rouen

Amiens

BRABANT

Le Mans

PICARDY

HAINAULT

VALOIS

Limburg

BLOIS

ÎLE DE FRANCE

Paris

Orléans 1429

Reims

Orléans

CHAMPAGNE

Sens

Troyes

HOLY

NEVERS

DUCHY OF BURGUNDY

Dijon

ROMAN

BERRI

BOURBON

Besançon

COUNTY OF BURGUNDY

EMPIRE

Basel

Lyons

SAVOY

Geneva

DAUPHINÉ

Milan

Joan of Arc and the end of the Hundred Years War

A revival of the Hundred Years War in the early 15th century led to French military disaster and the occupation of Paris by the English. But the defeatism that had marked the French cause was swept away in 1428 by a miracle; the inspiration of a peasant girl named Joan of Arc. By 1460 the English were defeated and, apart from Calais, all of France was back in French hands.

Below: *Joan of Arc (the Maid of Orléans) leads the attack on Paris in September 1429, from a French book illustration of c.1498.*

There was no real chance that the Treaty of Brétigny (1360) would end the war between France and England. When Charles V (1364–80) succeeded to the French throne he felt powerful enough to renew the conflict, although he tried to avoid direct open battle. Aquitaine was held by the Black Prince as a vassal of the French king, and in 1369 Charles declared the province forfeit to the Crown. The English responded by besieging the French city of Limoges and the war was renewed.

For the next decade the English conducted raids into French territory, while their opponents systematically reduced English-held castles. By the end of the 14th century, Aquitaine was securely in French hands and English Gascony was reduced to a narrow coastal enclave. Edward III, Charles V, and the Black Prince all died between 1376 and 1380, leading to a break in hostilities. This was extended by the declaration of a 20-year truce in 1396.

The war was renewed shortly after Henry V of England (1413–22) was crowned. In 1415 he crossed the English Channel with a small army and captured Harfleur. He then marched toward Calais, where he planned to re-embark his army, but at Agincourt he found his way blocked by a French army. Against all common sense the

French repeated the mistakes of Poitiers and charged, only to be cut down by English archers. For the third time in a major battle a compact English army had defeated a larger French one.

The greatest loser was the Armagnac party, one of two contending for the regency of France during the last years of the reign of the insane Charles VI (1380–1422). The English went on to capture most of Normandy while Duke John of Burgundy controlled the French court. In 1420 the Treaty of Troyes restored a kind of peace, favorable only to the English and the Burgundians. When Henry V and Charles VI both died in 1422, English governors were appointed to oversee the French royal demesne in the name of the infant Henry VI (1422–61), while the rest of France south of the River Loire and east of Gascony recognized the Dauphin as their rightful king. In simpler terms, the northern portion of France became the independent territory of the Duke of Burgundy, a central portion (including Paris) was garrisoned jointly by the English and Burgundians, while the southern half of France remained loyal to the Valois monarchy.

The crisis deepens

A malaise seemed to have overcome the French, and their reluctance to meet the English in battle paralyzed their military efforts. In 1428 the English under John, Duke of Bedford made a move against the Loire fortresses, besieging the key city of Orléans. The Dauphin's army made almost no attempt to relieve the city, and its fate seemed inevitable. At the same time a local nobleman in the province of Champagne was being lobbied by a peasant girl who claimed she had a vision. Joan of Arc claimed that God had told her to help relieve Orléans, and then to escort the Dauphin to Reims for his coronation.

She was sent to Chinon, where she continued her lobbying, this time with the Dauphin himself. With nothing to lose, he sent her to Orléans with a relief expedition. Faith in her vision created a miracle of inspiration, and an emboldened French army linked up with the garrison and routed the English, chasing them back to the outskirts of Paris. Joan then persuaded the Dauphin to travel to Reims to be crowned Charles VII (1422–61) in 1429. Joan of Arc was subsequently captured by

the Burgundians, who passed her to the English. She was duly tried on charges of heresy, and burned at the stake.

In 1435, the Duke of Burgundy switched sides

and signed the alliance treaty with France known as the Treaty of Arras. English occupation was untenable, and English garrisons withdrew into Normandy and Gascony. Without serious military intervention by Henry VI, their remaining strongholds were captured by the French. Following two English defeats at Formigny in Normandy (1450) and Castillon in Gascony (1453), the English gave up the contest. Only Calais remained in English hands, and while English monarchs still laid claim to the French throne until the 18th century, their cause was a lost one.

Above: *The trial of Jean II, Duke of Alençon (d.1476) in 1458, who—although he was an alleged friend of Joan of Arc—was accused of plotting with the English against France.*

England Divided: The Wars of the Roses

Just as England was disentangling herself from a century of conflict with France, the country was plunged into a new series of dynastic wars between the rival royal houses of York and Lancaster. Because the two parties were identified with white and red roses respectively, the conflict became known as the Wars of the Roses. After 30 years of slaughter, the issue was decided in favor of Henry Tudor.

Facing:
Henry VII at the Tower of London. The first Tudor king is seen greeting a guest at the door, while also looking down on the scene from a window, and then again inside signing a document. From a manuscript of poems of Charles, Duke of Orléans.

Right: *The death of King Henry V, left the future of the English throne in doubt, since his son's sanity was precarious.*

When Henry V of England (1413–22) died, his son Henry VI (1422–61) was only nine months old. The regency fell to the infant king's two uncles, the Dukes of Bedford and Gloucester. For the next decade the regents ruled England and occupied France until Bedford's death in 1435 and the discrediting of Gloucester six years later. The Duke of Somerset and the Earl of Suffolk became the new regents and they continued to manage the kingdom following Henry VI's majority and marriage to Margaret of Anjou, since it had become clear that the king was mentally unfit to rule. The English defeats in France caused a revolt against the two royal advisors, and although Suffolk was murdered, Somerset and the queen still dominated the country and the king.

In 1450 Richard of York took up the cause against the king's advisors and gathered supporters, as did Somerset and the queen. In 1453 Richard of York was named Protector of the Realm by parliament, but in a moment of sanity the king stripped him of his office and reinstated Somerset to power.

The political conflict became a military one in May 1455 when the two sides clashed at St. Albans. Richard of York, assisted by Richard, Earl of Warwick, triumphed; Somerset was killed in the battle and Henry VI captured. The conflict decided little; the queen took over the reins of government and reclaimed Henry. Fighting broke out again in 1459, and over the next five years several major battles were fought (including Northampton, Wakefield, and the second St. Albans), with both sides claiming victories. Richard of York was killed in 1460 and Warwick became the leading Yorkist nobleman. The decisive confrontation of the war was finally reached at Towton (1461). This was the bloodiest battle fought on British soil, and resulted in a decisive Yorkist victory. The royal family fled to

Scotland and Warwick ensured that the Yorkist Edward of March was crowned Edward IV (1461–83). Further rebellions were crushed and, by 1464, the Lancastrian faction was no longer a serious threat to the realm.

Henry returns

Edward IV proved to be a less than ideal monarch: he married a queen who created her own faction, and fell out with Warwick the Kingmaker. In 1467 Warwick rebelled against Edward, but was forced to flee to France for his own safety. Once there, he formed an alliance with his old enemy, the former queen, Margaret of Anjou. Warwick invaded England in 1470 and Edward was forced to flee the country.

Henry VI was brought back to sit on the throne, but in the spring of 1471 King Edward returned and brought Warwick to battle at Barnet (1471). Warwick was killed, and the unstable King Henry escaped to join his wife and son, Prince Edward. The Lancastrian royal family gathered another army, but were defeated at Tewkesbury (1471). The prince was killed in battle, the queen was imprisoned, and the king was quietly murdered, ending the direct Lancastrian line of succession. At long last, a period of peace descended on England, although recriminations and executions continued for some years.

Edward IV died in 1483, leaving a 12-year-old son, Edward V, under the regency of the kingdom's most powerful noble, Richard, Duke of Gloucester. Richard, who had a strong claim to the English throne imprisoned Edward and his younger brother, first in Ludlow Castle and then in the Tower of London. After arranging for Edward V to be declared illegitimate, the regent was crowned as Richard III (1483–85). To safeguard his position, he had the two princes murdered.

Richard only reigned for just over two years. The Lancastrian faction was now led by Henry Tudor and in mid-1485 he landed in Wales with a mercenary army. He marched into England, gathering support, and met Richard III at Bosworth (1485). The Yorkist king was killed, and Henry remained the sole royal contender. Henry VII (1485–1509) was the founder of the Tudor dynasty and, after a decade of minor rebellions, he restored peace to the troubled kingdom and brought to a close one of the most convoluted periods in English history.

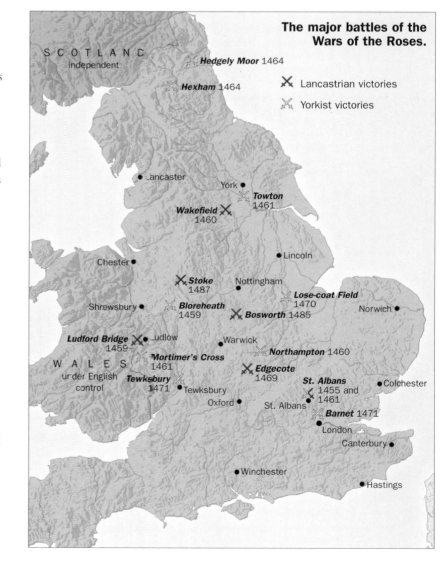

The major battles of the Wars of the Roses.

SCOTLAND independent

✗ Hedgely Moor 1464

✗ Hexham 1464

✗ Lancastrian victories

✗ Yorkist victories

Lancaster

York

✗ Towton 1461

Wakefield ✗ 1460

Chester

Lincoln

✗ Stoke 1487

Nottingham

Shrewsbury

✗ Lose-coat Field 1470

Norwich

✗ Bloreheath 1459

✗ Bosworth 1485

Ludford Bridge ✗ 1459

Ludlow

Warwick

WALES under English control

✗ Mortimer's Cross 1461

✗ Edgecote 1469

✗ Northampton 1460

Tewkesbury ✗ 1471

Tewksbury

St. Albans ✗ 1455 and 1461

Colchester

Oxford

St. Albans

✗ Barnet 1471

London

Canterbury

Winchester

Hastings

Manufacturing

The end of the feudal period brought a demand for specialized products from all over Europe: Flemish wool; Italian armor; German metals; and French wine. Manufacturing centers became increasingly specialized, and both artisans and merchants took full advantage of the opening up of European markets.

Throughout the medieval period there was nothing approaching industry on a large scale. The Arsenal in Venice represented the largest industrial establishment, but since it only built warships for the Venetian Republic, it was not a commercial enterprise. Some armorer's workshops were large enough to employ a sizeable workforce of artisans, but by necessity their work to produce individual pieces of merchandise was labor-intensive. When a large order was required (for instance the production of weaponry during a war), merchants frequently had to sub-contract other manufacturers to supply the entire quota required.

In most cases, the typical late medieval artisan's workshop was a single small building and the craftsman would employ one or more apprentices. Many were members of guilds, protective institutions that ensured the quality of production within a city, regulated prices, and adjudicated in disputes between merchants or customers. Products often went through several workshops before completion, with each artisan working on his particular section. Merchants, bankers, or guilds acted as agents, taking orders, allocating production quotas to the artisans, and then collecting the finished product and shipping it, for a suitable fee.

Birth of the mining industry

Raw materials were usually brought from a region close to the areas of production, and therefore certain types of products were produced in towns close to the best mines, woods, quarries, or ports. One exception to the generally small unit of production was in the mining industry. Previously, mines had been operated by small groups of less than a dozen miners, usually working on a cooperative basis, but by the 15th century the mining of silver and iron ore in Germany had become a major business. Financial backers provided funds for machinery, workers, and transportation, allowing wider and deeper seams to be dug than before. The largest mining centers in Europe were in Saxony, Bohemia, and the Balkans, but smaller-scale mining operations continued in France, England, Spain, and Scandinavia.

Once goods were manufactured or mineral resources mined, the material had to be transported to market. During the late medieval period, transportation as well as communication was limited by the lack of good roads, which were almost non-existent outside the north of Italy. Merchant goods were transported by cart or by sea and, until the late 14th century, there was almost no sea communication between the Mediterranean and the North Sea. Within these separate regions, mercantile shipping communities, such as the Hanseatic League in the Baltic and the North Sea, or the maritime city-states of Venice and Genoa, provided shipping that could transport a greater volume of goods than had ever been possible before.

The breaking of feudal bonds during the 14th century permitted freer movement of the peasant population around the countryside, although medieval horizons were not broad—journeys

Below: *The process of distilling grew in importance in manufacturing. This illustration from* Liber de arte distillandi de simplicibus *shows three distillation units sitting on a furnace fueled by the central pillar.*

Left: *Separating lead from silver or gold in a cuppelation furnace, from a 16th-century illustration in* De re metallica.

were limited to visiting the regional towns, religious centers, or merchant fairs. Even at the height of the feudal system, peasants frequently left their feudal obligations behind to go on pilgrimage, to Rome, Santiago de Compostela, or even to Jerusalem. The development of regular trade and pilgrimage routes led to the establishment of regular roads, maintained by the local nobility either for reasons of charity or profit.

By the 14th century regular transport routes crossed Europe and roads, graded and improved, allowed carts to cross even the Alpine passes. The river systems were also widely used, and the burgeoning river trade during the 14th century led feudal lords to establish toll castles and barriers to take full advantage of this traffic, never more so than on the German Rhine. The decline in economic demand in the aftermath of the Black Death provided a check to trade and industry, but by the 15th century a partial recovery led to a resumption of widespread commerce.

The late 15th century city had broken free from the constraints of feudalism, and had partially recovered from the ravages of the previous century. The concentration of capital in the hands of a few merchants (who combined the roles of manufacturers, traders, and bankers), a continental market for the supply and demand of produce, and the creation of private or state-run monopolies laid the groundwork for the advent of capitalism.

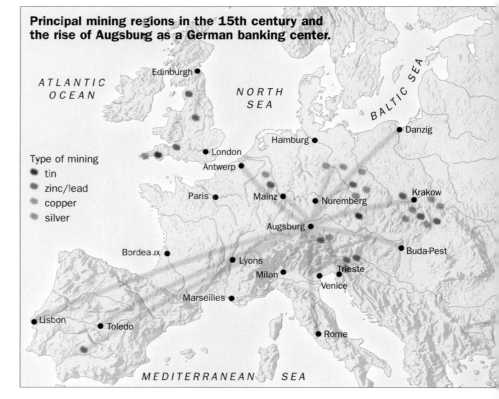

Principal mining regions in the 15th century and the rise of Augsburg as a German banking center.

ATLANTIC OCEAN

NORTH SEA

BALTIC SEA

Edinburgh

Danzig

Hamburg

London

Antwerp

Paris

Mainz

Nuremberg

Krakow

Augsburg

Bordeaux

Buda-Pest

Lyons

Trieste

Milan

Venice

Marseilles

Rome

Lisbon

Toledo

MEDITERRANEAN SEA

Type of mining
tin
zinc/lead
copper
silver

The Struggle for Control of the Church

Despite the reunification of the Church under one Pope in 1417, the problems facing the Roman Catholic establishment were far from over. The greatest of these were the rising tide of religious dissent and the constitutional stability of an establishment shaken to its very foundations by the Great Schism. Strong leadership was needed to combat the rising tide of heresy and secular disenchantment.

The Conciliar movement which began with the Council of Constance in 1414 eventually solved the problems of the Great Schism, but it also had to deal with the religious reformers who had thrived during the previous century. These dissidents questioned the very legitimacy of the institutions of the Church, pointing to the corruption and avarice among the late medieval clergy. Most prominent were

Below: The reformer John Wycliffe, who questioned the Church's doctrine of transubstantiation, became leader of the Lollards ("Mumblers," from the Dutch).

Englishman John Wycliffe (c.1329–1384) and the Czech reformer John Huss (*pages 166–167*), who shared many of Wycliffe's views.

Wycliffe was an Oxford theologian who rose to prominence through his attacks on the avarice of the clergy, and his call for secular control of Church property. This stance obviously found favor among the princes and nobles, who shielded Wycliffe from any papal backlash. His argument centered around the statement that true dominion belonged to God alone, and only the virtuous could exercise the right to own property in God's name. This view of the virtuous priest was similar to that adopted by the heretics of the 12th century, and enraged the late medieval Church.

Although condemned by the Pope and the Archbishop of Canterbury, Wycliffe's patrons prevented an arraignment on charges of heresy until his death.

Pressure on the papacy

The Council of Constance set a precedent whereby ecclesiastical problems were sent to a council of the clergy rather than the Pope. In other words, the papacy was encountering the same infringement of its divine right to govern as were the monarchs of 15th-century Europe. Pope Martin V (1417–31) owed his position to the Council, and at first he supported their authority to administer ecclesiastical affairs. However, his only achievement was to prevent any further reform within the Church by temporarily dissolving the Council in 1423, but he was forced to convoke a new meeting in Basel in 1431.

His successor, Pope Eugenius IV (1431–47), vowed to deal with the matter head-on, but encountered reformers whose stance exceeded the position taken at Constance. They emphasized the authority of their assembly over the Pope, who was unable to dissolve the Council. The papal position was saved by a stroke of good fortune. The Byzantine Empire, which in 1437 was on the verge of being overrun by the Turks, offered to heal the old split between the Roman and Orthodox Churches in return for military assistance. Eugenius convened a Council of Unity in Ferrara where he had the upper hand because, since the Greeks refused to negotiate with anyone other than the Pope, Eugenius controlled the Council.

However, no firm treaty was signed, and

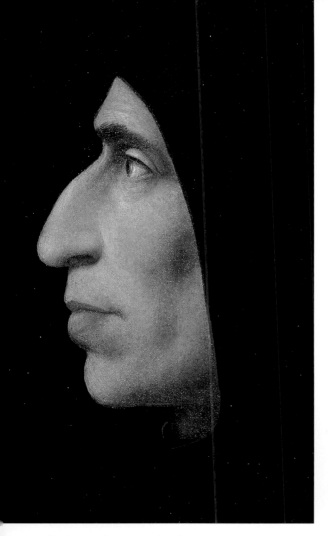

avarice of both ecclesiastical government and that of Lorenzo de' Medici.

When in 1492, two years after Lorenzo's death, the Florentines expelled the Medici to establish a republic, Savonarola became virtual dictator. His teachings brought him into conflict with Pope Alexander VI, who eventually excommunicated him. A disillusioned Florence turned its back on Savonarola and he was arrested, tried for heresy, and condemned to be hanged and then burned.

The Conciliarists had managed to end the Great Schism and introduce constitutional debate, but their eventual failure to introduce representative government to the Church, along with the enduring examples of Wycliffe, Huss, and Savonarola, would lead to the Reformation movement.

Left: *The fiery Dominican preacher Girolamo Savonarola brought austerity to the flamboyant Florence of the ruling Medici family, and prefaced the coming Reformation of the Church.*

Below: *Wycliffe's translation of the Bible into English made the Holy Book available to a wider audience.*

leading reformers refused to go to Ferrara, even going as far as to elect their own Pope (or Antipope), Felix V (1439–49). The rebellion against papal authority grew more serious when reformers in Basel gained the support of several German princes. This blow to papal authority followed close on the heels of another setback. In 1438 the French Church had adopted the Pragmatic Sanction of Bourges, which limited papal interference in their church, and supported a link to French secular authority. Louis XI of France (1461–83) now effectively controlled the French Church.

The following year the Pragmatic Sanction of Mainz similarly benefited the German princes. In 1449 the Pope reached a compromise with both groups: in return for withdrawing support for the Antipope and the Basel reformers, the rulers could appoint their own national clergy, so long as papal revenues from their lands were assured.

The Conciliar movement was weakened by its division between moderates and radicals, and failed to accomplish any lasting reforms. More important, the rulers of Europe did not want to establish a Conciliar precedent that might be applied to their own realms. Their failure led to further dissidents, such as Girolamo Savonarola (1452–98), becoming vocal. A Dominican friar, Savonarola began teaching theology at Florence in 1482 and became a fiery preacher against the

The Duchy of Burgundy

A series of land gifts, marriage treaties, and diplomatic alliances led to the creation of a new power in western Europe during the late 14th century. The Duchy of Burgundy became a political state during the 15th century, and its dukes developed a skill for pitching France and England against each other for their own ends.

In 1361 the Duke of Burgundy died without any clear successor. The Duchy became the ward of King John the Good of France (1350–64). John's youngest son, Philip, managed the Duchy, and when John's eldest son, Charles V (1364–80), succeeded to the French throne, he made his young brother the new Duke of

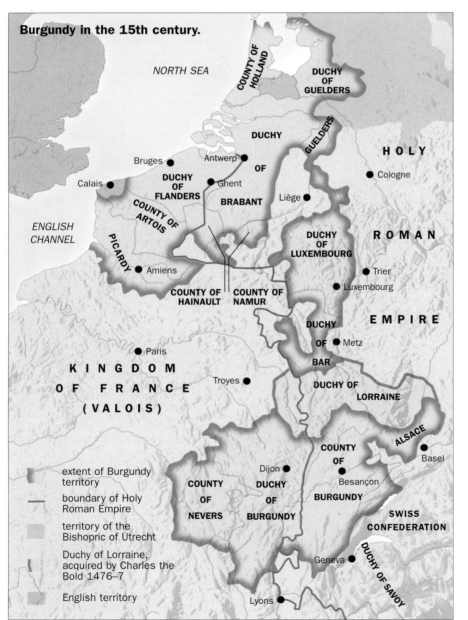

Burgundy in the 15th century.

NORTH SEA

COUNTY OF HOLLAND

DUCHY OF GUELDERS

DUCHY OF FLANDERS

GUELDERS

HOLY

Bruges •   Antwerp •

• Cologne

Calais •

• Ghent

Liège •

COUNTY OF ARTOIS

BRABANT

ENGLISH CHANNEL

DUCHY OF LUXEMBOURG

ROMAN

PICARDY

• Amiens

• Trier

Luxembourg •

COUNTY OF HAINAULT   COUNTY OF NAMUR

EMPIRE

DUCHY OF BAR

• Metz

• Paris

KINGDOM OF FRANCE (VALOIS)

Troyes •

DUCHY OF LORRAINE

ALSACE

COUNTY OF

Basel •

Dijon •

Besançon •

COUNTY OF NEVERS

DUCHY OF BURGUNDY

BURGUNDY

SWISS CONFEDERATION

extent of Burgundy territory

boundary of Holy Roman Empire

territory of the Bishopric of Utrecht

Duchy of Lorraine, acquired by Charles the Bold 1476–7

English territory

Geneva •

DUCHY OF SAVOY

Lyons •

Burgundy. Duke Philip the Bold (1364–1404) was ambitious, and engineered a marriage with Margaret, daughter of the Count of Flanders. The wedding took place in 1369, and when the Count died in 1384, Philip succeeded him.

His lands now included the Duchy of Burgundy, the Counties of Flanders, Artois, Nevers, and the Franche Comte (the County of Burgundy). During this period Philip remained loyal to his Valois brother, and the duke and king supported each other when required (his successors would not prove so loyal, however). His energy, ambition, and royal lineage allowed him to pass on to his son a powerful state. Up to that point Philip's allegiance to the Crown had masked the powerful political entity his domain had become.

Philip's son, Duke John the Fearless (1404–19), was linked to the murder of his cousin, Louis, Duke of Orléans (the brother of King Charles VI of France [1380–1422]). The French king was evidently insane, and the murder had been part of a family struggle for power within the French court. John's next rival was the Count of Armagnac, the brother-in-law of Duke Louis. When a minor civil war erupted, both parties sought an alliance with the English against their opponents. John kept Burgundy out of the Agincourt campaign (1415), which proved disastrous for the French cause.

Strategic alliances

By 1419 John was virtually running the French court, supported by the king's wife. His only rival was Charles the Dauphin (son of the king), and a meeting was arranged between the two. In September 1419 the two parties met at Montereau, and John the Fearless was assassinated, possibly on the Dauphin's orders. John had proved to be the most astute of the Valois Dukes of Burgundy, and an excellent strategist. During his reign he significantly increased the political and military independence of Burgundy.

Duke Philip the Good (1419–67) succeeded his father at the age of 23. Although married to the Dauphin's sister, he turned his back on the struggle for supremacy with France and, in the Treaty of Troyes of 1420, Burgundy allied itself with England. The Dukes of Burgundy would no longer have any influence in the French

court, but they bought independence and protection. Both Henry V of England and the insane Charles VI of France died in 1422. The Dauphin became Charles VII (1422–61), while England was ruled by a regent.

Philip refused to act as the English regent, so the post was given to John, Duke of Bedford. Bedford married Philip's sister and helped add the Duchy of Brabant to the Burgundian demesne, but relations between England and their new ally slowly deteriorated. A dispute over the inheritance of the Counties of Hainault, Holland, and Zealand brought Philip into armed conflict with Bedford's brother, but the English backed down, and the provinces became part of the Burgundian territory in 1433. Philip also acquired the lucrative Duchy of Brabant, which gave him control over most of what is now Holland, Belgium, and Luxembourg.

Philip's alliance with England become a burden when English fortunes fell. Although the Duke handed over Joan of Arc to the English authorities

in 1430, he began negotiations with Charles VI. In 1435, in the Treaty of Arras, Burgundy switched sides once more, in return for land, an apology for the murder of Philip's father, and exemption from feudal obligations. For the next 30 years Philip consolidated his gains, reorganized his estates, and played the role of one of Europe's leading figures.

He was a generous patron of the arts, and the Burgundian Ducal court became one of the most glamorous in Europe. When Philip the Good died in 1467 he was succeeded by his son, who became known as Duke Charles the Bold (1467–77), or even Charles the Rash. While his father Philip had been a gifted politician, a diplomat, and a soldier, Charles possessed none of these virtues. Under Philip, Burgundy reached the pinnacle of its power. Although his son added more territory, the political decline of the Burgundian state began on the death of his father.

FOCUS: SOCIETY
Late Medieval Art

During the 14th and early 15th centuries, an interest in perspective, the development of oil-based paints, and a new sense of realism led to a break with traditional approaches to religious art. This explosion of artistic skill reflected the re-evaluation of traditional views which was becoming common during the 15th century, and which developed into the cultural and intellectual flowering of the Renaissance.

Three distinct schools of painting existed in 15th century western Europe. The first developed at the papal court in Avignon during the last decades of the 14th century, but subsequently became a movement centered around

Paris. International Gothic spread from France throughout the continent by the mid-15th century. It was characterized by the bold use of color, the linear artistry of the late Gothic movement, and an emphasis on decorative detailing. In Italy, the artistic movement was established in Siena, and is best characterized by the work of the Sienese artist Stephano di Giovanni "Sassetta" (1392–1447). His surviving works include St. Thomas Aquinas (Museum of Fine Arts, Budapest) and St. Francis of Assisi (Musée Condée, Chantilly).

A particularly celebrated northern European example is the illuminated manuscript *Les Très Riches Heures du Duc de Berry*, a prayerbook produced for the brother of the French king in the early 15th century by the two Flemish Limbourg brothers. Each month contains a seasonal scene, painted with a vividness and esthetic beauty that is breathtaking. The existentialist work of Hieronymus Bosch (c.1450–1515) produced a later variation on this art form, as he broke away from the realism of the rest of the movement to produce fantastical landscapes and creatures.

Another school of painting developed in the Netherlands during the early 15th century, and this early Dutch school combined the use of true perspective with an exquisite rendering of detail, made possible by oil paint (*see* Rogier van der Weyden *on the previous page*). The first great practitioner of this form was Jan van Eyck (c.1385–1441), whose work includes *The Arnolfini Marriage* (National Gallery, London), *Madonna in the Church* (Dahlem, Berlin) and *Annunciation* (National Gallery of Art, Washington D.C.). Although his works contain symbolic references (such as the dog in *Arnolfini Marriage* symbolizing fidelity) that betray the artist's medieval roots, the style is a break with tradition. His works were realistic portrayals of the scenes they depicted and the people he featured. This Netherlands or Flemish school continued to develop through the late 15th and early 16th centuries, producing some of the most celebrated works of northern Renaissance art.

1401	1407	1414
The Baltic pirate Klaus Störtebeker is executed in Hamburg	Louis, Duke of Orléans murdered, prompting civil war in France	The Council of Constance is convened

Florentine artists

In Italy a Florentine school developed which broke even further from the religious painting styles that had gone before. The first of these Florentine artists was Giotto "di Bondone" (1266–1337) who rebelled against the Byzantine-influenced art favored in Italian religious painting of the period, and painted in a far more natural and realistic style. His style and use of color reflected an influence from the International Gothic movement, but he combined Gothic structures with a perspective and a new realism in features and in composition. His work includes the *Madonna Enthroned* (Uffizi, Florence) and the frescoes at Santa Croce (Florence). These frescoes and the similar sequence in Padua are regarded as his greatest works. Like many of the Renaissance artists who followed him, he combined the roles of painter, sculptor, and architect. This appreciation of three-dimensional structure is reflected in his painting.

In the early 15th century Masaccio "Tommaso di Giovanni di Simone Guidi"(c.1400–1428) followed in Giotto's footsteps, but the artist brought his own sense of dramatic perspective to bear. His works include *Virgin and Child with St. Anne* (Uffizi, Florence) and *Virgin and Child* (National Gallery, London). Together these Florentine artists created a painting tradition that made Florence the artistic center of Italy, and which led directly to the more celebrated works of the Italian Renaissance artists.

The accepted view is that the Renaissance developed in Florence, then expanded to embrace Italy, then Europe. During the 14th and 15th centuries it can be argued that an artistic influence flowed the other way. The light and dramatic style developed by French, Dutch, and Flemish artists and which incorporated Gothic perspectives was almost certainly an influence on the work of the first celebrated Florentine artists: Giotto, Monaco, and Martini. The International Gothic style was the forerunner of both the Florentine and Netherland schools, and therefore earns itself a special place in art history. While Renaissance classicists derided Gothic style in architecture, the same movement provided a cultural foundation for the greatest artists of the 15th and 16th centuries.

Opposite: Jan van Eyck's *Arnolfini Marriage*. This new painting technique would soon find its way to northern Italy.

Below: *Madonna Enthroned*, c.1305, by Giotto di Bondone, is painted with tempera on wood. Florentine and Venetian artists would soon embrace the new oil paints.

FOCUS: LEADERS
Charles the Bold

When he succeeded to the ducal throne in 1467, Duke Charles the Bold of Burgundy (1467–77) inherited a virtually independent state at the height of its power. Although he managed to expand its frontiers, his lack of diplomatic and military skill contributed to a decline in Burgundian power. In 1476 he went to war with the Swiss, and within a year he had lost his army, his state, and his life. It is little wonder that he was also known by historians as Charles the Rash.

Below:
Switzerland's most celebrated battle saw off the power of Burgundy at the edge of Lake Morat, near Bern. The walled town of Morat (Murten in Swiss-German) still retains much of its 15th-century character.

Revenue from the commercial centers of Flanders made Burgundy one of the richest states in Europe, and under Philip the Good the ducal court had become the center of an efficient administration, and a great patron of the arts. Charles also inherited a realm that was disjointed. The Burgundian lands were a patchwork of counties acquired through marriage, inheritance, or coercion. Charles wanted to create a more geographically unified realm, stretching from the North Sea to the Alps. The Duke's marriage to Margaret, the sister of the Yorkist Edward IV of England (1461–83) in 1468 was a direct threat to Louis XI of France (1461–83), and the alliance earned the Duke the enmity of the French king. Louis stirred up a revolt against Charles in the Flemish town of Liège, and during a meeting between the two leaders at Peronne in 1468, Charles imprisoned the French monarch. Louis was released on the promise that he would help the Duke defeat the rebels. By now, the two were mortal enemies.

Charles continued his expansion by gaining the Duchies of Alsace and Lorraine in 1469, with the approval of the German Emperor Frederick III (1440–93). The Dutch province of Guelders was added in 1473, although by this stage internal revolts were beginning to disrupt the unity of the Burgundian domains. Charles reformed his army along non-feudal lines, and the resultant increase in taxation caused resentment among his subjects. In 1474 the Duke was deeply in debt, and revolts in the Flemish cities and Alsace only added to his financial discomfiture. A series of Burgundian diplomatic blunders led to the French king and the German emperor dividing Alsace and Lorraine between them. This resulted in open warfare between France

1429	1431
Joan of Arc relieves the siege of Orléans	Joan of Arc burned at the stake at Rouen

Duke of Lorraine regarded them as useful allies against the Burgundians.

The Burgundians captured the town of Grandson on Lake Neuchatel, but before Charles could resume his advance on Berne at the start of March, he was defeated by a Swiss army. The Burgundians retreated into the Franche Compte to reorganize, while the Swiss awaited developments. In June Charles advanced around the south side of lake Neuchatel, and reached the walled town of Morat (Murten). The Burgundians laid siege and the Swiss marched to the town's relief. In the ensuing Battle of Morat, the Burgundians were decisively defeated.

Charles retreated with the remains of his army to the Franche Compte, then moved north in response to attacks on Burgundian garrisons in

Left: *A twin portrait of Charles the Bold and his wife Isabella of Bourbon, by an unknown painter of the 15th century.*

and Burgundy in 1475. The war fizzled out and a truce was signed, but it was evident that King Louis had completely outmaneuvered Charles the Bold in the political arena. While overt warfare had ended, Louis continued to incite revolts within Burgundian territories, and to forge anti-Burgundian alliances with the Swiss and the Duke of Lorraine.

Charles makes fatal errors

The Swiss, Austrians, and Lorrainers began to attack garrisons inside the County of Burgundy as early as 1474, and a skirmish at Hericourt (1474) prompted Charles the Bold to plan a retaliatory invasion of the Swiss Confederation. In the winter of 1475–6, Charles marched south at the head of a substantial army to invade them. The Swiss Confederation had come into being during the previous century as a series of communities bound together for mutual protection. By 1476 the Confederation consisted of ten *cantons* and was virtually independent of the German Empire, although traditionally the region had formed part of the Austrian ducal domain. The Swiss had already demonstrated their military prowess during their wars against the Hapsburgs, and both the French king and the

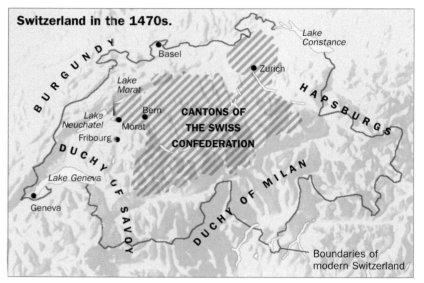

Switzerland in the 1470s.

Lorraine. During October he tried to besiege Nancy, and Duke Renatus of Lorraine recruited Swiss mercenaries to relieve the siege. In January 1477 the allies attacked the Burgundians and massacred the army. Charles the Bold was killed during the battle, and with his death his Burgundian domain fell apart. Charles's daughter was married to Maximillian, the heir to the German Empire, who added the Low Countries to his German estates King Louis seized the southern regions of Burgundy and the Franche Compte in 1478. Charles the Bold, the last Valois Duke of Burgundy, almost succeeded in carving out a new and lasting kingdom between France and Germany. The historical ramifications if he had succeeded have intrigued historians ever since.

FOCUS: WARFARE
Gunpowder v. Chivalry

By the middle of the 14th century mounted knights had dominated the European battlefield for more than 200 years, but now this dominance was being challenged. In several pivotal battles infantry proved victorious, and the advent of gunpowder completed the knight's demise by the end of the century. Chivalry had little place in the age of firepower.

The knight was the epitome of chivalric warfare, a heavily armored warrior supported, like a modern tank, with a skilled crew who helped him perform his task. As one of an upper caste in the pyramid of feudal society, the knight was the aristocratic ruler of a number

his attendant men-at-arms were still important on the 14th-century battlefield, they could no longer claim to represent the decisive military arm. Increasingly, foot soldiers were demonstrating the fallibility of the chivalric knight, and new technologies hastened their extinction.

In 1314 a small Scottish army defeated an English feudal host at the battle of Bannockburn by using formed bodies of spearmen (*shiltrons*). A similar disaster had befallen the French nobles at the hands of Flemish rebels at the Battle of Courtrai a dozen years before. The two victories marked a turning point in medieval warfare. Infantrymen, who had long been regarded as supernumeraries, were beginning to come into their own on the battlefield. In the early 15th

of retainers, and when called to go to war, he did so at the head of his retinue, or feudal contingent. By the 14th century this feudal military structure had begun to fracture. An army contained fewer true knights than previously, and the cost of equipping a knight and his retinue had increased. Although the mounted knight and

century the spears used by the Scots and Flemings were replaced by pikes, and the abilities of closely packed ranks of pikemen were first demonstrated in Flanders. During the Burgundian Wars (1475–77) the Swiss defeated the mounted gendarmes of the Burgundians in a series of battles based around their blocks of

1464	1467	1473	1476	1477	1485	1490	1490
Death of Cosimo de' Medici, the ruler of Florence	The first ballad about the Swiss national hero William Tell is written	Cyprus comes under the control of Venice	Charles the Bold of Burgundy defeated by the Swiss at Morat (Murten)	Charles the Bold's defeat and death at Nancy lead to the breakup of Burgundy	Richard III killed at Bosworth, marking the end of the Wars of the Roses	Europe's first orphanages are established in Italy and the Netherlands	Portuguese convert King of Congo to Christianity

highly trained pikemen. Cavalry no longer ruled the battlefield.

In Wales, a new weapon was developed that could achieve even more and at a longer range. The longbow dominated the battlefields of the Hundred Years War (*see pages 124–125*), but highly trained archers were required to use the weapon. During the second quarter of the 14th century gunpowder weapons began to find their way onto the battlefield. Gunpowder (or black powder) was a ground-up mixture of roughly four parts of saltpeter to one of carbon and one of sulfur.

A new firepower

The first guns are recorded in a Florentine manuscript of 1326, and an English manuscript written by Walter de Milemete provides an illustration of one of these early artillery pieces; a bronze vase-like tube. By the late 14th century artillery was in common use in siege warfare,

Smaller guns are also mentioned, and around the end of the century the first handheld firearms made an appearance. In the 15th century, cannons comprised two types: large bronze muzzle-loading pieces, or smaller wrought-iron breech-loading guns. Some of these big bronze guns were truly massive siege guns, designed to knock down the walls of medieval castles and cities. In the 1470s light field carriages were invented that enabled the unwieldy cannons to accompany armies on the march.

Early handguns grew in popularity during the 15th century and, unlike the longbow, they could be used with little or no training. The early handgun (known as a *hackbut* or *arquebus*) was a crude weapon, with little accuracy. While earlier versions were ignited by hand, firearms in the 15th century usually incorporated a primitive form of ignition system.

By the late 15th century, commanders would be forced to integrate the knight into a

Below: *The chivalrous era of the medieval knight in armor came to an end when the might of the English longbow put infantry to the forefront of the battle, and gunpowder gave princes a terrifying new form of artillery.*

particularly by the French, whose kings maintained a powerful train of siege guns. Chroniclers mention large cannons firing massive iron shot, and these bronze or wrought-iron guns were usually set on the ground and surrounded by heavy timber frames to absorb the recoil when they were fired.

combined arms force, which used mounted shock troops alongside blocks of pikes, supported by bowmen, handgunners, and field artillery. A century later the mounted knight or man-at-arms would still be an important part of an army, but by 1600 they had become an anachronistic legacy of a bygone chivalric age.

1492	1492	1492	1494	1495–97	1497–98	1499	c.1500
The Spanish conquer Granada, driving the Moors from Spain	Ferdinand and Isabella of Spain back Columbus	Charles VIII of France invades Italy	Beginning of the Italian Wars between France and the Hapsburgs	Leonardo da Vinci paints *The Last Supper* in Milan	Vasco da Gama sails to India	Vespucci explores the northeast coast of Brazil	Extinction of Norse Greenland colony

CHAPTER NINE
Ottomans and Slavs

The Byzantine Empire never recovered from the capture of Constantinople by western European crusaders in 1204. Although the Empire survived for over two more centuries, it became a shadow of its former self, with territories divided between squabbling Greek regional rulers and the colonies of rival Christian maritime states. The rise of the Ottoman Turks during the 14th century upset the regional balance of power, and while the Empire was distracted by dynastic disputes and civil disturbances, the Turks created a powerbase in western Anatolia (now Turkey). When the Empire called on Ottoman troops to help them fight their enemies in the Balkans, its fate was sealed. Within a decade Constantinople was a city surrounded by Muslim enemies, and her final conquest in 1453 was a foregone conclusion. The Byzantine Empire, which had survived for a millennium, was replaced by an expansionist Muslim empire in the southeast corner of Europe.

The sprawling states of eastern Europe had existed in seclusion for centuries, but increasingly they became involved in the events that were shaping the German Empire. While the Hungarian, Polish, and Lithuanian states all developed into significant late medieval kingdoms, each was subjected to external threats; marauding German crusaders, Muslim invaders, or dynastic aspirations by neighboring states. While all these countries adopted the doctrines of the Roman Church, their neighboring kingdom of Bohemia had become a center for religious dissent by the start of the 15th century. These Bohemian heretics openly opposed their feudal overlords and the power of a Church that they saw as corrupt beyond measure. The Hussites defied the power of Church and emperor for much of the century, adding to the political decline of the Holy Roman Empire and laying the foundation for the Protestant reformers of a century later. By the end of the 15th century the map of eastern Europe had changed considerably. Beyond the crumbling German Empire a series of powerful eastern European kingdoms maintained a barrier between the rest of Europe and the growing powers of the East; the Empire of the Ottoman Turks and the latent giant of Muscovite Russia.

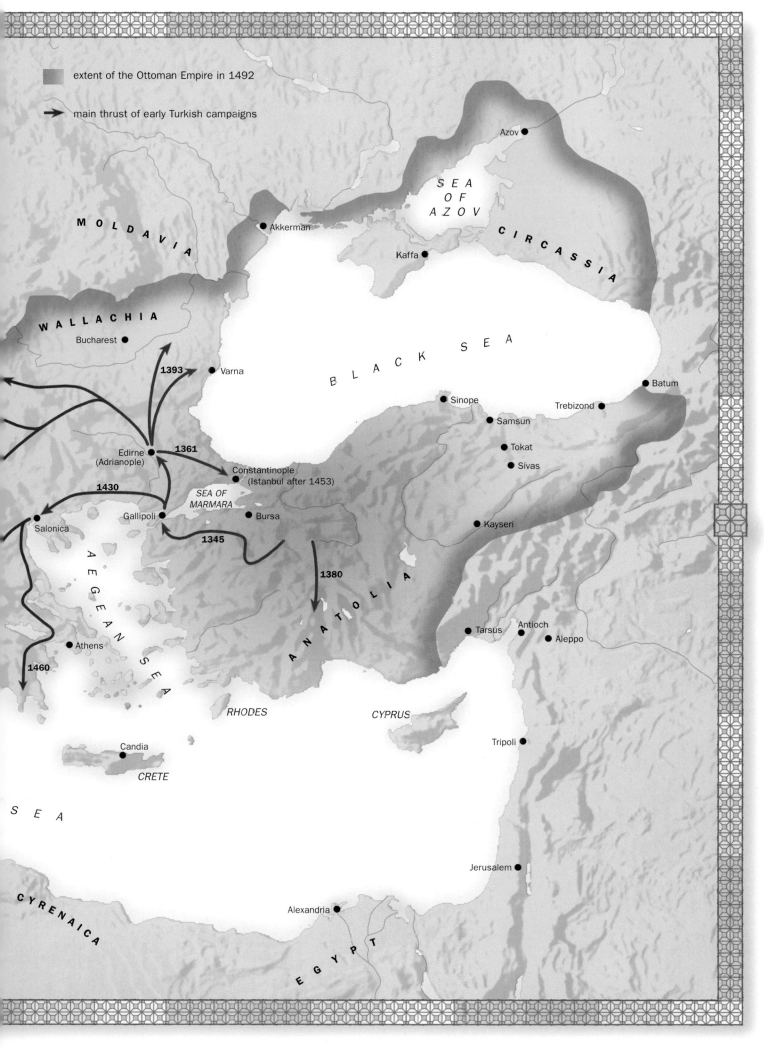

extent of the Ottoman Empire in 1492

main thrust of early Turkish campaigns

MOLDAVIA

WALLACHIA

Bucharest

Akkerman

CIRCASSIA

SEA
OF
AZOV

Azov

Kaffa

BLACK SEA

1393

Varna

Sinope

Batum

Trebizond

Samsun

1361

Edirne
(Adrianople)

1430

Constantinople
(Istanbul after 1453)

SEA OF
MARMARA

Tokat

Sivas

Gallipoli

Bursa

1345

Salonica

AEGEAN SEA

1380

Kayseri

ANATOLIA

Tarsus

Antioch

Aleppo

Athens

1460

RHODES

CYPRUS

SEA

Candia

CRETE

Tripoli

S E A

CYRENAICA

Jerusalem

Alexandria

EGYPT

The Rise of the Ottoman Empire

During the 14th century a Turkish dynasty took shape in Asia Minor that threatened the survival of the last remnants of the Byzantine Empire. By 1400 the Ottoman Turks had bypassed Constantinople to sweep through Greece and the southern Balkans, defeating every army sent against them. Constantinople was now surrounded by Muslim enemies, and was only spared from conquest by the timely arrival of a Mongol army.

The Ottoman Turks derived their name from the founder of their dynasty, Osman I (1259–1326), the son of a Seljuk general who inherited the small Turkish province of Bithynia in western Asia Minor (Anatolia) in 1281. His strength came from his association with Muslim militant crusaders known as *Ghazis*, who saw in him the opportunity to repeat the Islamic expansion of the early medieval period. During the late 13th century Seljuk power had declined in Anatolia, allowing the Ghazis to create semi-autonomous emirates. Osman and his successors helped to unite these emirates into a homogenous Ottoman (or Osmanli) state.

By his death in 1326 Sultan Osman had consolidated his powerbase in northwestern Anatolia and captured the Byzantine city of Brusa (1326). He was succeeded by his son Sultan Orchan (1326–62), who continued his expansion through an alliance with Byzantine Emperor John VI Cantacuzenus (1341–55). The Byzantine ruler was engaged in a dynastic dispute and asked Osman for mercenary troops to help him. During the mid-14th century Turkish troops campaigned in northern Greece while Ottoman troops occupied much of the Byzantine Empire in Anatolia. Nicomedia and Nicaea became Turkish cities. The Turks had reached the edge of Asia, and their military experience in Greece showed them the potential offered by an invasion of Europe.

In 1356 the Turks gained control of a fortress at Gallipoli, which gave them control of the sea approaches to Constantinople, and although the Ottomans were engaged in expansion elsewhere in Anatolia, their sultan had already decided that their future lay in Europe. Although Byzantine Constantinople would survive until 1453, its fate was sealed a century earlier.

A region ripe for invasion

During the mid-14th century Greece and the Balkans were a patchwork of former Byzantine provinces, Latin (western) enclaves, Venetian trading posts, and autonomous domains, such as the Serbian kingdom of King Steven Dusans. The Byzantines controlled Constantinople and very little else. Ottoman access to Europe via the Dardanelles meant that the Turks could expand into Thrace and Rumelia without hindrance. By 1362 the Ottomans had occupied Thrace with little serious opposition, and Constantinople was

Below: *Serbia's subjection to Turkish rule began at the Battle of Kosovo, June 28, 1389 at Kosovo Polje (Field of Blackbirds). Although a decisive Turkish victory, it cost Sultan Murad I his life.*

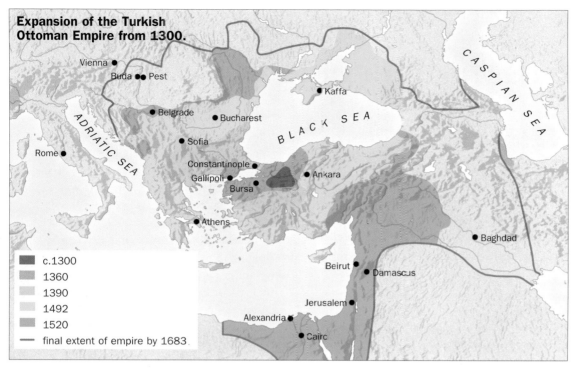

Expansion of the Turkish Ottoman Empire from 1300.

c.1300
1360
1390
1492
1520
— final extent of empire by 1683.

surrounded by Muslim territory. Three years later Sultan Murad I (1362–89) moved his capital to Adrianople (Edirne), and what began as an independent Ghazi migration became a conquest.

Thrace was now securely held as a Turkish province, and military strength in the province built up, ready for further conquests. By 1370 the Turks were on the move again. Murad defeated a Serbo-Bulgarian army and the Bulgarian capital of Sofia fell in 1382. Macedonia and Thessaly also fell to the Ottomans, and then the armies marched northwest, into the land of the Serbs. The city of Nis was besieged and captured, then the Serbian army was decisively defeated at Kossovo Polje (1389), a victory that cost the sultan his life.

A similar policy of expansion was taking place in Anatolia. Under Sultan Beyezit I Yilderim (Thunderbolt) this conquest of Anatolia quickened, as a succession of independent Seljuk emirates became amalgamated into the growing Ottoman Empire. In 1396 he laid siege to Constantinople, only to hear that an army of European crusaders stood on his Danube River frontier. In the battle of Nicopolis (1396) his Turkish army slaughtered the crusaders and, in doing so, effectively ended any further possibility of western intervention on behalf of the Byzantine Empire.

Europe was spared from further conquest by the appearance of a Mongol army on the eastern border of Anatolia. The invaders were led by Tamurlane the Great

(1346–1405). When Tamurlane captured the Anatolian town of Sivas, he massacred the garrison, including Beyezit's eldest son. The Ottoman Sultan marched east to give battle, but was defeated at Angora (Ankara) in 1402. Beyezit was captured and committed suicide in captivity three years later. The Mongols reached the Aegean coast before they returned to the Asian steppes, leaving the Ottoman emirs and the sultan's successors to reclaim what was left of their empire.

Constantinople had a reprieve, but its effects would only be temporary. A dynastic struggle was fought over the sultanate that lasted a decade, but from it Sultan Mehmet (Mohammed) I (1413–21) emerged as the undisputed head of the Ottoman Empire. With the Ottoman Empire united once more, the fall of Constantinople would only be a matter of time.

Below: *The great mass of Hagia Sofia (Santa Sofia) still dominates Istanbul's (formerly Constantinople) skyline in modern Turkey. A Byzantine might still recognize the church's exterior, but the Ottomans added the Muslim minaret towers when it was converted into a mosque.*

The Fall of Constantinople

In the mid-15th century the city of Constantinople was surrounded by the lands of the Ottoman Turks. When Sultan Mehmet II came to power in 1451 he vowed to capture the city, and two years later his army was camped outside its walls. In less than two months the last bastion of the Byzantine Empire had fallen, and what had been the center of Orthodox Christianity became the capital of a Muslim Empire.

Below: *The Turkish army camps before Constantinople, from an illustration of 1455 by Jean Mielot.*

During the 14th century the Byzantine Empire had shrunk to the confines of its once-great capital city, Constantinople, and a handful of small towns and islands in the Aegean Sea. Although no longer the wonder it had been

before its sack by crusaders in 1204, Constantinople was still one of the most important cities in the Mediterranean. It was ruled by the emperor, who in 1451 was Constantine XI Paleologus (1449–53). His imperial title was, however, only a hollow reminder of former Byzantine greatness. Although the city was strongly fortified the Byzantine defenders were heavily outnumbered. Appeals for help from western Europe came to nothing, and it was clear that if the Ottoman Turks chose to attack, the Byzantines would have to defend Constantinople on their own.

In 1451 Sultan Murad II died and was succeeded by his son, Mehmet (Mohammed) II (1451–81). The 19-year-old sultan felt vulnerable and, fearing the intrigues of court, he elected to divert his enemies by launching an attack on Constantinople. In April 1451 he began building the castle of Rumeli Hisar (Strait Cutter) on the Bosphorus, which was designed to cut Constantinople off from the Mediterranean (and western relief). In August he sank a Venetian ship that refused to stop, and decapitated the crew.

Emperor Constantine sent out final desperate appeals for help, and even agreed to reunite his Orthodox Church with Rome, but it was too late. While this was taking place the sultan commissioned the construction of massive bronze siege guns and gathered his army. By the end of March 1453 the guns were in place in front of the city and Turkish forces sealed Constantinople off from the outside world. The defenders strengthened their defenses and waited.

On April 5, 1453, Mehmet called on the Byzantines to surrender. When no answer came by the next day he ordered his guns to open fire. The 7,000 defenders were outnumbered by an overwhelming margin. Constantinople sat at the end of an eastward-facing peninsula, surrounded by the waters of the Golden Horn, the Sea of Marmara, and the Bosphorus. Its base was defended by a powerful land wall, while subsidiary walls ran along its shores, and an older land wall lay behind the first. Protected harbors on the southern side were further protected by booms, while across the Golden Horn the suburb of Galata was also linked to the city by a boom, preventing access to the Golden Horn. The Ottoman siege guns were positioned facing the center of the land wall.

The defenses are breached

The bombardment caused considerable damage, and the defenders struggled to repair their walls after each shot and to detect tunnels dug under their walls. Four Genoese ships fought their way through the blockading Turkish squadrons to deliver supplies, which caused embarrassment to the Turkish sultan, who began his own maritime venture. From the commencement of the siege his engineers had been busy constructing a road around the suburb of Galata from the Bosphorus to the Golden Horn. On April 22 a fleet of Turkish warships was transported along the road and set sail in the Golden Horn. The defenders now had to contend with a possible naval attack against their vulnerable northern seawall.

Surrender talks broke down, and the siege dragged on into late May. Finally, Mehmet judged that the breaches would allow a full assault, and plans were laid for an attack to take place during the early hours of May 29. Both sides braced themselves for the assault, which came amid a clamor of noise. Two waves were launched at the wall to weaken the defenses, then the sultan sent in his elite Janissaries. The fighting on the walls continued until dawn when the defenders were overwhelmed.

A party of Turks captured an open gate in the inner walls and the besiegers streamed into the city. While some defenders fled for the ships and tried to fight their way through the Turkish

blockade, the rest were slaughtered in the streets. The last Byzantine Emperor died defending his city. Sultan Mehmet entered the ruins the next morning as a conqueror, marking the end of a Byzantine Empire that survived the fall of Rome by a millennium.

Above: *The city of Constantinople after its capture by Turks, from original plans drawn in 1522.*

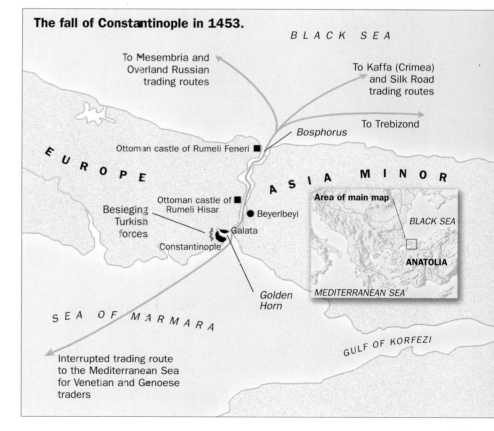

The fall of Constantinople in 1453.

BLACK SEA

To Mesembria and Overland Russian trading routes

To Kaffa (Crimea) and Silk Road trading routes

To Trebizond

Bosphorus

Ottoman castle of Rumeli Feneri ■

EUROPE

ASIA MINOR

Area of main map

Ottoman castle of Rumeli Hisar ■

● Beyerlbeyi

Besieging Turkish forces

Galata

Constantinople

BLACK SEA

ANATOLIA

MEDITERRANEAN SEA

Golden Horn

SEA OF MARMARA

GULF OF KORFEZI

Interrupted trading route to the Mediterranean Sea for Venetian and Genoese traders

Poland, Lithuania, and Muscovy

For centuries the states of eastern Europe struggled under Mongol domination or internal disorder. From the 14th century Poland, Lithuania, and Muscovy emerged as dynamic and expanding territories, resisting pressures from the Teutonic Knights and the Tartars alike to forge their political boundaries.

Below: *Icon of The Holy Trinity by Andrei Rubljov (c.1360–1427).*

To the east of the Holy Roman Empire lay a large area of Europe that was divided into kingdoms existing in relative isolation from the rest of Europe. Centuries of internal fighting, barbarian invasion, and dynastic ambition had restricted economic and political growth, but by the early 14th century external forces began to influence the political geography of eastern Europe. In 1300 King Wenceslas II of Bohemia was crowned as King of Poland, and when he also claimed the Hungarian crown in 1301 he raised the prospect of a new central European empire.

A nationalist movement sprang up in Poland, and by 1320 the rebel leader Wladyslaw I the Short was crowned the new king of Poland by the Pope. Although Poland had previously lost territory (Silesia and Pomerania), the state survived as a political entity, providing a basis for Polish expansion during the 15th century.

The biggest threat to Poland's security came from fellow Christians, the Order of the Teutonic Knights. From 1229 the knights gained control of the province of Kolm on the Vistula river, and campaigned against the pagan peoples of Prussia. Within two decades the Teutonic Knights controlled Prussia and were campaigning actively in Lithuania. Crusades into Lithuania and Russia continued until 1308, when the knights conquered the Polish province of Pomerania. While the war between the Poles and the Teutonic Order continued for another 14 years, the Poles were unable to recover their lost territory for another century.

When Wladyslaw Jagiello (1386–1434) was crowned King of Poland, the war was renewed. At Grunwald (1410) the power of the Teutonic Order was broken, and by 1470 the Poles had reclaimed Pomerania and safeguarded their northern border. By this stage, the Polish king had formed an alliance with the Lithuanians, who were expanding into Russia. By 1450 the Polish-Lithuanian allies occupied territories stretching from Danzig to Smolensk, and maintained indirect control of Moldavia and Prussia. King Wladislaw III was killed in battle with the Turks at Varna (1444) but under his brother Casimir IV (1447–92) the Poles consolidated their control over the remains of the Teutonic Order's stronghold of Prussia, and strengthened the alliance with Lithuania, which would continue into the 18th century. By 1500 Poland was a large and respected kingdom, with a healthy economy and a stable government. As a Catholic country, she also provided a bulwark for the Roman Church against the Muslim Tartars and Orthodox Russians beyond her eastern frontiers.

The growth of Russia

For much of the medieval period the southern region of what is now Russia formed the territory of a Mongol successor state, the Khanate of the Golden Horde. In the early 15th century the Khanate splintered into three provinces, based around Khazan, the Crimea, and the lower Volga river. Ottoman Turkish pressure led to the loss of most of the Khanate's coastal territories, while Lithuanian expansion had extended her territories to the Black Sea coast by 1363. While the Lithuanians had also expanded into Russian territory on the Dnieper river during the late 14th century, they were simply taking advantage of growing divisions within the region. The Ukrainians (Little Russians) and the Byelorussians (White Russians) further north looked toward Europe for salvation from the Mongols, but the Russians of Greater Russia looked to Moscow for protection.

Under Prince Alexander Nevski of Vladimir (1246–63) the Russians defeated the Teutonic Knights at Lake Piepus (1242), and established peaceful relations with the Mongols (or Tartars). By the 14th century Moscow had established a supremacy over Vladimir, and the building of the stone fortress of the Kremlin in 1368 symbolized the power of the new Muscovite State. Although unable to prevent the Tartars from sacking Moscow in 1382, the Muscovites benefited from the break-up of the Khanate. Under Grand Duke Vasili II (1425–62), Muscovite power was extended to include the ducal "fiefdom" of Ryazan and a buffer zone was created to the south of Muscovy to protect the region from further Tartar attacks. Ivan III (1462–1505) stamped his autocratic authority over his "feudal" nobility and took steps to ensure that the duchies of Ryazan and Novgorod were consolidated as part of the Muscovite state. By 1500 Muscovite Russia was an established state, although still isolated by its Lithuanian and Tartar neighbors. This Russian expansion would continue during the following century, and the

coronation of Duke Ivan IV the Terrible as Tsar of all Russia in 1547 confirmed Russia's position as a significant eastern European power.

Above:
Russian imperial and ecclesiastical costumes.

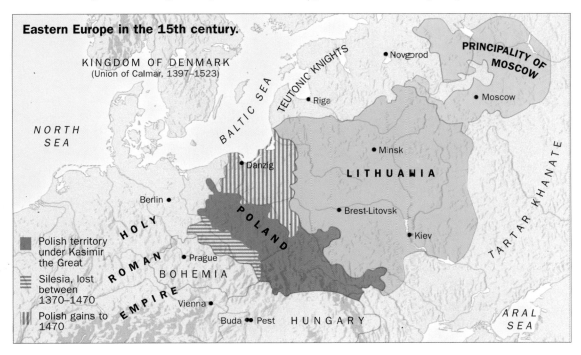

Eastern Europe in the 15th century.

KINGDOM OF DENMARK
(Union of Calmar, 1397–1523)

NORTH SEA

BALTIC SEA

TEUTONIC KNIGHTS

• Riga

• Novgorod

PRINCIPALITY OF MOSCOW

• Moscow

• Danzig

Berlin •

HOLY ROMAN EMPIRE

POLAND

• Minsk

LITHUANIA

• Brest-Litovsk

TARTAR KHANATE

Prague •

BOHEMIA

Vienna •

• Kiev

Buda •• Pest   HUNGARY

ARAL SEA

Polish territory under Kasimir the Great

Silesia, lost between 1370–1470

Polish gains to 1470

The Hussite Revolt

A cleric in early 15th century Prague combined reforming beliefs with a brand of Czech nationalism so effectively that he was excommunicated, tried, and burned at the stake. His death led to the birth of a militant heretical movement in Bohemia. These Hussites defied the German "crusading" armies sent against them for over a decade through a combination of skilled leadership and radical tactics.

At the start of the 15th century Bohemia was a relatively stable and prosperous feudal kingdom. Following a period of dynastic turmoil in the 14th century, the King of Bohemia became closely linked to the affairs of the Holy Roman Empire. The capital of Prague was a thriving commercial center, whose wealth was derived from mining and trade, but the city was also a cultural capital, boasting the first university in the Holy Roman Empire (1348). The kingdom was ruled by Wenceslas IV (1378–1419), the son of the German Emperor.

About 1400 a group of church reformers built a chapel in Prague and in 1402 Jan (or John) Huss (c.1375–1415) was appointed its preacher.

He quickly developed a reputation as a convincing orator. As a moderate reformer, Huss approved of some of John Wycliffe's teachings, and was opposed to the corruption and worldliness of the Church. He also called for lay involvement in the Eucharist, and mirrored some of the English reformer's views on the involvement of secular authority in religious affairs. As a former student of Prague University he campaigned against its domination by German academics, and in the process helped espouse the cause of Bohemian nationalism. King Wenceslas ruled in favor of the reformer and Huss was elected to be the university's rector in 1409. This earned him the enmity of German theologians, who saw Prague as a hotbed of heretical reform.

In 1410 Huss openly condemned the selling of indulgences, and was excommunicated by the Pisan Pope John XXIII (1410–15) in 1412. Wenceslas now expelled Huss and the other Czech reformers from Prague, so the preacher continued his sermons in the Bohemian countryside, while recording his beliefs in *De Ecclesia* (On the Church). In 1414 the Council of Constantinople was convoked and Huss willingly

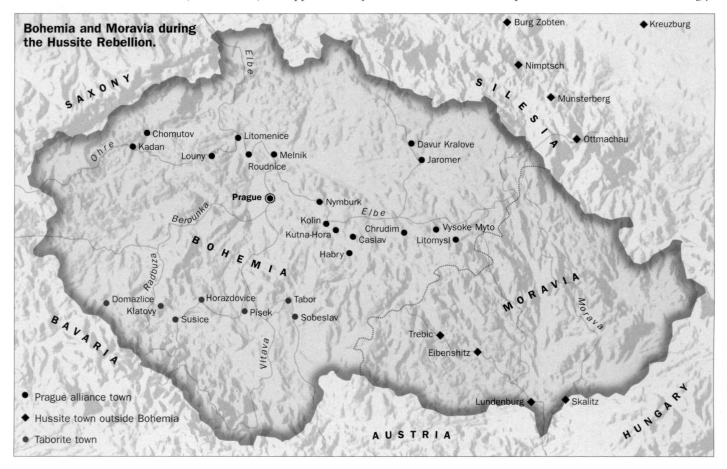

Bohemia and Moravia during the Hussite Rebellion.

- ● Prague alliance town
- ◆ Hussite town outside Bohemia
- ● Taborite town

went to present his case to the Conciliarists, guaranteed safe conduct by King Wenceslas's brother, Emperor Sigismund I (1410–37). Huss was immediately imprisoned, then tried for heresy. He was finally condemned and, under Sigismund's orders, he was burned at the stake in July 1416.

A catalyst for revolution

His execution sent shock waves through Bohemia. Many saw Huss as a victim of the clergy he had campaigned to reform. He was also seen as a Bohemian (or Czech) nationalist, and support for the martyr grew among reformers and a cross-section of secular society. King Wenceslas allied himself with the Pope, and in 1419 the Hussites revolted in Prague and seized the city, slaughtering royal officials in the process. Wenceslas was deposed, and Emperor Sigismund became the new King of Hungary (1419–37). Sigismund declared a crusade against the rebels and marched on Prague, only to be defeated by the Hussites at Vyehrad (1420). For the next 14 years the Hussites defied the might of the Holy Roman Empire.

However, without the guidance of Jan Huss the Hussites splintered into sects divided along doctrinal and theological lines, but dominated by the moderate *Orebites* (or *Utraquists*) and the more heretical and extremist *Taborites*. The division was partly an urban and rural split, with the moderates being centered around Prague and its university. The Hussites also found commanders who were able to consistently outwit the imperial crusaders sent against them. The greatest was the half-blind Jan Ziska, and after his death the Orebites were commanded by the gifted Procop the Short. Their tactics revolved around the use of fortified wagons, which combined mobility with protection, and these could be used both offensively and defensively.

The Hussites also placed a heavy emphasis on firepower, mounting cannons in some of their wagons, and making extensive use of handheld guns to defeat the crusading knights sent against them. Decisive Hussite victories at Kutna-Hora (1421), Habry (1422) and Taussig (1426) proved

that the heretics were unbeatable on the battlefield, but internal divisions between the sects led to an agreement between the Orebites and the Church in 1434. The moderates and the imperialists formed the Bohemian League, and their forces defeated the Taborites at Lipan (1434). Two years later Sigismund entered Prague, but following his death in 1437, factional fighting continued in various forms throughout the rest of the century. Although the revolt was ultimately a failure, the Hussite victories forced the Church to adopt a pragmatic compromise, although religious differences continued to split Bohemia until the 17th century.

Above: *The martyrdom of Jan Huss began a rebellion against Catholicism in Bohemia, and his Hussite followers held off the might of both Church and Holy Roman Empire for two decades.*

FOCUS: SOCIETY

Byzantine Art and Architecture

The Byzantines saw themselves as the successors to the Roman Empire after the fall of Rome in the early fifth century. Their art and architecture reflected some Roman traditions, but became more eastern over the centuries. As the center of the Orthodox Church, Constantinople produced some of the best religious art of the medieval period, although the ravages of crusaders, Turks, and time itself have left little trace of the Byzantine Empire's artistic legacy.

Below: *This figure of Christ, a mosaic from the Karibye Mosque, Istanbul, typifies the later Byzantine style.*

The Byzantine buildings of Istanbul bear testimony to the grandeur of what was once the capital of an empire. When Emperor Theodosius I (379–92) made Christianity the official religion of the Eastern Roman Empire, he formed a link between the Church and State that would remain until 1453. This was reflected in Byzantine art, with the majority of surviving pieces being religious, although a few depicted the secular rulers of senior noble families. Since the emperor was effectively the head of the Church, the two were interrelated.

The influence of Middle Eastern art and architecture became suffused with this Roman element to produce the architecture that survives throughout the former Byzantine Empire. Religious architectural masterpieces such as the Church of Hagia Sofia and the Church of St. John of the Studion combined spacious domed structures with a wealth of internal decoration: mosaics, marble decoration, and ornamental metalwork, and traces of their former sumptuous nature can still be seen. Both were built during the reign of Emperor Justinian I (527–65); a period that is regarded as a golden age of Byzantine religious art and architecture.

By the time of the collapse of the Roman

1223	1229	1237	1242	1242	1280	1281	1294
The Mongols reach the borders of Russia	Teutonic Knights establish bases on the Baltic coast	The Mongols conquer Russia	Teutonic Knights defeated by Alexander Nevski at Lake Piepus	The Khanate of the Golden Horde established in the Ukraine	The Bulgarian State collapses, divided between Serbs and Byzantines	Ottoman rule established in the Anatolian province of Bythnia	Hanseatic League led by Lübeck dominates Baltic trade

Empire a particular form of Greek religious art had developed, which drew inspiration from regional Greek traditions. By the sixth century this had merged with Middle Eastern forms, which were more symbolic, to create a uniquely Byzantine style that appeared in several forms, particularly icons, mosaics, or illuminations in Greek manuscripts.

A blend of cultures

Mosaic evolved into a particularly Byzantine art form; the majority of works were religious, but some secular examples remained. Byzantine mosaic artists were particularly fond of portraiture, although artistic traditions veered toward a formal, eastern style of depiction. In most examples the rigid figures are portrayed facing the viewer, a style which was repeated in both iconography and illuminated works.

This two-dimensional nature of Byzantine art reflected a religious argument, which stated that a more realistic depiction detracted from the spiritual quality. As a consequence of this belief, three-dimensional sculpture was rare in Byzantine art and, more commonly, carving was restricted to miniature relief in the form of book covers, decorative boxes, or metalwork. Ivory was also a popular material. One exception was the bronze Lions of St. Mark, looted from Constantinople in 1204 (together with a hoard of other treasures) and transported to Venice.

Painted religious icons became an integral part of the Orthodox Church until the Iconoclastic Controversy of the ninth century. Although these images of religious figures and scenes were banned by Church decree, and thousands of examples were destroyed after 843, sufficient examples survive to compare with the set techniques and rigid composition that remained in use in Russian iconography throughout the medieval period.

The Byzantine emphasis on spiritual grace and color seen in icons and mosaics was reflected in illumination on Byzantine manuscripts. The color and compositional forms seen in surviving Byzantine illuminations is breathtaking in the charming and esthetic way it conveys the spiritual nature of the subject. Although the Church was the source of inspiration for much Byzantine art, secular works were also produced, and several examples of domestic mosaics survive, together with decorative domestic items, secular books, and even statues. Favored methods of decoration in Byzantine decorative art include the use of enameled metal or glass, fine metalwork, and ivory relief.

Following the sack of Constantinople by the crusaders in 1204, the Byzantine Empire fragmented into numerous small Latin states. Although Constantinople was recovered from the crusaders during the 13th century, the Empire was no longer a source of religious and secular patronage. Many Byzantine artists and artisans sought employment with their new Italian overlords (principally in Venice and Genoa), while others enjoyed the patronage of Muslim rulers. Although the Byzantine Empire ended with the fall of Constantinople in 1453, the influence of the Byzantine artistic community was felt elsewhere, particularly in Italy, where it has been described as one of the sources of inspiration for the artists and architects of the Italian Renaissance.

Above: *The Byzantine style exercised a strong influence over the artists of Constantinople's trading partner, Venice. This version of* The Lion of St. Mark, *painted by Donato Veneziano (1344–82), uses the two-dimensional profile common to Byzantine art.*

1295	1308	1320	1356	1362	1362	1382	1389
Marco Polo returns to Italy from China	Teutonic Knights conquer Polish Pomerania	Polish nationalist movement asserts independence of region	The Ottoman Turks gain control of the Dardanelles	Ottoman Turks occupy Thrace	Construction starts on the Kremlin in Moscow	Moscow sacked by the Tartars	The Serbs are defeated by the Turks at Kossovo Polje

FOCUS: LEADERS
Mehmet the Conqueror

Best remembered as the Ottoman ruler who conquered Constantinople in 1453, Mehmet II was a dynamic leader who more than doubled the size of Ottoman Turkish territory in Europe during his reign. Although his conquest of Europe was halted at Belgrade in 1456, he subdued all of the Balkans and created a religious rift in the region that continues to plague Europe today.

Below: *Title page of* Schildtberger's Travels. *Captured by Turks in 1396, Schildtberger traveled around Asia for 22 years. On his return home in 1421, he was an acknowledged expert on Turkish and Tartar customs and warfare.*

Mehmet (or Mohammed) was born in 1432, the son of the Ottoman Sultan Murad II (1421–51) and an unknown slave girl from the harem. His eldest half-brother died when he was seven, and when his younger brother was strangled and Mehmet duly named as the heir apparent, he was only 12. When his father died in 1451, the 19-year-old heir became Sultan Mehmet II (1451–81). His first official action was to have his new infant half-brother murdered, to reduce the likelihood of a palace coup, and from this incident fratricide became established Ottoman policy.

Mehmet was an educated monarch, versed in several languages, and read Greek and Roman history. He also acquired a reputation for brutality, earning him a fearsome reputation in western Europe. Prisoners were frequently executed (often by being sawn in half), and during his campaigns against the Walachians in the 1460s both sides decapitated their prisoners and mounted the heads on spikes by the thousand.

His most celebrated military achievement was the capture of Constantinople in 1453, when he demonstrated a shrewd skill for siege warfare in outflanking the Byzantine defenses by transporting galleys overland, and judging the Byzantines' weakest moment to launch his final decisive attack. The victory earned him the epithet "the Conqueror," but at 21 his military reputation was only starting to grow. His victory won him a crossing point into Europe, a vital economic center, and unified the two parts of the Ottoman Empire.

1396	1402	1402	1410	1412	1416	1419	1421
Crusaders defeated at Nicopolis. End of western help for the Byzantine Empire	The Mongols capture much of Turkish Anatolia	Jan Huss appointed as a preacher of a reformist Church in Prague	Power of the Teutonic Knights is broken at the Battle of Grünwald	Jan Huss excommunicated by the Pope	Jan Huss burned at the stake, prompting a heretical revolt in Bohemia	The Hussites capture Prague and massacre the Imperial officials	Hussites decisively defeat an army of imperialist crusaders at Kutna-Hora

Both the Asian (Anatolian) and European (Rumelian) portions of Mehmet's empire were administered by a *beylerbeyi*, a son of the sultan, who in turn controlled a number of *sancaks* (counties), each administered by a local *bey*. With the administration of his empire secure under this feudal arrangement and augmented by a growing bureaucratic body, Mehmet was free to continue his military conquests. For the rest of his reign he fought a virtually ceaseless series of expansionist military campaigns in Europe and Asia.

The last remnant of Byzantine power was the Empire of Trebizond, an enclave on the Black Sea in northern Anatolia. Mehmet's army crushed local resistance, enslaved the population, and imprisoned the Greek emperor. His next targets were the despotic petty kingdoms and trading enclaves of southern Greece, the remains of both the Latin states founded after 1204, and the southern outposts of the Byzantine Empire. In 1460 he crossed into the Pelopennese to conquer the territories of the Greek despots Thomas and Demetrius, and the last Byzantine traces were destroyed within a year. Mehmet's most ambitious campaigns were along the northern frontier of Rumelia.

The limits of expansion

In 1456 he invaded Hungary. The Ottomans advanced up the River Danube to Belgrade in Serbia, but were repulsed after bitter street-fighting with Hungarians and crusaders led by Janos Hunyadi. This was the first serious check to Ottoman expansion, and although Mehmet reformed his army, other defeats were to follow at the hands of the Albanians at Abelena (1457) and the Wallachians led by none other than Count Dracula in 1462. However, these setbacks ran against the stream of Turkish conquest, and by 1459 the whole of Serbia was in Ottoman control; the rest of Greece fell in 1461. Following the death of Albanian leader Scandler Beg in 1468, Ottoman armies established control of Albania, Herzegovina, and Bosnia, and by 1481 only Montenegro and Venetian trading enclaves remained in Christian hands on the Adriatic coast. From Bosnia Muslim troops raided deep into Croatia and Carinthia, where the smoke from burning villages was reportedly seen in Venice in 1477.

Above:
Constantinople 30 years before its capture by the Turks under Sultan Mehmet II, from original plans of 1422. The city's defenses are clearly visible, including the double walls on the landward side. Santa Sophia (Hagia Sophia) is the large building to the right in the center of the map.

Facing top:
Although an educated and cultured ruler, Mehmet II secured his rule with the murder of his infant half-brother.

Ottoman power was based on the army, which became one of the most highly organized military forces in Europe. While much of the Turkish force consisted of lightly-armed levies, the military elite were the feudal Spahi cavalrymen and the Jannisaries (New Army), a professional body recruited from the subject Christian population. Mehmet also maintained a powerful artillery train and a substantial navy, which fought its own campaign against the Greek islands in the Aegean. Although the Ottoman navy was unable to capture the Christian stronghold of Rhodes during Mehmet's reign, it succeeded in turning the Black Sea into a Turkish lake. By the time he died in 1481, Mehmet's empire was a unified entity, possessed of the most powerful army in Europe, and was a serious threat to Christian Europe.

1434	1437	1453	1456	1468	1470	1526	1529
Hussite moderates make peace with Church, extremists defeated in battle	King Sigismund of Bohemia dies; renewal of Hussite rebellion	Constantinople falls to the Turks, marking the end of the Byzantine Empire	The Turks are defeated at the gates of Belgrade	The Turks conquer Bosnia and Albania	The Poles reclaim Pomerania, gaining access to the sea	The Ottomans defeat Hungary	The Ottomans besiege Vienna

CHAPTER TEN

The Birth of Renaissance Europe

The traditional view of the Renaissance was that it began in Florence, then spread through Italy to the rest of western Europe. Although this is essentially true, it is a dangerous simplification of a cultural trend that can be traced as readily in the Low Countries of northern Europe as in Italy. The advantage Italian city-states, such as Florence, possessed was that the art was accessible to the whole of society. The development of the humanist study of the classics and its dispersal throughout society inspired a revolution in art, thought, architecture, and even warfare, but many of these changes would have been impossible had it not been for the encouragement of secular patrons, such as the Medicis in Florence. This in turn was the result of the incredible wealth created by the transformation of the European economy during the 14th and 15th centuries. By the end of the century a network of mercantile and financial institutions united Europe in a way that was unimaginable a century before.

The spread of knowledge led to an end to the dark introspection that had plagued medieval Europe since the Black Death. European merchants and explorers were probing further into the unknown, and before the end of the 15th century European sailors had reached both the Americas and the Far East, ushering in the era known as the Age of Discovery. As scholars were creating a renaissance (or rebirth) of European thought and culture, the horizons of the continent were being expanded to embrace the entire world. While the humanist scholars of the 15th century liked to turn their backs on the previous millennium of European history, the Renaissance was less a miraculous rebirth of classical ideals than the culmination of the long and painful process of European cultural, political, and spiritual development. In this light, the Renaissance was the final product of the medieval world.

Europe in 1499.

Aragonese territory 1430

nominally English territory 1430

Hungarian temporary gains 1477–90

Venetian territory

Genoese territory

Hapsburg territory 1430

■ printing centers

• Portuguese African bases

NORWAY

Oslo
(Christiania)

KINGDOM OF DENMARK
(UNION OF CALMAR)

SWEDEN

Helsinki

Stockholm

Calmar

PRINCIPALITY
Novgorod

OF NOVGOROD

Moscow

MUSCOVY

BALTIC SEA

TEUTONIC KNIGHTS

Riga

Copenhagen

Lübeck

Vilna

Bremen   Hamburg   Stettin

Deventer   BRANDENBURG

Amsterdam

Cologne   Berlin

Danzig

Warsaw

POLAND-LITHUANIA

THE
KHANATE OF
GOLDEN HORDE

Leipzig

SAXONY

SILESIA

HOLY ROMAN EMPIRE

Frankfurt

Mainz   Bamberg   Prague

Nuremberg   BOHEMIA

Krakow

Lemberg

Kiev

Strasbourg

BAVARIA

Augsburg

Basel   Munich   Vienna

SWISS
CONFED.   Zurich   Salzburg   AUSTRIA

Geneva

Buda   Pest

MOLDAVIA

SEA OF
AZOV

Kaffa

SAVOY   Milan

Venice

Zagreb

HUNGARY

TRANSYLVANIA

BLACK SEA

Genoa

Pisa   Florence

Zara

Belgrade

WALLACHIA

Trebizond

Siena   PAPAL
STATES

SERBIA

BOSNIA

Varna

CORSICA

Rome

ADRIATIC SEA

Nish

Sofia

BULGARIA

Naples   NAPLES
to Aragon 1442

BENEVENTO

SARDINIA

ALBANIA

MACEDONIA

Adrianople

Istanbul
(Constantinople)

Ankara

OTTOMAN   EMPIRE

TURKISH EMIRATES

Palermo   Messina   Reggio

SICILY

AEGEAN SEA

Athens

Tarsus

Tunis

MALTA

TUNIS

RHODES
(Knights of
St. John)

CYPRUS

Tripoli

Candia   CRETE

Damascus

MEDITERRANEAN   SEA

MAMLUKE
SULTANATE

Jerusalem

Alexandria

Humanism and the Florentine Renaissance

From the mid-14th century scholars looked to the classics of the ancient world as an inspiration for the improvement of their own. They saw the era in which they lived as one of rebirth, where classical values were resurfacing after a thousand-year hiatus. In Florence, these humanist scholars popularized such views and created a cultural revival that would lead to the flowering of the Renaissance.

Petrarch (1304–74), the son of a minor city official, was born at Arezzo, to the southeast of Florence. After studying in France he attended the university at Bologna, where he studied law. In 1326 his father died and Petrarch gave up his studies to support his mother in Avignon, the seat of Pope John XXII (1316–34). The following year he was so inspired by a young lady he saw in a church that he began to compose poetry. The beauty and virtues of *Laura* became a dominant theme in his poetic writing, but he was also increasingly acknowledged as a scholar.

During his 30s he traveled extensively throughout Europe, studying classical Latin texts, and these works increasingly influenced his writings. In 1340 he was invited to Rome to become the poet laureate of the city, and his work reached a wider audience. He continued to be influenced by classical writers, although his poetry also reflects contemporary events such as the ravages of the Black Death on Italy. He influenced other Italian writers, including Boccaccio, and by the time of his death in Padua Petrarch had inspired a revival of interest in the ancient classics, earning him the posthumous title of Father of Humanism.

Shortly before Boccaccio died in 1375, he wrote that the muses had long been banished from Italy, but Dante had opened the way for their return and Petrarch restored them. Influential Italian writers following in the footsteps of Petrarch believed that they were living in an age of cultural rebirth, a revival of classical values after the ignorance and darkness of the medieval period. It was hoped that through the study of classical works and the vision of inspired secular leaders, artists, and writers, the "lost light of antiquity" could be restored to the world.

Florence eclipses Rome

The writings of Florentine humanist (or classicist) scholars developed this notion of a cultural renaissance around 1400. This vision was applied to art, and in 1430 Matteo Palmieri stated that before Giotto, painting was dead, as were true leaders and masters of men. This artistic extension of humanist beliefs encouraged other artists to experiment with new techniques, inspired by classical rather than religious influences.

The material prosperity of the city-states of Italy reached their zenith in the 14th and 15th centuries, encouraging patronage of the arts, and

sponsorship of scholars, universities, and publications. In the mid-14th century the leading humanist writer and exponent of the notion of a cultural rebirth was Coloccio Salutati. In 1375 he was appointed Chancellor of Florence at a time when the city was (in the words of Giovanni Villani) "rising and achieving great things, whereas Rome was declining." Florentine humanists saw their city as a cultural successor to ancient Rome. This eulogy for Florentine culture, prosperity, and government was reflected in the writings of

Filippo Villani, when he produced a study of famous Florentines, including Petrarch, Dante, and Giotto, "the grandfather of Italian art."

Italian humanism was essentially an academic literary movement, existing outside the political and social context of contemporary society. Early humanists, such as Petrarch, praised solitude as a state that encouraged scholarship. What changed during the 15th century was that humanist study was increasingly seen to have a purpose beyond that of purely academic scholasticism. In Florence, patronage of humanist scholars made humanism an accepted element in Florentine thought, and therefore in everyday life. Humanist scholars performed public duties on behalf of the state, such as writing official statements and speeches.

The chancellor died in 1406 and the Florentines named his humanist disciple Leonardo Bruni to be his successor in 1410, although papal duties in Rome prevented his full acceptance of the chancellorship until 1426. Bruni wanted to renew the ideals of the ancient Roman Republic, and used his humanist views to integrate his philosophy with Florentine political life. When he dedicated his translation of Plato's *Letters* to Cosimo de' Medici he was saluting a new breed of Florentine leaders created in the classical likeness. This particularly Florentine merging of cultural and social humanism was the catalyst that made the academic concept of a rebirth into the reality of the Renaissance.

Left: *The best known of Giovanni Boccaccio di Certaldo is the* Decameron, *which he wrote between 1348–53.*

Facing: *A painting of Francesco Petrarch by Justus van Gent, probably done after 1476.*

Below: *A wall enclosing the Forum of Augustus. Florence may have eclipsed Rome in the early Renaissance, but Rome was still full of Imperial Roman ruins, whose classical orders and wealth of sculpture inspired the new Italian artists.*

Early Renaissance Art in Italy

The humanist writers of the 14th and 15th centuries created an environment in Italy where the classical world was viewed as a model for the present day. Humanism was to have a profound influence on the artists, sculptors, writers, and architects of 15th- and early 16th-century Italy.

Early Renaissance art differed from all that had come before it because of several major influences. The first was a technical one: new paint pigments allowed artists to experiment with colors and textures their predecessors could only

dream of. Additionally, early 14th-century artists found a better understanding of the human form and of artistic construction than previously. From the early 15th century this developed into dramatic use of perspective, depth, and composition. The new learning of the humanists inspired painters to turn toward literature, the classics, and even philosophy for ideas, and the choice of subjects became infinitely broader.

The forerunner of the amalgam that these influences produced is usually considered to be Giotto di Bondone (*see page 153*). The Florentine painter was an innovator, and his works evoked a sense of realism lacking in earlier religious art. His artistry was praised by humanist scholars, who saw a spark of classical genius in him. During the first half of the 15th century the works produced by Italian (mainly Florentine) artists represented a striking break with the medieval past. Painters adopted the innovations introduced by Giotto, combined them with the new humanist approach, and turned them into the artistic rebirth of the early Renaissance.

From about 1380 the wealth of the city-state was controlled by an oligarchy, although the Medici family retained the reins of Florentine power for most of the 15th century itself. While Florentine patrician families supported humanist scholars, such as Salutati, they also provided patronage for painters working in the humanist style, commissioning a substantial body of secular and classically inspired painting.

A blend of developments

Masaccio (1410–28) painted in a style that was clearly influenced by Giotto. Lorenzo Monaco, whose *Adoration of the Magi* was painted c.1425, produced work that was little different from the paintings of the late 14th century. By contrast, Masaccio developed along more radical lines; his work was clearly influenced by near-contemporary Gentile de Fabriano (c.1370–1427), who became a leading exponent of the International Gothic style. The difference between the two and the true genius of Masaccio was his emphasis on realism in his depiction of the human figure at the expense of esthetic beauty.

Brunelleschi (d. 1446) was inspired by more blatantly classical subjects, while Andrea Mantegna (1431–1506) of Mantua introduced classical forms of composition into his largely religious art, combining a vivid realism with older medieval artistic conventions in a striking manner, centered around his daring foreshortening of perspective. Fra Angelico (1387–1455), a Dominican friar from Rome, combined a stylistic approach to religious painting that followed the tradition of Giotto with experimentation in the use of space and light, which inspired the later Renaissance artists.

Perhaps the greatest of the Florentine artists of the 15th century is Sandro Botticelli (1445–1510). For his use of color alone he was a master craftsman set above his Florentine peers, but he combined this with subtleties of observation and detail. In his great allegorical work *Primavera* he depicted the coming of spring, and the painting became linked to the notion of cultural rebirth or renaissance. The allegorical imagery continues throughout the painting, which in itself is inspired by the classical writings of Ovid. His *Birth of Venus* conveys a wealth of humanist imagery, much of which is lost to the modern viewer. The classical goddess is carried on her shell to the waiting arms of the Spring, representing (in its most simplistic form) the recapture of the sensual beauty of the classic form by the enfolding cloak of the Renaissance. In other words, Botticelli encapsulated the ideals of the early humanists in a visual form.

From Giotto to Botticelli the artistic transformation inspired by the humanism of the late medieval classical scholars is striking. Even more impressive was the burst of artistic creativity produced during the century following the death of Plutarch, and the appointment of Salutati as Chancellor of Florence (1374/5). In the same way as humanism affected public life in Florence and then Italy, it similarly inspired patrons and artists of the same time and place, and created a cultural flowering that has remained unmatched ever since.

Facing: *The new classically inspired art found daring form in the work of Andrea Mantegna. His* Saint Luke Evangelist *shows off his daring foreshortening of perspective.*

Below: *The painting that became most closely linked to the cultural rebirth— Sandro Botticelli's* Primavera (Spring).

The Portuguese and the Age of Discovery

Under the patronage of Prince Henry the Navigator (1393–1460), Portuguese explorers took their first tentative steps beyond the shores of Europe and the Mediterranean. From 1432–60 Prince Henry encouraged his sea captains to explore further south down the coast of Africa. By the end of the 15th century Portuguese explorers had reached India and carved out a new route to the Orient, while the Spanish were establishing their first tentative colonies in the Americas.

Above: *Prince Henry the Navigator of Portugal taught navigational skills and commissioned sailors to explore and open up Portugal's trade routes to the Far East.*

During the Reconquista of Spain and Portugal from the 11th century, as the Spanish recovered territory from the Moors, they also captured Arab centers of learning. These Arab centers contained copies of Greek scholarly works that had been lost to Christian Europe for centuries. Along with Arab scientific works they were translated into Latin, and provided a wealth of knowledge on astronomy, cartography, mathematics, and navigation. As these were being digested a revolution in late medieval shipbuilding produced the *caravel*, a small and responsive vessel that was well suited to the challenges of lengthy voyages. This became the principal type of ship used on 15th-century voyages of discovery, although it was eventually replaced by the larger carrack (or *não*). The twin tools of better ships and navigational knowledge were now available to the 15th-century mariner.

Prince Henry, the son of King João (John) I of Portugal (1385–1433), turned his back on the politics of the Portuguese court to provide patronage for maritime exploration, and to further the study of navigation and cartography, and in the process encouraged his small nation to become a leading maritime mercantile power. Although he never left Portugal, he became the leading exponent of voyages of discovery as a means of expanding European secular power.

His first commissioned voyage of exploration was in 1431, when he sent Gonçalo Cabral to find some mythical islands in the Atlantic. Over the next decade, while Cabral discovered the Azores and claimed them for Portugal, Gil Eannes ventured down the African coast by way of Madeira and the Canary Islands, and by 1434 passed the psychological barrier of the Sea of Darkness (now Cape Bojador on the northwest African coast). A dynastic dispute in Portugal brought a temporary halt to Prince Henry's patronage, but in 1455 he commissioned Alvise da Cadamosto to sail past Cape Bojador and explore further down the coast. Like all of the prince's voyages, the expedition was to pay for itself through trading with the people they encountered. In 1456 a storm blew his ships out into the Atlantic, where the Portuguese explorer discovered the Cape Verde Islands. By the death of Prince Henry in 1460 the explorer Diogo Gomes had pushed the limits of European exploration as far south as the Gambia river and the Guinea Coast.

The pace quickens

Portuguese patronage of exploration was continued after Henry's death by his nephew, Alfonso V and his son, João II the Perfect (1481–95). It was under the sponsorship of the latter that the great breakthroughs of Portuguese exploration were made. In June 1482 Diogo Cão passed the limits set by Diogo Gomes, rounded the corner of West Africa, and reached the mouth of the Congo. His ship had been supplied with stone markers, or *padrãos*, inscribed with the king's name, to reinforce Portugal's claim to the territory discovered. He erected one at the mouth of the Congo, then continued south down the African coast, reaching Cape Santa Maria in modern Angola before turning for home in late 1483. Four years later Bartolomeu Dias passed the southernmost *padrão* and reached the Cape of Good Hope, on the southern tip of Africa. Dias even ventured further east into the Indian Ocean before his crew refused to go any further.

The voyage of Christopher Columbus in 1492–93 convinced the Spanish that the Genoese explorer had discovered the fabled spice islands of the Indies, although he had actually found the Bahamas. Eager to protect their discovery, the Spanish urged the signing of the Treaty of Tordesillas (1494) which divided the world into Spanish and Portuguese spheres: Spain could explore to the west of a line bisecting the Atlantic Ocean, leaving Portugal everything to the east. The race to find a sea route to the Indies had started. In 1497 the Portuguese explorer Vasco da Gama rounded the Cape of Good Hope and entered the Indian Ocean, reaching the Indian port of Calicut in May 1498. Eighteen months later the explorer returned to Lisbon with the first spices carried from the Orient by ship. In the process he broke through the medieval boundaries that had existed for a thousand years, and began a process of European involvement with the rest of the world… for better or for worse.

MADEIRA

Lisbon

CANARY ISLANDS

Cape Bojador

Lagos

Cape Blanc

Portuguese explorers of Africa

→ Gil Eannes 1433 and 1434
→ Alvise da Cadamosto 1455 and 1456
→ Diogo Gomes 1458
→ Diogo Cão's first voyage 1482–3
→ Diogo Cão's second voyage 1485
→ Bartolomeu Dias 1487–8
⚑ Padrãos placed by Cão and Dias

Cape Palmas

Axim
Elmina

Right: *Gil Eannes was one of Henry the Navigator's explorers and the man who first passed the barrier of the "Sea of Darkness."*

ATLANTIC OCEAN

Mouth of the Congo
1. Diogo Cão

Cape St. Mary
2. Diogo Cão

Monte Negro
3. Diogo Cão

Diogo Cão perished to the south of Cape Cross.

Cape Cross
4. Diogo Cão

Cape Derberg
1. Bartolomeu Dias

Cape of Good Hope
3. Bartolomeu Dias

2. Bartolomeu Dias

INDIAN OCEAN

The Renaissance Dawn

The Renaissance was born in late 14th century Florence, and it came of age in 15th-century Italy, then matured toward the end of the century as it swept through the rest of Europe. At the same time a similar cultural transformation was taking place in northern Europe, inspired by French and Flemish humanists. By the close of the 15th century the Renaissance had transformed Europe into the cultural base on which modern European civilization is founded.

Below: *The Flagellation of Christ by Piero della Francesca is a work indicative of the new cooler look of Renaissance painting before the advent of Leonardo da Vinci, Raphael, and Michelangelo.*

Taken in its most basic form, humanism revolved around the study of human affairs, a new breed of academic scholarship grounded in the classic writings of the ancient world. This emphasis on language, philosophy, and literature can be traced to the influence of Petrarch (1304–74), particularly in Italy, but other humanist influences were at work that ensured that the "new learning" of these scholars reached beyond the confines of Florence or the Italian peninsula. Although the traditional view is that the cultural upheaval of the Renaissance began in Florence, other parts of Italy proved receptive to humanist ideas.

Rome was dominated by the Vatican and the

reconcile the doctrines of the Church with the overt paganism of the classical world.

The Neopolitan court provided patronage to humanist scholars, such as Antonio Beccadelli and Lorenzo Valla, who combined the classical studies of northern scholars with an appreciation of Arab humanism. Further north, the Sforza Dukes of Milan encouraged classical study from 1450, particularly under the guidance of Ludovico Sforza during the last decades of the century. In neighboring Venice, despite the city's contacts with Greek humanists, a lack of patronage delayed its particular cultural renaissance until the Venetian renaissance flowered during the early 16th century.

Renaissance gathers pace

In northern Europe, Paris, London, Oxford, Strasbourg, Brussels, and Deventer all became centers of humanist development, most developing independently of the classical revival in Italy. This northern strain of humanism culminated in the scholarship of Erasmus (c.1466–1536) and contributed to its own artistic and architectural revival. The earliest French humanist writings date from the late 14th century, although the work of scholars like Jean de Montreuil in Paris had little impact on French society. Paris became a true center for humanist study in the mid-15th century when Gregorio Tifernate's teachings influenced the French court in Paris.

Unlike the Italians, many French humanists had problems reconciling the study of pagan classical writers with Christianity, and debated the relationship between the two throughout the late 15th century. The French humanists were dominated by Guilaume Budé (1468–1540), one of

Church, which provided patronage for artists and writers, as long as they adhered to accepted doctrines. Humanists such as Poggio Bracciolini worked for the papal curia and helped to

the leading classical philologists of the century. In England humanism centered around the study of Greek, with Thomas Linacre (c.1460–1524) proving to be one of the greatest Greek scholars of his age, but the approach taken by Thomas More (1478–1535) was radically different; he emphasized humanism as a means of seeking truth, and therefore of achieving Christian revelation.

Scholastic humanism was slow to develop in the Netherlands and Germany, where it was used to harness a growing sense of nationalism and opposition to Roman influence. The influence of the Dutch-born Erasmus consolidated this northern approach to humanism as a vehicle for religious understanding. Like More, he was loyal to the established Church, but his works exposed the flaws in the Catholic system, and provided ammunition for the reformers who followed him. The humanism of these northern scholars also inspired an artistic and architectural revival, although most of this post-dates the end of the 15th century.

The work of Dutch, German, and Flemish painters such as Jan van Eyck (c.1390–1441), Geertgen (c.1460–90), and Hans Holbein the Elder (1460–1524), as well as the mid-15th century triumph of the International Gothic movement, shows an independence of Italian renaissance development that is often overlooked by art historians seeking a clear linear development of Renaissance art. These artists painted from a human perspective, even in religious works, making them true practitioners of humanist art. Albrecht Dürer (1471–1528) brought an uncompromising realism to his art (*see picture on page 183*), and his painting was demonstrably influenced by the development of his native Nuremberg into a center for the printing of humanist texts. For it was in Nuremberg, in 1455, that Johannes Gutenberg developed moveable type and thus founded the process of modern mechanical printing, capable—unlike the monks of the past—of producing multiple identical copies of a book for mass consumption. A revolution of unparalleled import, it firmly shut the door on the medieval era.

Following the production of the Gutenberg Bible, Germany became a leading producer of printed books, and from 1470 humanist texts were the best-sellers of their day. This in turn led to the establishment of northern Europe as the center for humanist thought and renaissance culture from the end of the 15th century. By 1500 the cultural Renaissance had covered the whole of western Europe, ushering in a new phase of European history; replacing the scorned values of medievalism with the humanity of the new age.

Left: *Many consider Michelangelo's* David *to be the finest expression of a humanist sensibility that began in the later medieval period, although it is also clearly an expression of the new classicism in Renaissance art.*

FOCUS: SOCIETY
Banking

During the period from 1150 to 1400, financial transactions developed from simple money-lending into a complex network of international banking institutions. Investment, exchange, and loans were all introduced during the late medieval period, resulting in a financial sophistication that answered the developing needs of an increasingly complex medieval economy.

Banking first emerged during the 12th century as a result of the growing level of trade within feudal Europe. From the fall of Rome in the fifth century until the 11th century, Europeans had struggled for survival, and the agrarian and subsistence-based economy did little to foster economic growth. The urban revival of the 11th century created a demand for economic institutions that could support this growth. Since the Church condemned the practice of usury (lending money and charging interest on the loan) among Christians, Jews performed the valuable role of money-lenders to nobles and the Crown, until such time as pogroms throughout Europe ended their activities. From then on, the international religious orders serviced the needs of Europe's rulers, but these were unsuited to the needs of new mercantile communities, and getting around the Church's proscription would require a more sophisticated approach

By the mid-12th century several money-lenders in northern Italy had developed into formal banking institutions. "Bank" derives from the Italian *banca* (table), reflecting the makeshift nature of these first banking enterprises, set up in the squares of Florence, Genoa, and Venice. Early bankers safeguarded the money of their customers and provided a means of local exchange. The real breakthrough came when bankers used the deposits they received for investment. This, combined with a network of alliances with other bankers, set the scene for the development of medieval banking.

By 1300 Italian bankers were accepting deposits, investing money in business or property, transferring funds from one banking house to another, and extending loans or credit to merchants and rulers. The Italian city-states created legal safeguards to monitor these transactions through public notaries, and contracts between bankers and their clients were enforced by the city judiciary, which created a level of confidence in banking houses. Although a client took the risk that a banker might fail, he was assured that he could not be defrauded by him.

The Church tries to intervene

The Church prohibition of usury extended to payment of interest by a bank to a client who had deposited money. The impetus for deposits to be made came through the development of formal business agreements between depositors and bankers. An agreement of this kind (known as a *commenda*) involved one party providing capital for a venture, while the other guaranteed a return on the investment. Designed for commercial

Below: *A mint at work; an engraving after a woodcut of c.1487.*

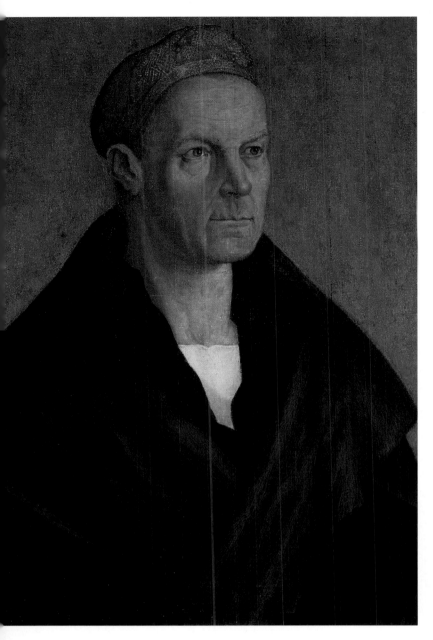

maintained agreements with one other. It meant that a merchant could agree to pay an artisan for goods without either party handling money (like the modern checking system).

By the 14th century a number of the larger Italian and Flemish banks maintained agreements with each other and with subsidiary financial houses in France, England, and Germany, principally those of the Fugger family. This created a European network of banking and permitted the transfer of funds from one country to another. Because of the need to deal in different currencies, the agreement between the various banks included details of exchange rates. In theory, exchange rates would remain static if the various national coins remained on comparable levels of parity. The realities of foreign exchange was that secular rulers occasionally devalued their coinage (for instance by reducing its silver content), which in turn led to a readjustment of these international exchange rates.

enterprises, the system was applied to banking, and by paying interest on an investment rather than on a deposit (which the Church regarded as a loan), no religious transgression was made.

This system of investment banking created a climate where clients wished to deposit money with the banking houses, because it generated money, whereas keeping it in a safe did not. This form of banking was by no means universal, and in many cases the client benefited from the initial deposit (the principal) by taking advantage of other services that the bank offered. Temporary loans (overdrafts) could be made, and funds could be transferred without the client needing to physically handle any money. The transfer system worked within the banking house itself, that is, between the accounts of individual clients, or between different banking houses who

From the 15th century investors in one country could support ventures in another, and rulers could borrow money from banks in other countries. Bills of Exchange became common between banks in different countries, and leading bankers had to constantly update these international agreements in line with the latest political or financial developments. The growing complexity of international investment banking created phenomenal wealth for banking families such as the Medicis, but also led to spectacular crashes, particularly when foreign rulers defaulted on loans. By the end of the medieval period banks had become institutions able to control the well-being of countries, and this laid the groundwork for the growth of a post-medieval capitalist economy.

1408	1412	1420	1425	1426	1431	1434	1434
Donatello produces his statues of *David* and *St. John*	Filippo Brunelleschi produces his *Rules of Perspective*	Brunelleschi creates the cupoa of Florence Cathedral	Lorenzo Monaco paints the *Adoration of the Magi*	Leonardo Bruni becomes full-time humanist Chancellor of Florence	Henry the Navigator sponsors first Portuguese voyage of exploration	Portuguese pass through the Sea of Darkness off the West African coast	The Medici family gain control of Florence

Lorenzo de' Medici

The Medici governed Florence for more than a century—a dynastic rule founded on banking and political acumen rather than on force. Lorenzo de' Medici the Magnificent used his skills as a politician and statesman to dominate Florence and, as a patron of the arts, encouraged the development of the Florentine Renaissance.

The Medici rose to prominence in the 14th century as merchants and city administrators. At the death of Giovanni di Bicci de' Medici (1360–1429), who established the family fortune, the Medici Bank was one of the most powerful financial institutions in Italy. Florence—a republic in name only in the early 15th century—was dominated by the oligarchy of the Albizzi. Cosimo de' Medici (1389–64), who succeeded Giovanni, challenged Rinaldo Albizzi for control of the city. In 1434 he succeeded and began a domination of Florence that lasted 30 years.

Cosimo never ruled directly, but preferred instead to govern through loyal supporters. Both the Medici banking empire and the city prospered under his stewardship, and the family became one of the most influential in Italy. His patronage also encouraged artists, sculptors, and writers of the time to make Florence their home.

Following his death in 1464, Florentine and Medici affairs were run for five years by his gout-ridden eldest son Piero, whose financial policies proved unpopular and harmed the bank's prestige. Piero married his son Lorenzo into the Orsini family, one of the oldest patrician families of Rome. A year later, Piero died and young Lorenzo became head of Medici Florence in 1469.

Lorenzo de' Medici (1449–92) has become closely associated with the development of the Renaissance, but he only followed the family's policy of patronage. He, too, preferred to control the government from a distance… at least, at first. Lorenzo commissioned fine new buildings, and held a series of carnivals and tournaments. He encountered no serious opposition until 1478, when members of the old Florentine family of Pazzi conspired against him.

The Pazzi joined forces with Girolamo Riario, nephew of the Pope, and attempted to assassinate Lorenzo and stage a coup. Lorenzo, who was celebrating Easter Mass, barely escaped with his life, but his brother Giuliano was murdered at the cathedral altar. The Florentine mob, loyal to the Medici, hunted down and killed the Pazzi conspirators, and the Archbishop of Pisa, who had supported the coup, was summarily hanged. Pope Sixtus IV (1471–84) was complicit in the plot and he retalliated by excommunicating the whole Florentine State. Florence declared war on Sixtus, and papal and Neopolitan troops invaded Tuscany. It looked as though Florence might fall, until Lorenzo escaped and negotiated a peace with King Ferrante of Naples. Stripped of his ally, the Pope was forced to make peace with Florence.

Dictatorial control

The Pazzi crisis marked a watershed in Lorenzo's administration. His legislation of 1480 institutionalized Medici control and from that point he ruled Florence directly and also expanded his interest in the arts. In commissioning artists like Verrocchio, Botticelli, and Lippi, he established himself as the leading patron of early Renaissance painters, while the humanist scholars Politian, Scala, Pulci, and Ficino had a pervasive influence on Florentine life · through his support.

His patronage came at a price, however. Through neglect of his banking interests, by his death in 1492 the Medici empire was virtually bankrupt. Two years later, the whole family was exiled from Florence in a French-backed coup, leaving Girolamo Savonarola (*page 149*) as virtual dictator. More than for his achievements as a statesman, Lorenzo de' Medici is remembered as the patron who inspired the cultural whirlwind that blew away the medieval world and replaced it with the wonders of the Renaissance.

Facing: *Lorenzo de' Medici earned his soubriquet of "the Magnificent" as much for his patronage of writers, painters, sculptors, and architects—who transformed Florence into Europe's most glorious city—as for his skill as a politician. Bust by Antonio Pollaiuolo (c.1430–1498).*

1435	1452	1455	1456	1456	1460	1460	1469
Rogier van der Weyden paints his *Descent from the Cross*	Birth of Leonardo da Vinci	Production of the Gutenberg Bible (The Constance Mass)	The Cape Verde Islands discovered	Paolo Uccello paints *The Battle of San Romano*	Diogo Gomes discovers the coast of Guinea	Work begins on the Palazzo Pitti in Florence	Lorenzo de' Medici effectively becomes the ruler of Florence

FOCUS: WARFARE

The Swiss—Mercenary Masters of Warfare

When King Charles VIII of France (1483–98) marched into Italy in 1494, he changed the course of both warfare and history. While his army still retained medieval characteristics, such as its emphasis on armored knights (*gendarmes*), the power of his army was concentrated in two new military tools; a train of powerful mobile artillery, and divisions of Swiss pikemen, regarded as the finest infantry in Europe.

The Swiss established their military reputation when they defeated the invading army of Duke Charles the Bold of Burgundy in 1475–7. It was enhanced by a string of victories in the Italian Wars that followed Charles's invasion of 1494, and continued until their defeat by a Spanish and German army at Bicocca (1522). Swiss mercenaries were in operation as late as the 18th century, and still form the bodyguard of the Pope within the Vatican City today.

The origins of the Swiss Confederation lay in the Eternal Alliance forged in the Treaty of Rütli (1291), which united the cantons of Schwyz, Uri, and Unterwalden. A defensive arrangement, it helped resist Hapsburg Austrian domination of the region and, following the Confederate victory at Morgarten (1315), other cantons joined the alliance. During the 14th century the three "Forest Cantons" were joined by Lucerne (1319), Zurich (1351), Glarus and Zug (1352), and Bern (1353). In the face of this unity, the Hapsburgs renounced any claims over the Swiss.

By the time of the Burgundian Wars the original cantons were closely allied with neighboring ones, and maintained military alliances with the states of Lorraine and Strasbourg. The Swiss Confederation crushed the Burgundians in a series of three battles; Grandson (1476), Morat (1476), and Nancy (1477), demonstrating a ruthless mastery of the battlefield.

1477	1478	1480	1482	1484	1484	1485-95	1487
Sandro Botticelli paints *Primavera*	Foundation of the Spanish Inquisition	Russians stop paying tribute to Mongols	Diogo Cão reaches the mouth of the Congo river	Botticelli paints *The Birth of Venus*	Albrecht Dürer paints his *Self Portrait*	Ivan III brings Italian architects to Moscow	Bartolomeu Dias discovers the Cape of Good Hope

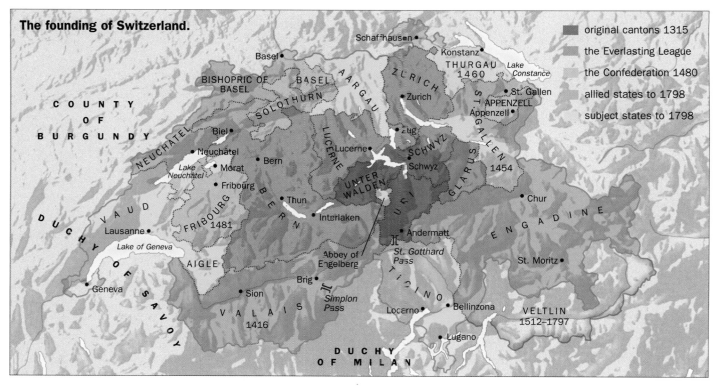

The founding of Switzerland.

The founding of Switzerland.

original cantons 1315
the Everlasting League
the Confederation 1480
allied states to 1798
subject states to 1798

Schaffhausen
Konstanz
Basel
THURGAU *Lake*
1460 *Constance*
BISHOPRIC OF BASEL
BASEL
ZÜRICH
AARGAU
SOLOTHURN
Zurich
St. Gallen
Appenzell
APPENZELL
ST. GALLEN
COUNTY OF BURGUNDY
NEUCHÂTEL
Biel
Zug
LUCERNE
Lucerne
Schwyz
SCHWYZ
GLARUS
1454
Neuchâtel
Bern
UNTER WALDEN
URI
Lake Neuchâtel
Morat
Chur
ENGADINE
Fribourg
Thun
VAUD
DUCHY
BERN
Interlaken
Andermatt
Lausanne
FRIBOURG
1481
Abbey of Engelberg
St. Gotthard Pass
St. Moritz
Lake of Geneva
AIGLE
Brig
TICINO
OF
Geneva
Sion
Simplon Pass
Locarno
Bellinzona
VELTLIN
1512–1797
SAVOY
VALAIS
1416
Lugano
DUCHY OF MILAN

Following the Burgundian Wars, the Swiss Confederation expanded to include the cantons of Fribourg and Solothurn (1481), Basel and Schaffhausen (1501), and Appenzel (1513). Alliances were also forged with neighboring French- and Italian-speaking regions (such as Ticino, Vaud, and the Valais) and these were eventually incorporated into the Swiss Confederation.

A fierce reputation

The demonstration of Swiss military skill against the Burgundians led to offers of mercenary employment from other states. In 1479 an agreement with Louis XI of France (1461–83) led to the hiring of 6,300 Swiss, and by the end of the 15th century the French Crown was the greatest employer of Swiss mercenaries. Switzerland—largely mountainous—was a poor region, and the income from mercenary employment proved attractive for the Swiss cantonal governments over the next half-century.

The qualities the Swiss brought to the late 15th century battlefield included a high level of morale (the Swiss had a reputation for never running away from a fight), professionalism, ferocity (refusing quarter to the enemy), and new tactical doctrines. Primarily the Swiss soldier was a pikeman, and formations of successive ranks of Swiss pikemen presented a hedge of these 12–16-foot-long weapons that was impenetrable to cavalry. Their favored formation was a deep block

of men, with the pikemen supported by crossbowmen and handgunners.

Unlike other European troops of the period, the Swiss used the pike as an offensive weapon. Their favorite tactic was a rapid advance, a unique combination of speed and crushing impact that negated any firepower advantage the enemy might have. As with all mercenaries, Swiss loyalty could be bought and sold The phrase *Point d'argent, point de Suisse* (no money, no Swiss) became common by the end of the century and, as the best foot troops in Europe, the Swiss demanded a high price for their services.

The 1494 French invasion of Italy marked a transition. For most of the 15th century successive French monarchs were concerned with enforcing their authority over powerful and virtually independent French nobles, such as the Duke of Burgundy. Charles VIII was the first French king who was able to influence external affairs, and his aspirations to the Kingdom of Naples mark the start of a French involvement in Italy that continued well into the 16th century. It also marked an end to the isolation of the Italian states. The French army that marched through Italy to Naples in 1494 alarmed the rest of Europe by its modern composition (Swiss pikemen, handgunners, cavalry, and artillery) and its professionalism. Charles VIII's invasion raised the curtain on a new age of warfare, where shining knights and chivalry no longer had a place. The medieval period of Europe was finally over.

Facing: *Arnold von Winkelried, a Swiss patriot at the Battle of Sempach (July 1386), by engaging as many Austrian spearmen as possible, allowed his comrades to push through a breach in the Austrian lines and win a decisive victory. From an illustration published in London c.1890.*

1492	1492	1494	1494	1495	1498	1498	1519
Christopher Columbus discovers the Bahamas	Leonardo da Vinci draws his flying machine	End of Medici domination of Florence	The treaty of Tordesillas is signed between Portugal and Spain	Leonardo da Vinci paints *The Last Supper*	Michaelangelo produces his sculpture of the Pietà	Vasco da Gama reaches India, establishing a sea route to the Indies	Death of Leonardo da Vinci

187

GENEALOGICAL TABLES

The Descendants of Charlemagne the Great

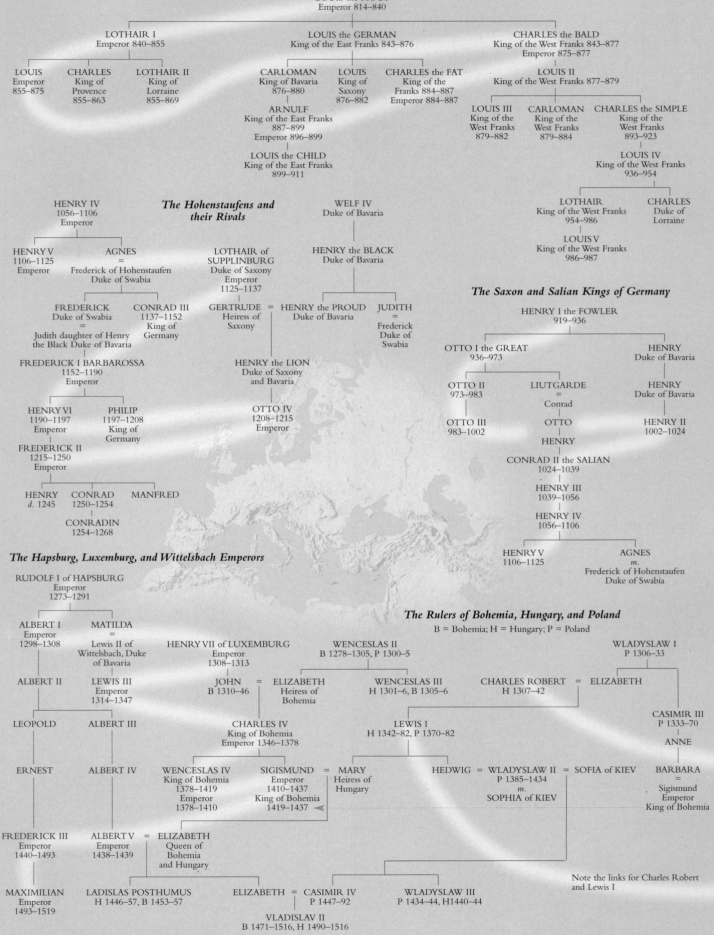

CHARLEMAGNE
King of the Franks 768–814
Emperor 800–814

LOUIS the PIOUS
Emperor 814–840

LOTHAIR I
Emperor 840–855

LOUIS the GERMAN
King of the East Franks 843–876

CHARLES the BALD
King of the West Franks 843–877
Emperor 875–877

LOUIS
Emperor
855–875

CHARLES
King of
Provence
855–863

LOTHAIR II
King of
Lorraine
855–869

CARLOMAN
King of Bavaria
876–880

LOUIS
King of
Saxony
876–882

CHARLES the FAT
King of the
Franks 884–887
Emperor 884–887

LOUIS II
King of the West Franks 877–879

ARNULF
King of the East Franks
887–899
Emperor 896–899

LOUIS III
King of the
West Franks
879–882

CARLOMAN
King of the
West Franks
879–884

CHARLES the SIMPLE
King of the
West Franks
893–923

LOUIS the CHILD
King of the East Franks
899–911

LOUIS IV
King of the West Franks
936–954

LOTHAIR
King of the West Franks
954–986

CHARLES
Duke of
Lorraine

LOUIS V
King of the West Franks
986–987

The Hohenstaufens and their Rivals

HENRY IV
1056–1106
Emperor

HENRY V
1106–1125
Emperor

AGNES
=
Frederick of Hohenstaufen
Duke of Swabia

**LOTHAIR of
SUPPLINBURG**
Duke of Saxony
Emperor
1125–1137

WELF IV
Duke of Bavaria

HENRY the BLACK
Duke of Bavaria

FREDERICK
Duke of Swabia
=
Judith daughter of Henry
the Black Duke of Bavaria

CONRAD III
1137–1152
King of
Germany

GERTRUDE =
Heiress of
Saxony

HENRY the PROUD
Duke of Bavaria

JUDITH
=
Frederick
Duke of
Swabia

FREDERICK I BARBAROSSA
1152–1190
Emperor

HENRY the LION
Duke of Saxony
and Bavaria

HENRY VI
1190–1197
Emperor

PHILIP
1197–1208
King of
Germany

OTTO IV
1208–1215
Emperor

FREDERICK II
1215–1250
Emperor

HENRY
d. 1245

CONRAD
1250–1254

MANFRED

CONRADIN
1254–1268

The Saxon and Salian Kings of Germany

HENRY I the FOWLER
919–936

OTTO I the GREAT
936–973

HENRY
Duke of Bavaria

OTTO II
973–983

LIUTGARDE
=
Conrad

HENRY
Duke of Bavaria

OTTO III
983–1002

OTTO

HENRY II
1002–1024

HENRY

CONRAD II the SALIAN
1024–1039

HENRY III
1039–1056

HENRY IV
1056–1106

HENRY V
1106–1125

AGNES
m.
Frederick of Hohenstaufen
Duke of Swabia

The Hapsburg, Luxemburg, and Wittelsbach Emperors

RUDOLF I of HAPSBURG
Emperor
1273–1291

ALBERT I
Emperor
1298–1308

MATILDA
=
Lewis II of
Wittelsbach, Duke
of Bavaria

HENRY VII of LUXEMBURG
Emperor
1308–1313

The Rulers of Bohemia, Hungary, and Poland
B = Bohemia; H = Hungary; P = Poland

WENCESLAS II
B 1278–1305, P 1300–5

WLADYSLAW I
P 1306–33

ALBERT II

LEWIS III
Emperor
1314–1347

JOHN =
B 1310–46

ELIZABETH
Heiress of
Bohemia

WENCESLAS III
H 1301–6, B 1305–6

CHARLES ROBERT =
H 1307–42

ELIZABETH

LEOPOLD

ALBERT III

CHARLES IV
King of Bohemia
Emperor 1346–1378

LEWIS I
H 1342–82, P 1370–82

CASIMIR III
P 1333–70

ANNE

ERNEST

ALBERT IV

WENCESLAS IV
King of Bohemia
1378–1419
Emperor
1378–1410

SIGISMUND =
Emperor
1410–1437
King of Bohemia
1419–1437 ◄

MARY
Heiress of
Hungary

HEDWIG = **WLADYSLAW II** = **SOFIA of KIEV**
P 1385–1434
m.
SOPHIA of KIEV

BARBARA
=
Sigismund
Emperor
King of Bohemia

FREDERICK III
Emperor
1440–1493

ALBERT V =
Emperor
1438–1439

ELIZABETH
Queen of
Bohemia
and Hungary

MAXIMILIAN
Emperor
1493–1519

LADISLAS POSTHUMUS
H 1446–57, B 1453–57

ELIZABETH = **CASIMIR IV**
P 1447–92

WLADYSLAW III
P 1434–44, H1440–44

Note the links for Charles Robert
and Lewis I

VLADISLAV II
B 1471–1516, H 1490–1516

GENEALOGICAL TABLES

The Capetian Kings of the Senior Line

HUGH CAPET
987–996

ROBERT II the
PIOUS 996–1031

HENRY I
1031–1060 — ROBERT
Duke of Burgundy

PHILIP I
1060–1108 — HUGH
Count of Vermandois

LOUIS VI the FAT
1108–1137

LOUIS VII
1137–1180 — ROBERT
Count of Dreux — PETER
Lord of Courtenay

PHILIP II AUGUSTUS
1180–1223 — ROBERT
Count of Dreux

LOUIS VIII
1223–1226 — ROBERT
Count of Dreux — PETER
Duke of Brittany

LOUIS IX
(ST. LOUIS)
1226–1270 — ROBERT
Count of Artois — ALPHONSE
Count of Poitiers
Count of Toulouse — CHARLES
Count of Anjou
Count of Provence
King of Sicily

PHILIP III
1270–1285 — ROBERT
Count of Clermont

PHILIP IV the FAIR
1285–1314 — CHARLES
Count of Valois — LOUIS
Count of Evreux

LOUIS X
1314–1316 — PHILIP V
1316–1322 — CHARLES IV
1322–1328 — ISABELLE
=
Edward II
King of England — PHILIP
Count of Valois
King of France
1328–1350 — PHILIP
Count of Evreux
=
Jeanne
Queen of Navarre

JEANNE
Queen of Navarre

EDWARD III
King of England
Claimant to throne
of France

CHARLES the BAD
Count of Evreux
King of Navarre

The Norman and Early Plantagenet Kings of England

WILLIAM I the CONQUEROR 1066–1087

ROBERT
Duke of
Normandy — WILLIAM II
1087–1100 — HENRY I
1100–1135 — ADELE
=
Stephen
Count of Blois

WILLIAM
Duke of
Normandy

WILLIAM — MATILDA
=
Geoffrey
Plantagenet
Count of Anjou — STEPHEN
1135–1154

HENRY II
1154–1189

HENRY
The Young
King — RICHARD I
1189–1199 — GEOFFREY
Duke of
Brittany — JOHN
1199–1216 — MATILDA
=
HENRY the LION
Duke of Saxony and
Bavaria

ARTHUR
Duke of
Brittany — HENRY III
1216–1272 — RICHARD
Earl of Cornwall
King of Germany — OTTO IV
Emperor

EDWARD I
1272–1307 — EDMUND
Earl of Lancaster

EDWARD II
1307–1327 — THOMAS
Earl of Lancaster — HENRY
Earl of Lancaster

EDWARD III
1327–1377

HENRY
Duke of Lancaster

BLANCHE
=
John of Ghent

The Valois Kings of France

PHILIP VI
1328–1350

JOHN the GOOD
1350–1364

CHARLES V
1364–1380 — LOUIS
Duke of Anjou — PHILIP the BOLD
Duke of Burgundy

LOUIS
Duke of Orléans — CHARLES VI
1380–1422 — LOUIS
Duke of Anjou — JOHN the
FEARLESS
Duke of Burgundy

CHARLES
Duke of Orléans — CATHERINE
=
Henry V
King of England — CHARLES VII
1422–1461 = MARY — RÉNE the GOOD
Duke of Anjou
Duke of Lorraine
Titular King of Naples — LOUIS III
Duke of Anjou — PHILIP the GOOD
Duke of Burgundy

LOUIS
Duke of Orléans
King of France
1498–1515 — HENRY VI
King of
England — CHARLES
Duke of Berry — LOUIS XI
1461–1483 — MARGARET
=
Henry VI
King of England — CHARLES the BOLD
(the RASH)
Duke of Burgundy

CHARLES VIII
1483–1498

The Later Plantagenet Kings of England

EDWARD III
1327–1377

EDWARD
The Black Prince — LIONEL
Duke of Clarence — EDMUND
Duke of York — JOHN of GHENT
Duke of lancaster

RICHARD II
1377–1399 — PHILIPPA
=
Edmund Mortimer
Earl of the March — EDWARD
Duke of
York — JOHN BEAUFORT
Marquis of Somerset — HENRY IV
1399–1413

ROGER MORTIMER
Earl of the March — JOHN BEAUFORT
Marquis of Somerset — HENRY V
1413–1422

EDMUND
MORTIMER
Earl of the March — ANNE MORTIMER = RICHARD
Earl of
Cambridge — MARGARET
BEAUFORT
=
Edmund Tudor — HENRY VI
1422–1461

RICHARD
Duke of York

EDWARD IV
1461–1483 — RICHARD III
1483–1485

EDWARD V
1483 — RICHARD
Duke of York — ELIZABETH = HENRY VII
1485–1509 — EDWARD
Prince of Wales

Succession to the Kingdom of Naples and Sicily from Charles of Anjou

CHARLES II
King of Naples
and Sicily

CHARLES MARTEL — ROBERT
King of Naples
and Sicily — JOHN
Duke of
Durazzo

CHARLES ROBERT
King of Hungary — CHARLES
Duke of
Calabria — CHARLES
Duke of
Durazzo — LOUIS
Duke of
Durazzo

LEWIS I
King of Hungary — JOANNA I
Queen of Naples — MARGARET = CHARLES III
King of Naples
King of Hungary

LADISLAS
King of Naples — JOANNA II
Queen of Naples

189

GENEALOGICAL TABLES

The Spanish and Portuguese Kings from the Tenth to the Thirteenth Century

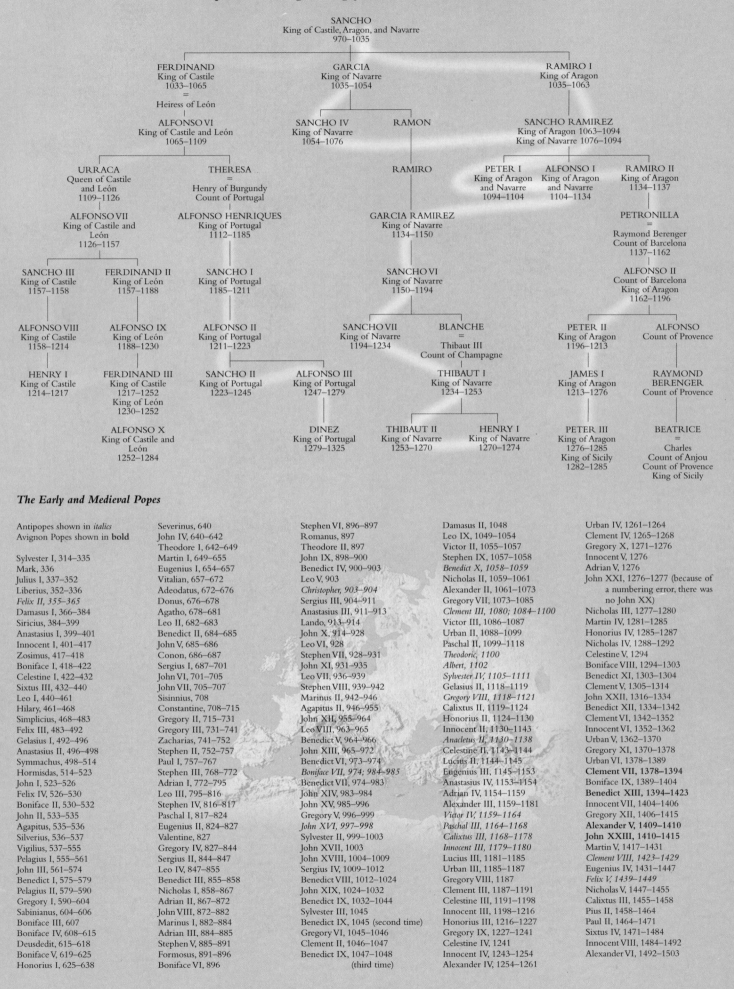

SANCHO
King of Castile, Aragon, and Navarre
970–1035

FERDINAND
King of Castile
1033–1065
=
Heiress of León

GARCIA
King of Navarre
1035–1054

RAMIRO I
King of Aragon
1035–1063

ALFONSO VI
King of Castile and León
1065–1109

SANCHO IV
King of Navarre
1054–1076

RAMON

SANCHO RAMIREZ
King of Aragon 1063–1094
King of Navarre 1076–1094

URRACA
Queen of Castile
and León
1109–1126

THERESA
=
Henry of Burgundy
Count of Portugal

RAMIRO

PETER I
King of Aragon
and Navarre
1094–1104

ALFONSO I
King of Aragon
and Navarre
1104–1134

RAMIRO II
King of Aragon
1134–1137

ALFONSO VII
King of Castile and
León
1126–1157

ALFONSO HENRIQUES
King of Portugal
1112–1185

GARCIA RAMIREZ
King of Navarre
1134–1150

PETRONILLA
=
Raymond Berenger
Count of Barcelona
1137–1162

SANCHO III
King of Castile
1157–1158

FERDINAND II
King of León
1157–1188

SANCHO I
King of Portugal
1185–1211

SANCHO VI
King of Navarre
1150–1194

ALFONSO II
Count of Barcelona
King of Aragon
1162–1196

ALFONSO VIII
King of Castile
1158–1214

ALFONSO IX
King of León
1188–1230

ALFONSO II
King of Portugal
1211–1223

SANCHO VII
King of Navarre
1194–1234

BLANCHE
=
Thibaut III
Count of Champagne

PETER II
King of Aragon
1196–1213

ALFONSO
Count of Provence

HENRY I
King of Castile
1214–1217

FERDINAND III
King of Castile
1217–1252
King of León
1230–1252

SANCHO II
King of Portugal
1223–1245

ALFONSO III
King of Portugal
1247–1279

THIBAUT I
King of Navarre
1234–1253

JAMES I
King of Aragon
1213–1276

RAYMOND
BERENGER
Count of Provence

ALFONSO X
King of Castile and
León
1252–1284

DINEZ
King of Portugal
1279–1325

THIBAUT II
King of Navarre
1253–1270

HENRY I
King of Navarre
1270–1274

PETER III
King of Aragon
1276–1285
King of Sicily
1282–1285

BEATRICE
=
Charles
Count of Anjou
Count of Provence
King of Sicily

The Early and Medieval Popes

Antipopes shown in *italics*
Avignon Popes shown in **bold**

Sylvester I, 314–335
Mark, 336
Julius I, 337–352
Liberius, 352–336
Felix II, 355–365
Damasus I, 366–384
Siricius, 384–399
Anastasius I, 399–401
Innocent I, 401–417
Zosimus, 417–418
Boniface I, 418–422
Celestine I, 422–432
Sixtus III, 432–440
Leo I, 440–461
Hilary, 461–468
Simplicius, 468–483
Felix III, 483–492
Gelasius I, 492–496
Anastasius II, 496–498
Symmachus, 498–514
Hormisdas, 514–523
John I, 523–526
Felix IV, 526–530
Boniface II, 530–532
John II, 533–535
Agapitus, 535–536
Silverius, 536–537
Vigilius, 537–555
Pelagius I, 555–561
John III, 561–574
Benedict I, 575–579
Pelagius II, 579–590
Gregory I, 590–604
Sabinianus, 604–606
Boniface III, 607
Boniface IV, 608–615
Deusdedit, 615–618
Boniface V, 619–625
Honorius I, 625–638

Severinus, 640
John IV, 640–642
Theodore I, 642–649
Martin I, 649–655
Eugenius I, 654–657
Vitalian, 657–672
Adeodatus, 672–676
Donus, 676–678
Agatho, 678–681
Leo II, 682–683
Benedict II, 684–685
John V, 685–686
Conon, 686–687
Sergius I, 687–701
John VI, 701–705
John VII, 705–707
Sisinnius, 708
Constantine, 708–715
Gregory II, 715–731
Gregory III, 731–741
Zacharias, 741–752
Stephen II, 752–757
Paul I, 757–767
Stephen III, 768–772
Adrian I, 772–795
Leo III, 795–816
Stephen IV, 816–817
Paschal I, 817–824
Eugenius II, 824–827
Valentine, 827
Gregory IV, 827–844
Sergius II, 844–847
Leo IV, 847–855
Benedict III, 855–858
Nicholas I, 858–867
Adrian II, 867–872
John VIII, 872–882
Marinus I, 882–884
Adrian III, 884–885
Stephen V, 885–891
Formosus, 891–896
Boniface VI, 896

Stephen VI, 896–897
Romanus, 897
Theodore II, 897
John IX, 898–900
Benedict IV, 900–903
Leo V, 903
Christopher, 903–904
Sergius III, 904–911
Anastasius III, 911–913
Lando, 913–914
John X, 914–928
Leo VI, 928
Stephen VII, 928–931
John XI, 931–935
Leo VII, 936–939
Stephen VIII, 939–942
Marinus II, 942–946
Agapitus II, 946–955
John XII, 955–964
Leo VIII, 963–965
Benedict V, 964–966
John XIII, 965–972
Benedict VI, 973–974
Boniface VII, 974; 984–985
Benedict VII, 974–983
John XIV, 983–984
John XV, 985–996
Gregory V, 996–999
John XVI, 997–998
Sylvester II, 999–1003
John XVII, 1003
John XVIII, 1004–1009
Sergius IV, 1009–1012
Benedict VIII, 1012–1024
John XIX, 1024–1032
Benedict IX, 1032–1044
Sylvester III, 1045
Benedict IX, 1045 (second time)
Gregory VI, 1045–1046
Clement II, 1046–1047
Benedict IX, 1047–1048
(third time)

Damasus II, 1048
Leo IX, 1049–1054
Victor II, 1055–1057
Stephen IX, 1057–1058
Benedict X, 1058–1059
Nicholas II, 1059–1061
Alexander II, 1061–1073
Gregory VII, 1073–1085
Clement III, 1080; 1084–1100
Victor III, 1086–1087
Urban II, 1088–1099
Paschal II, 1099–1118
Theodoric, 1100
Albert, 1102
Sylvester IV, 1105–1111
Gelasius II, 1118–1119
Gregory VIII, 1118–1121
Calixtus II, 1119–1124
Honorius II, 1124–1130
Innocent II, 1130–1143
Anacletus II, 1130–1138
Celestine II, 1143–1144
Lucius II, 1144–1145
Eugenius III, 1145–1153
Anastasius IV, 1153–1154
Adrian IV, 1154–1159
Alexander III, 1159–1181
Victor IV, 1159–1164
Paschal III, 1164–1168
Calixtus III, 1168–1178
Innocent III, 1179–1180
Lucius III, 1181–1185
Urban III, 1185–1187
Gregory VIII, 1187
Clement III, 1187–1191
Celestine III, 1191–1198
Innocent III, 1198–1216
Honorius III, 1216–1227
Gregory IX, 1227–1241
Celestine IV, 1241
Innocent IV, 1243–1254
Alexander IV, 1254–1261

Urban IV, 1261–1264
Clement IV, 1265–1268
Gregory X, 1271–1276
Innocent V, 1276
Adrian V, 1276
John XXI, 1276–1277 (because of
a numbering error, there was
no John XX)
Nicholas III, 1277–1280
Martin IV, 1281–1285
Honorius IV, 1285–1287
Nicholas IV, 1288–1292
Celestine V, 1294
Boniface VIII, 1294–1303
Benedict XI, 1303–1304
Clement V, 1305–1314
John XXII, 1316–1334
Benedict XII, 1334–1342
Clement VI, 1342–1352
Innocent VI, 1352–1362
Urban V, 1362–1370
Gregory XI, 1370–1378
Urban VI, 1378–1389
Clement VII, 1378–1394
Boniface IX, 1389–1404
Benedict XIII, 1394–1423
Innocent VII, 1404–1406
Gregory XII, 1406–1415
Alexander V, 1409–1410
John XXIII, 1410–1415
Martin V, 1417–1431
Clement VIII, 1423–1429
Eugenius IV, 1431–1447
Felix V, 1439–1449
Nicholas V, 1447–1455
Calixtus III, 1455–1458
Pius II, 1458–1464
Paul II, 1464–1471
Sixtus IV, 1471–1484
Innocent VIII, 1484–1492
Alexander VI, 1492–1503

INDEX